The Stage Door

THE STAGE DOOR

Kurt Collins

authorHOUSE®

AuthorHouse™
1663 Liberty Drive
Bloomington, IN 47403
www.authorhouse.com
Phone: 1-800-839-8640

Published by AuthorHouse 02/18/2012

ISBN: 978-1-4678-8945-2 (sc)
ISBN: 978-1-4678-8946-9 (e)

This book is printed on acid-free paper.

Contents

CHAPTER ONE

It Begins

Kurt lived in a typical end-of-terrace former council house, which he'd brought a few years ago. He was quite a popular guy with a typical British sense of humour. Most of the time he was the clown of the group, but occasionally his personality would change, as he was not alone.

In the daytime he worked as a painter and decorator for a London company, and most Friday and Saturday evenings he could be found working in one of the local night clubs as a DJ. Music, it has to be said, was the number one passion in his life. It kept him going and fired his soul, so to speak.

He met his current girlfriend Nicola at a talent contest in north London. It was a chance meeting that would ultimately change the course of his life! For better or for worse, this is where it all began.

* * *

Hi, I'm Kurt. Let's go back to the above statement, "He was not alone." It doesn't embarrass me to say it, although others seem to think it a bit strange. Now you're completely confused, aren't you? We'll let me explain. This is what I truly believe, honestly.

My philosophy in life is that the body is a vessel that carries the soul, which is who and what we are. When the body dies, the soul moves on to the next body, and then the next, and so on, until "you" that is your soul gains enough life experience to ascend to your ultimate life.

The problem is that I seem to have an extra soul in this body that I now reside in.

I know it sounds daft, but when I was three years old, I lived in a big old house which my parents owned in Clacton-on-Sea, and in my bedroom there was a large wardrobe that had the usual array of toys and teddies on top.

Once the lights went out at night I would always look up and see shadows on the wardrobe that would scare me. One day I decided to scale the wardrobe to investigate. Unfortunately, whilst I was climbing, it fell down on top of me, injuring me severely. I was rushed to hospital and later died for a few seconds, before the doctor managed to revive me. Luckily, I went on to make a full recovery.

The reason I'm telling you this is because I believe that in the moment that my heart stopped beating, another soul entered my body, maybe as a guide to help in the transition of my soul to its next destination. Unfortunately, before he could leave, the doctor revived me, trapping him inside me and effectively forcing this poor unfortunate soul to be with me for the rest of my life.

Generally, I'm a run-of-the-mill type of guy, but there is another side to me that's a little bit reckless—you might say a bit of a rebel who takes chances and acts on the spur of the moment, so to speak. I've always called that side of me Colin. Don't ask me why. I don't know that myself.

I can often be found chatting away to myself, and friends would often say, "Are you talking to yourself again?"

"No, I'm talking to Colin," I would always reply. This would normally bring fits of laughter.

I would often put it down to my being a Gemini. You know—split personality and all that. Sometimes I'm in control, and other times Colin takes over. I know everybody talks to themselves, but the scary thing is that Colin answers back! Please don't read too much into this as it's not really an integral part of the story. I'm just trying to show you how my mind works.

Going back to the night in question, the night when I met Nicola . . .

It was about 9.30 p.m., and I was sitting in the front row of a north London theatre waiting for my turn on the talent stage. Three others had gone before me, a pretty blonde girl and two other guys. None of them could sing. Well, that was my opinion anyway, but I guess you could say I was biased.

I remembered seeing a sign for a bar as I'd come into the theatre, so naturally I thought that a drink for Dutch courage would help. I approached the bar and ordered my usual—a Baileys and ice. The girl behind the bar ignored me, so I repeated my order a little louder this time, but she ignored me again! Great night this was turning out to be, eh? So I clicked my fingers at her. That was a mistake. She launched herself the whole length of the bar and drowned me in a pint of Carlsberg.

"If you want my service in here, you'll ask nicely. Don't demand and don't click your fingers at me, okay?

"Oh, that's just fucking great." This just wasn't going to be my night. I heard a voice inside my head saying, "It can't get any worse, can it?" so I turned to face the barmaid and said, "Look, I'm sorry if I offended you. It wasn't my intention."

She seemed shocked by my response, half-expecting me to go mad at her. "It's not what you said, it's the way you said it. And clicking your fingers at me was the last straw."

There was a silent pause between us, and then we both burst into laughter. I hadn't really looked at her properly before, as I was too preoccupied in my own thoughts. She was about five-foot eight tall with long straight brown hair, very attractive, and she had quite an intoxicating smile.

"Let's start again. I'm Kurt, a wet singer trying to get up a bit of Dutch courage before I go on stage."

"Oh my god! I'm really sorry, but you did deserve it. I'm Nicola. Pleased to meet you," she chuckled.

A voice crackled through the speakers in the bar. "Next up on stage is Kurt Collins." That's my stage name. It comes from my split personalities, Kurt and Colin.

"That's me. Wish me luck, Nicola," I said.

"That's for luck," she replied, blowing me a kiss.

I'd been involved in music in one way or another since I'd won a talent contest at Butlin's Holiday Camp when I was only five years old. Since then I'd sung and played guitar in various bands that were going nowhere fast, but the experiences were great and I enjoyed them immensely. After that I moved on to working in studios, producing music for other bands and, of course, working in the evenings as a DJ. I guess you could say that I liked to keep myself busy. This contest was giving me the chance to perform, which I loved doing. Anyway, here goes nothing . . .

The compère introduced me, and I slid up to the microphone in my lager-soaked clothes. I was singing an old classic of Sam Cooke's called "Touch the Hem of Your Garment." It's not as well-known as some, but it's a beautiful song none the less. I sailed through the song, delivering it with the passion it deserved, and as I finished several people clapped. I had to strain my eyes to see who was at the back of the hall clapping, and I was pleased to see that among them was Nicola, the fiery barmaid I'd met earlier.

She walked towards me smiling. "Hiya, I thought I owed it to you to at least watch. You were pretty good."

"Thanks, I know," I replied, laughing. "The truth is you just couldn't resist my charms and natural good looks, could you?"

Nicola pulled a face and laughed as she replied. "Modest bastard, aren't you? So are you going to buy me a drink then?"

"Sure, if you promise not to throw this one at me." Nicola laughed again and said she'd try not to.

We sat and had a drink and chatted for about half an hour. She was a single girl with her own flat, working in the day as a hairdresser with the occasional evening shift behind the bar. She was very confident, but with a sensitive side to her. We just seemed to click.

It turned out I'd come runner-up to the pretty blonde girl in the contest.

"Oh well, you can't win them all," she commiserated.

"Yeah, I guess you're right, but what the hell! It's the taking part that counts, and anyway, if I hadn't come down here tonight I wouldn't have met you, so I guess I'm a winner after all, eh?"

We had a few more drinks and then went on to a club until the early hours. Eventually we went back to Nicola's place.

Thinking about that night, I thought that we'd had a great time. It was as if I'd known her for a very long time. I have to say, I've had many girlfriends over the course of my life, none of whom lasted very long. If I got past four weeks in a relationship with a girl, it was very unusual. The problem is that I seek more than just good looks and great sex, and as most people know, on its own that's a combination that's notoriously difficult to find. So after I'd had my wicked way with them a few times, I'd start getting bored and then look around for my next sexual conquest.

Anyway back to the night in question . . .

There was definitely something about this feisty barmaid that intrigued me. I couldn't really put my finger on it, but she seemed different from the others. I mean, sure, she had the looks and the figure, but there was something else about her, an instant attraction to her personality maybe. She had a drive and a confidence about her, yet I sensed a trace of insecurity. I felt compelled to be in her company.

We entered her flat and went into the front room. "Can I fix you a drink?" she asked.

"Sure! Baileys and ice, thanks, or if you haven't got that, I'll have a brandy and lemonade with ice—whichever you have."

"No Baileys, I'm afraid, but I do have a bottle of Courvoisier brandy."

"Great! That's my favourite brandy."

She smiled and gave me a very sexy look. Seems like it might be my night after all, I thought to myself.

"Make yourself comfortable. I'll be back in a second, okay?" With that she went off into the kitchen, returning a few moments later, drinks in hand. "I'll just put some music on. Who are you into musically?"

"Something soft and sensual," I replied.

"What about some R&B?"

"Sure, sounds good to me." She turned the stereo on and stuck in a CD. Then she sat down next to me and placed the drinks on the table. Leaning towards me, she said, "Well are you just going to sit there all night, or are we going to warm it up a little?"

She had that sexy look in her eyes again, so I leaned over and gently kissed her on the lips.

"Mmm, that was nice. Kiss me again, a little harder this time," she whispered in my ear.

I pulled her close to me, cupping the back of her head in my hand. Our tongues entwined in a deep passionate kiss, and after what seemed like an eternity, our lips finally parted. Nicola stood up, took me by the hand, and led me to the bedroom.

As I walked into the room the first thing that caught my eye was the bed. Surprise, surprise, I hear you say. It was one of those four poster-beds that you sometimes see in magazines with all the trimmings.

"Wow, very sexy!" I blurted out. If I wasn't turned on before, I was now!

Before we knew it we were both on the bed kissing, laughing, and fooling around. I reached forward and unbuttoned the front of her blouse to reveal a white lacy bra. My whole body was tingling in anticipation of what was to come.

She slipped my shirt off and pressed her warm body against me. I pulled her long brown silky hair to one side and then after gently biting on her ear, I kissed the soft flesh on her neck.

"I like that," she said, giggling.

"You know I give a wicked massage," I said.

"Mmm, you really know how to please a girl, don't you, Kurt?"

"I try my best," I replied.

Nicola laughed and lay face down on the bed. "There's a bottle of baby oil on the side," she said.

I began rubbing the oil into her, caressing her shoulders and massaging her lower back. She had great skin and was covered in freckles, which I'd have to say was a tremendous turn on for me. I worked my way down her sexy body, slipped her skirt off, and caressed every part of her skin that I could get to. After a lot of pleasurable foreplay, we made love to each other until the early hours of the morning. It was fantastic.

We eventually fell asleep in each other's arms, both thoroughly content and totally exhausted.

I woke the next day to the smell of bacon in the air. Nicola was cooking. There's nothing like a fried breakfast to get the energy levels back up after a great night's shagging, I thought to myself. I got up and made my way into the kitchen.

"Morning, sleepy head," she said.

"Morning, gorgeous," I replied, kissing her.

"Hey, pack it in! I've got to go to work."

"That's a shame coz I've got the day off. Can't you ring in sick?"

"I wish I could, babe, but unfortunately I've got bills to pay, and I'm trying to put some money away for a holiday I'm going on in about six weeks' time"

"Oh, really? Where are you going?" I asked her.

"Spain. With three girlfriends of mine. We planned it ages ago. I've never been before, and I'm really looking forward to it."

"Yeah, I know what you mean. It's great to get away sometimes, and it helps to recharge the batteries, although I've never been to Spain either. I've heard it's quite wild out there"

"That's what we're hoping. Anyway I've really got to go, as much as I'd love to stay and fool around a bit more, so give me a call later, babe, okay? There's plenty of hot water if you want a shower."

Nicola kissed me goodbye and then she was gone. I took her up on the offer of a shower and then left her flat and went home to collect a change of clothes before going down the gym for a light workout.

I couldn't stop thinking about what had happened last night, and no matter how much I tried to concentrate, I just couldn't get Nicola out of my mind. I don't know why, but I guess I felt a little bit jealous about the fact that she was going on holiday to Spain with a group of girls and what she'd be getting up to when she got there. This was a bit weird for me, as normally it's the other way around.

Well, that's how our relationship started.

I saw her every night over the next few weeks, spending fun days out and passionate nights in. it was a hectic time in my life, but a hell of a lot of fun all the same.

It was now only two weeks before Nicola and her friends were going on holiday. I couldn't forget it, as the closer we got, the more she would go on about how excited she was.

As I've said before, I've never been to Spain although I've always fancied going, and to be quite honest, with all that talk about holidays, I really wanted to go myself now, but I didn't let on, as I wasn't sure how she would feel about me tagging along on an all-girl holiday.

Later that evening Nicola received a phone call from her friend Sharon. She was one of the three girls who were going with her. She called to say that unfortunately she would have to pull out of the trip due to some personal problem. Nicola looked quite disappointed but told Sharon not to worry as these things happen. She wished her well and then hung up the phone.

Nicola turned to me with half a smile on her face.

"Penny for your thoughts," I said.

"Well, the holiday is paid for, and it would be a shame to waste it. So how would you feel about going in Sharon's place?"

"I'd love to come. You know that, but are you sure it would be okay with the other two girls?"

"There wouldn't be a problem with you going, honestly."

"What about the sleeping arrangements?"

Nicola told me that she really wanted me to go with her and reassured me that there wouldn't be a problem with her friends as they had booked two double rooms and I could double up with her.

"Great then, you've convinced me. I'll start packing tomorrow."

"Terrific! I can't wait," she replied.

I couldn't believe my luck. For once I'd actually got what I wanted without even trying.

A beautiful girl and a holiday to Spain . . .

Everything was falling into place. This was a strange feeling for me. Usually in my life, I'd try hard to get things to work out, but something would always pop up and throw my best-laid plans into chaos.

Strangely, at this moment in time everything felt right, as if it was destined to be. Well, they do say that you should go with your instincts, and to be quite honest, every fibre of my body was saying that this was right.

So how could I possibly resist?

CHAPTER TWO

The Holiday

The next two weeks passed by very quickly, and before we knew it the holiday was upon us. It was now Saturday morning, and we were flying out from Luton airport in less than ten hours' time.

Nicola was cooking breakfast and generally trying to do about ten things at once. She was a very organized girl. You know the type—everything in its place and a place for everything. Well, this was the total opposite to me. I'm more laidback and casual. I've never really planned ahead, as I've always done things on the spur of the moment.

Anyway, we sat down to breakfast and Nicola pulled out a list of what we were going to do today.

"First we need to go shopping for clothes," she said. Nicola was in her element when she was spending money. She just loved to shop, and like all women she'd go around every store to look for clothes, only to go back to the first shop she'd been in to get what she wanted. I've never really understood that about women. When a guy goes shopping, he sees what he wants and buys it straight away. Women can be so indecisive sometimes!

Anyway, next on the list was the travel agent's to sort out some currency, and finally on to the hairdresser's for a cut and highlights for the both of us. After doing all that, we met up with the other two girls at the airport, checked our bags in, and made our way into the departure lounge.

Everyone was really upbeat and excited now. The two other girls couldn't stop talking about what they were going to get up to when they got there. Nicola laughed and joked with them about how many guys they were going to shag, but then she turned to me and whispered, "Don't worry. I've only got eyes for you, lover," as if to reassure me in some way.

"I'm not worried. We're going to have a great time too," I replied. She just looked at me with that intoxicating smile of hers beaming across her face.

After a while they announced over the tannoy that our flight was about to board, so we made our way down to the departure gate and boarded the plane, found our seats, and sat down. I could feel butterflies in my stomach, and I asked Nicola if she was feeling nervous about flying. She said she was, but she was more concerned about being in confined spaces, so she couldn't wait to get off of the plane.

The flight took about two and a half hours to get there, but the time passed quickly, and we eventually landed at Malaga airport. As soon as the plane doors were opened, Nicola was up, pushing her way down the aisle. As she said, she hated confined spaces. We collected our bags and walked through the exit doors of the airport. It was about 9 p.m. Spanish time, and the first thing that hit us was the heat. We didn't expect it at this time of night.

We found our way onto the coach, which took us to our hotel. It was situated about half an hour down the road in a place called Fuengirola. Our hotel was right in the middle of town, adjacent to the port and beaches.

We were all buzzing with excitement now. We waited for another twenty minutes to get our room key, before eventually going up to our apartment. Everything inside was so clean—marble floors with whitewashed walls and pine woodwork. We had a balcony, a bathroom, and a huge double bedroom with fitted wardrobes. It was very impressive.

Within an hour we were unpacked, changed, and ready to go out and explore. We wanted to make the most out of every second here. We all met up in the lobby downstairs and headed out of the hotel. It was now 11.30 p.m. and the place was rocking with people. There was music coming from everywhere.

We crossed the road and went into the first bar we came to. It was called the London Bar, and it was packed wall to wall with people. They had a DJ booth at the side of the bar with a live compère hyping up the crowd. There were TVs hanging everywhere from the ceiling showing music videos, and there must have been at least half a dozen bar staff doing tricks with bottles and generally befriending the customers and making everybody feel welcome. There was also a small dance area—not that you needed it to dance, as most people danced where they stood. It was so friendly in there that for a moment you'd think you were dreaming.

By that I mean . . . well, it's just not like that in the UK any more, is it? Yet here we were surrounded by English people who were just having a great time. It was fantastic.

I wouldn't like to say how much alcohol we put away in there, but suffice to say, it was quite a lot. When you ask for a spirit out there, they don't measure it; they just fill a tall glass with ice and then pour your drink until the glass is full, so you're effectively getting three or four shots for the price of one in the UK.

We decided to move on after a couple of hours to look around for a bit. We made our way across the road to the port area, where there was a parade of smaller open terrace bars serving food and drinks and playing music. Nicola wanted to check them out, so we did just that, drinking and dancing all the way.

We were all getting on great and as you can imagine, we were quite loud and drunk by now. We'd met a few people in the bars with whom we'd got on really well, and they suggested that we go on to Linekers Bar, which was now opposite us at the front of the port, so we agreed and staggered over there.

It was a large sports bar with a huge terrace, and like the London Bar, it was packed with English tourists having a great time. Again, there were TVs everywhere blasting out MTV music videos. We approached the bar and ordered some drinks from the barmaid. It was unbelievable how friendly and full of energy everyone was.

The barmaid came back to us with a tray of drinks, saying, "Here you are. My name's Luciana. Have you just arrived?"

"Yes, we've only just got here tonight."

"I didn't think I'd seen you before." With that Luciana pulled out a handful of small shot glasses and mixed some cocktails and then set them alight. "This is a welcome-to-Fuengirola drink from Linekers, on the house." She gave us each a straw and told us to drink them as fast as possible through the straw. So that's what we did, and it was very strong.

"Another round of them, please," shouted Nicola.

This went on for quite a while, until we eventually ended up on the dance floor totally pissed, dancing, and singing along to every song that was played.

At about 2.30 a.m. they closed up, and we all made our way up to the Underground Nightclub that was situated under the London Bar where we were drinking earlier. There were lots of people hanging around chatting and larking about, as most of the bars in the surrounding area had also just kicked out. By this time the other two girls that we'd flown out with had hooked up with a couple of lads, and we were all waiting in the queue to get into the club when we spotted Luciana, the barmaid from Linekers.

Nicola shouted over to Luciana to get her attention, and she came running over and kissed us both on the cheek as if she'd known us forever.

"Are you going into the club?" asked Luciana.

"Yes, if we ever get through this queue."

"Don't bother queuing up. Come with us and we'll get you in quicker and without having to pay." Luciana and her mates grabbed me and Nicola and dragged us down the stairs past the waiting queue. She briefly spoke to the doorman, and the next thing we knew we were in!

"You've got to love this place. It's brilliant here," I said to Nicola.

"Yeah, I know what you mean. I can't believe I've never been here before."

It was quite dimly lit inside with a strong smell of damp in the air, but I'd have to say the atmosphere more than made up for it. There were four bars, three around the wall and one in the middle of the floor, which also housed the DJ booth. As you can imagine, it was a very lively place.

Luciana got the drinks in and then introduced us to her friends. The guys greeted me with handshakes, while the girls greeted us both with the double-kiss-on-the-cheek thing, which seemed to be customary out here. Luciana was quite a popular girl.

Next she introduced us to her boyfriend, Big Tony. He certainly lived up to his name. He was over six foot tall and built like a brick shit house. She told us that he also worked in Linekers Bar as the head doorman, and I've got to say that despite his size, he seemed really friendly and approachable.

We danced and chatted through the night, until we were kicked out at about 6 a.m. After saying our goodbyes, we staggered across the street to our hotel. I remember speaking to Nicola about what a great time we'd had that night. We both felt so at home here. Eventually we made it up to our apartment and fell into bed exhausted. We didn't made love that night; we just cuddled up in each other's arms, happy and contented. Thinking about it now, I guess our relationship took a step up that day.

We didn't wake up until about 6 p.m. that evening, and, yes, you've guessed it, we were both suffering from hangovers. In fact, to be honest to you, we'd have probably slept a lot longer if it wasn't for the intense heat in the apartment.

After a shower and a change of clothes, we both decided to try and find something to eat, so we made our way down to the parade of bars in the port area that we'd stopped at last night.

We sat down at a bar called Scottie's. It was by far the busiest bar in the parade, which is always a good sign. The owner of the bar was called Jimmy, and like everyone else around here, he was a very bubbly and friendly character with a lot of time for his customers. His bar was covered wall to wall with football shirts, which, he told us, were given to him by holiday-makers who had returned year after year. It has to be said that he was the perfect host and knew just how to get his customers to spend their money. The food was very good, and I must admit that we too found ourselves charmed into ordering afters. It was obvious to us why people came back here every year!

As we were still feeling a little hung-over, we decided that we'd give the late-night drinking a miss tonight and go on a shopping trip to Marbella instead. We'd heard so much about it, and it was only about twenty miles down the road.

The taxi cab pulled into Marbella high street at about 9.30 p.m. We half-expected most of the shops to be closed by now, but the cab driver had insisted on the drive down that it did stay open till late. All the same, we were quite surprised to see how busy it was. If we'd been in England, everything would have been closed by now, yet this place was teeming with people. All the shops were still open, and there was an open-air market setting up on the promenade. To us this seemed a little crazy!

As I've said before, Nicola just loved shopping, and this place was filled with every shop from designer boutiques to the usual high-street stores. I could literally taste the excitement in her. We must have been in at least forty shops, some of them several times, and of course we spent an obscene amount of money. But what the hell? We were here to have fun and enjoy ourselves.

The shops finally closed at around midnight, and we made our way down to one of the bars opposite the port for a well-earned drink after all the walking we'd done. The view was terrific, with all the boats in the port and the bars coming to life with people. It seemed a million miles away from our lives in England.

Eventually we caught a cab back to Fuengirola at about 1 a.m. to drop off all the bags of shopping. We both fancied one last drink but didn't want anyone else's company, so I volunteered to nip down to the London Bar to grab a bottle of vodka and a bottle of brandy to bring back to the apartment. On the way out of the bar I bumped into Tony and Luciana.

"Hi, Kurt, where's Nicola tonight then? I hope we didn't wear her out too much last night. It can get a bit hectic around here if you're not used to it," they chuckled.

"Yeah, I think I'd worked that one out already. We've decided to have an early night tonight, so we'll probably see you tomorrow if you're about"

"Okay, *hasta manana*. That means 'see you tomorrow.' You two have fun," said Luciana. She kissed me on the cheek and wished me well, and I returned the kiss and said goodnight to the both of them before making my way back up to the apartment to have a long and steamy night with Nicola.

I woke up at about 10 a.m. the next morning and just lay there next to Nicola watching her sleep. She looked so peaceful and content. She was so beautiful, and I felt like a very lucky guy. You know they say that there's a soul-mate out there for everyone, and although I'd only known Nicola for a short space of time, I felt in my heart that maybe she was the one for me. Time would tell, I guess, but for the moment at least I intended to fully enjoy the moment!

Nicola opened her eyes and let out a great big yawn. She looked up at me and smiled.

"Morning, sleepy head," I said.

"Morning, babe. You know I had the best time yesterday with my favourite sexy man."

I laughed and gave her a big hug and kissed her on the lips. "Shall we get up and go down the beach for a while?"

"Mmm, that sounds like a great idea. After all, it wouldn't be right to holiday in Spain and come back without a tan to prove it."

With that we got up, showered, got dressed, and then made our way down to the beach. Once there, we grabbed a couple of sun loungers to lie down on. It was so hot here, and because my skin does not tan easily, I liked to shade myself on and off to avoid being burnt by the sun. Nicola on the other hand had no problems there. She could lie out in the full heat of the sun, and her skin would just keep tanning. She asked me if I would mind if she went topless, as it was commonplace for a girl to do that out here.

"Sure, why would I mind?" I asked her.

"Well some people are funny about things like that."

"Hey, it's always a pleasure seeing you topless," I replied, laughing.

I looked across the beach, which was very busy. There were wooden sun loungers and parasols as far as the eye could see, and Nicola was right: there were topless girls everywhere. As a red-blooded guy I'd have to say that it was a great sight to see. That feeling of dying and going to heaven was coming back again, if you know what I mean.

I noticed a queue of people about two hundred yards along the beachfront waiting to go on the jet skis, and I thought I'd quite fancy having a go at them myself. I asked Nicola if she wanted to go on one, but she declined, saying she much preferred to sunbathe. However, she said that I should go on them if that's what I wanted to do.

"Bring me a drink back when you return, please. I'm really thirsty," she asked me. I kissed her and walked over to the jet ski hut. When I got there, I heard voices calling out my name. It was Tony and Luciana, and they were with a couple of friends.

"Hiya, Kurt, I take it you're going on the jet skis then?"

"Yeah, I thought I'd give it a go. How much is it?" Tony told me that it was about thirty pounds an hour, which seemed quite reasonable.

They asked after Nicola, and I told them that she was catching some rays on the beach. Luciana introduced me to her friends Kirby and Fallon. We all kissed and said hello. Kirby was from America and was nineteen years old with long brown hair. She had a cute face and was about five foot eight tall. Fallon came from Sweden. She was twenty-two years old and looked like your stereotypical Swede. You know the type—tall, blonde hair, and a body to die for. We all chatted while we were waiting to go on the jet skis.

Kirby and Fallon told me that they both worked at Linekers Bar, giving out fliers and generally trying to encourage as many people as possible into the bar. For this they were paid a basic wage and a commission. They also told me that they normally went home in the winter months and returned again each summer, as there wasn't enough trade out of season to keep them in work.

We finally got onto the water after a twenty-minute wait, and I can tell you that it was an exhilarating experience. Once our time was up, we all made our way back over to Nicola, who was still cooking in the sun and now noticeably tanning. I remembered that she wanted a drink, so I grabbed a couple of cans from one of the beach vendor's that constantly walked up and down.

"Hiya, gorgeous, look who I bumped into."

Nicola looked up and was pleased to see Tony and Luciana. We all sat down and started chatting. Luciana introduced the other girls to Nicola, and they inquired as to why she hadn't gone out on the jet skis with me. She told them that she didn't care too much for the sea although she could swim quite well; she just preferred to lie on the beach, take in the sun, and relax. Eventually we all said goodbye, and we arranged to meet up with them later that evening in Linekers, as apparently everyone had the evening off.

We went back to our apartment to freshen up and to get a change of clothing and then went out for something to eat, followed by several drinks, before making our way down to Linekers to meet up with the others.

It was very busy inside. The music was blaring, and there were quite a lot of people dancing and generally having a great time. We walked up to the bar and ordered our drinks. We couldn't see anyone in here yet that we recognized, so when the barman returned we asked him if he'd seen Tony or Luciana in here tonight.

"You must be Kurt and Nicola," he said in a strong Geordie accent. "They said you might be in here tonight. My name's Scott. I've heard a lot about the two of you."

"All good, I hope."

"Of course! They said that they would be in here at about 10.30 p.m."

We thanked him and made our way over to a table, put down our drinks, and then walked over to the dance floor, which is where we stayed until Nicola spotted Luciana entering the bar with Tony and a few friends.

Luciana came running over to us. She was very upbeat and excited to see us and gave out a loud girly scream as she hugged and kissed us both. Kirby and Fallon did the same, and Tony and I just looked at each other and laughed.

"Were really glad you guys came down tonight as we've got a great evening planned," said Luciana. The girls all sat down chatting as they do, while Tony and I made our way up to the bar to grab some more drinks. Tony told me that Scott, the guy that had served me earlier, was actually the manager and had got him the job here.

"So, what have you got in store for us tonight then?" I asked.

"That would be telling. But don't worry, it will be a good night, so don't expect to get home too early."

Everyone in here seemed to know Tony. I lost count of the number of people who came up to acknowledge him. Scott returned with the drinks and Tony went to pay him, but Scott would have none of it.

"These ones are on me," he said.

He told us that he would see us later, and with that we made our way back to the girls. The group had swollen by now, as a couple of lads had joined us. They turned out to be Kirby and Fallon's boyfriends. They both shook me by the hand and then introduced themselves.

Ricky had been going out with Kirby for a few months now and was in his early twenties. He was about five foot eight with short dark hair, and by his accent I could tell that he was also a Geordie lad. He said his parents had moved out here last year and had set up a breakfast bar just down the road in Los Boliches. Robbie was a London lad in his late twenties and was about six foot tall with fair hair. He had only been dating Fallon for a few weeks. He told me that he worked as a waiter in the London Bar. They both seemed very friendly and quite a laugh.

After about an hour Luciana suggested that we should move on, so we all got up and made our way over to a bar called Tramp's, which was situated right next door to the entrance of the Underground club and the London Bar. Apart from Linekers, this area of the town seemed to be the most popular with the English.

They had a karaoke night going on in there, and everything was in full swing already. After ordering a few drinks, Fallon asked me if I was going to sing a few songs tonight, as she'd heard from Nicola that I was quite good. "I might have a go later," I told her.

We were all laughing and joking around when the compère stopped the music to make an announcement. "This evening we've arranged a special treat for you. In the bar tonight is an English up-and-coming singer and DJ. His name is Kurt Collins. This is as much as a surprise to him as it is to you, so let's give him a very warm welcome." Everybody clapped and cheered as the spotlight fell on me.

I looked straight at Nicola, who had a suspiciously large smile across her face. "You bitch! I'll get you for this," I told her. Everyone just burst into laughter, and I was dragged up to the stage area. I couldn't believe it; I'd been well and truly stitched up.

The compère put a mike in my hand and then called up a couple of girls to help me. I had no idea what songs I was going to have to sing. I guess you could say that I was in a state of shock at the time, but as they say, the show must go on.

The compère picked up his mike and said that the songs that he'd chosen for me tonight would be from the rock 'n' roll era, so he wanted to see everyone on the dance floor enjoying themselves to show support for me. The first song came up on the monitor. It was an old Manfred Mann classic, and, yes, you've guessed it—"Do Wah Diddy". I knew that song quite well, so I was pleased for that at least. The music started and I burst into song with the girls backing me all the way. Everyone was singing and dancing along with the song. It was a great atmosphere, and the crowd cheered loudly as the tune came to an end. It was quickly followed by another well-known track by the infamous Chubby Checker called "The Twist". This got just about everyone going. I could see Nicola and our new-found friends giving it large by the bar. I stayed up there for another few songs, before finishing with the appropriate number for the evening, which was an absolute classic by Boney M. called "Hooray! Hooray! It's a Holi-Holiday".

Everybody was cheering and screaming when I finished, and the compère got back on the microphone and shouted, "How about that then? Was he great or what? Let's have one last round of applause for Kurt Collins!"

The compère thanked me for being such a great sport and told me that there would be a round of drinks waiting for me at the bar. After shaking his hand, I kissed and thanked the girls who were on backing vocals and left the stage to rapturous applause and made my way back through the crowd who were patting me on the back and congratulating me as I went. Eventually I reached the bar, where Nicola and all the others were waiting. They cheered and banged their glasses on the bar as I approached. They laughed as I cursed them for setting me up, and there were, of course, lots of kisses all around for me and a special hug from Nicola.

There seemed to be a real party atmosphere in here now, and it didn't stop there. The resident DJ came on to play all the best party songs and handbag classics you could think of, from "Living Next Door To Alice" to "Y.M.C.A." I didn't think it could get much better than we'd already experienced that night, but how wrong could I be? There seemed to be no end to the fun out here.

The place kicked out at about 2 a.m., and we all piled into the Underground nightclub next door. Kirby and Fallon told us that we were only going in there for an hour or so as we'd been invited to a party at Scott's villa, Scott being the manager of Linekers whom we'd met earlier.

The hour passed by quickly, and before we knew it we were making our way over to the taxi rank and driving up to Scott's place, which was a few miles inland in a small village called Mijas. The cabs pulled up outside his villa, and we followed Tony up some steps to the front door.

It was quite a big place with its own pool. Tony knocked on the door, and Scott answered and invited us in. There were quite a few people inside already, laughing and dancing to the music being played by one of the Linekers DJs, who was set up in the corner of the room. Everyone kissed and hugged each other, and Scott told us to help ourselves to food and drinks.

Nicola and the other girls started dancing together, and Scott introduced me to his DJ whose name was Danny. He told me that he'd been working out here for a couple of years now. We chatted for ages about music and what life was like in Spain. He said the English were like a big family out here; everyone looked out for each other. He said that when you have problems out here, people are always willing to help you out—unlike in the UK, where it's every man for himself. I agreed with him. It did seem like a big family out here.

Scott asked me if I'd like to spin a few tunes to see what I was like as a DJ, so I took Danny's place, stopped the music dead, and shouted out, "Okay, it's time to liven it up in here a bit, so I want to see everybody up dancing and having fun." With that I threw on some upbeat dance music, and everyone just went crazy, whooping with delight. I lost track of the time playing the music as I was now in my element. This was one of the things I loved doing.

Between me and Danny we played until dawn. Once we'd finished, we threw on a CD and went over to join the others for a well-earned drink. Most of the people started to leave, complimenting us on a great party as they went. Only about a dozen of us were left to talk about the things that had gone on that night.

Scott topped up the drinks, and Tony rolled a few joints to pass around. I liked to smoke pot occasionally to relax, but I'd never smoked it in front of Nicola before, so I asked her if she minded. She told me that she'd never smoked a joint before but didn't mind if I did. I asked her if she wanted to try some, and she said yes, so I passed it to her and she started smoking it like a cigarette, which made me laugh.

"What are you laughing at?" she asked me.

"You're supposed to inhale slowly and deeply, hold it in your lungs for a few seconds, and then exhale."

So that's what she did, coughing a little to start with, but she got used to it after a while. After several joints had been passed around, everyone started to feel a little stoned, including Nicola.

Scott said that he didn't think any of us were in a fit state to go home, so he suggested that we all stayed there. We staggered to our feet, and he showed us to one of the bedrooms. We said our goodnights and fell onto the bed laughing. I think it was about that time that the room started spinning for us, and I remember both of us saying that we would never touch another drink again.

The next thing I knew it was daylight. I glanced over to the clock and saw that it was almost midday. I was still feeling a bit rough, so I got up and made my way to the bathroom. I took off my boxers and walked up to the shower. Still half-asleep, I pulled the curtain to one side, not realizing that there was someone already in there. It was Fallon. She had just finished showering and was about to step out to dry herself off. I was a little embarrassed to say the least.

"I'm really sorry. I didn't realize that you were in there."

I half-expected her to go mad at me or scream or something, but to my surprise she did neither. Instead she told me not to worry about it, and anyway she said that she was sure that I'd seen plenty of naked girls before in my time.

We both laughed at the predicament that we'd found ourselves in. Fallon said that unless I wanted her to join me in the shower to wash my back or something, then I should pass her the towel so that she could dry herself off. As tempted as I was, I passed her the towel and wrapped another around my waist to cover my dignity.

As Fallon went to leave the bathroom she told me not to worry as she wouldn't say anything to Nicola. I smiled and gave her a hug to say thanks, and she left and closed the door behind her.

I jumped into the shower and then made my way back to the bedroom to get dressed. Nicola was just starting to stir now, and she asked me if I'd make her some coffee. She looked as fragile as I did when I'd first got up. After all, it wasn't that long ago that we were lying there watching the room spin from all the alcohol we'd put away the night before.

I kissed her on the lips and told her that I'd be back in a while. With that, Nicola got up and made her way to the bathroom, and I went into the kitchen to put the kettle on. Scott, Danny, Kirby, and Fallon were all sitting around the table eating breakfast, and I joined them while I was waiting for the kettle to boil.

Danny told me that he thought that the set we'd played last night was wicked and that everyone enjoyed themselves. Scott said that if I ever fancied working at Linekers, then I only had to ask and the job was mine. He thought that between me and Danny we could pack the place. I thanked him for his offer but told him that we were only here on holiday and hadn't planned on staying any longer, although I had to admit that I was tempted by his offer.

The kettle boiled and I finished making the coffee and went back to the bedroom to re-join Nicola. She finished getting ready, and we both went into the kitchen and chatted for a while longer. We thanked Scott for the party and for letting us stay, and then after saying goodbye we jumped into a cab and made our way back to our apartment in Fuengirola. We got changed and spent the rest of the day on the beach, avoiding alcohol like the plague. Then we got some food inside us and made our way back to the hotel for an early night.

I'd have to say that I was used to staying out late in the UK because of the lifestyle that I led, but even by my standards this had been a hectic few days, and it had taken its toll on the both of us.

We spent the next few days just exploring the area. We went everywhere from Torremolinos to Malaga and back. In the evenings we checked out most of the local English bars, making quite a few friends along the way. We didn't run into any of the Linekers crew again until the Friday night.

We had just sat down to look at the menu at the German restaurant on the port front, when Luciana, Kirby, and Fallon walked in with their boyfriends. Nicola spotted them and called them over to join us. They seemed really pleased to see us, and there were the usual hugs and kisses all around.

We sat down, ordered our meals, and chatted for what seemed like forever over dinner until about 9.30 p.m., when Tony and Luciana said they had to go as they had to start work at 10 p.m. They asked us to pop in and see them a bit later and then got up, said their goodbyes, and made their way back to Linekers. Robbie and Ricky were the next to go, leaving just the four of us chatting. We called the waiter over to ask for the bill, and Nicola and Kirby got up to go to the loo, leaving just me and Fallon together at the table.

"It's good to see you again. I thought you'd been avoiding me because of what happened at Scott's house."

"It's good to see you too and no, Fallon, I wasn't avoiding you. I've just been exploring the area and spending a few days with Nicola."

Fallon paused for a few seconds and then asked me if I'd liked what I'd seen in the shower at Scott's villa the other night. I smiled and told her that I thought that she had a very sexy body and of course, being a red-blooded male, how could I not like seeing a beautiful girl still wet from the shower standing naked in front of me. Besides, I was also standing there naked, so I would have thought that it was pretty obvious how I felt!

Fallon giggled and told me that she couldn't help noticing that something was stirring. She told me that she was kind of disappointed that I hadn't invited her to join me in the shower. We both laughed, and I told her to behave herself. I said that I had only recently met Nicola and that I felt that I had made a strong connection with her. I wasn't the type of person that cheated on people easily, so I wouldn't be looking for any extra activity at this time. She said that if ever I change my mind, I'd only have to ask and she was all mine. I leaned over to Fallon and gave her a gentle kiss on the lips and told her that I was flattered by her advances but I felt that I had to decline at this moment in time.

At this point Nicola and Kirby returned. We paid the bill and then all left together, making our way over to the London Bar for a while before moving on to Linekers. The terrace was packed with people, as there was a hypnotist show going on, so we grabbed one of the few remaining tables, and the girls sat down while I went up for the drinks. I said hello to Tony who was working on the door, got the drinks, and made my way back to the girls.

We all sat down and watched the show. It was very funny; they had people up doing all sorts of stupid things. The show finished at about midnight, after which most of the customers got up and went inside. Danny started playing the music, and Tony closed the terrace doors. He told me that they had to do this as they were not allowed to let the sound travel outside the bar after midnight. We stayed in Linekers until it closed at 2 a.m. and then made our excuses and went back to the hotel to crash.

Nicola woke me up at around 10 a.m., and we made our way down to Scottie's for breakfast, only to find that it was closed for the day, so we decided to walk along the coastline to try to find another place to eat. Eventually we came across a breakfast bar called Gina's. It was very much like all the others with an open terrace looking onto the sea front.

We sat down at a table and a woman came over to serve us. Whilst ordering our food, I noticed a for-sale sign in the window, and I asked the woman why she wanted to sell up. She told us that she had moved out here with her family six months ago to try to make a new life for themselves. They thought it would be very easy to do, but they were now finding it difficult to make a success out of the business. She also told us that in reality it was extremely hard work with long hours, which didn't suit them as they also had two young children living out here with them.

Out of interest, I asked her how much she was looking to sell the bar for. She told us that they were hoping to get twenty grand, which is roughly what they paid for it. With that, she went back inside to give our orders to the cook and to serve some other customers. We both thought the price was fairly reasonable, considering how much it would cost to set up a bar in England.

The conversation that we'd just had with the woman had definitely sparked our interest, so we decided to find out exactly what would be involved in setting up a business out here. Nicola suggested that we should check out a few estate agents to make some inquiries. We hadn't made any plans, so that's what we did for the rest of the day. By the evening we'd found out quite a lot. There were quite a few businesses for sale—mainly bars and cafes, ranging from ten grand and up, depending on where they were situated and how big they were. In most cases they were asking for a premium for the lease and then a monthly rent, but in some cases you could rent without paying a premium.

We also found out that to be able to work out here you simply had to go down to the local police station to register for a national insurance number, and then two weeks later you'd be up and running. You didn't even need to appear in front of a judge to get a drinks license; you just paid a fee to the town hall and the license was yours.

We eventually got back to our apartment at about 2 p.m. feeling exhausted. Our feet were sore from all the walking about that we'd done, so we slept for a few hours until about 6 p.m.

Since this would be our last Saturday night out here, we decided to go out for the night, so after getting ready we made our way down to the port area for dinner before going on to the London Bar for a drink to start the night off. The bar was only half full as it was still quite early, and anyway things never really kicked into gear out here until about 9.30 p.m.

Nicola made her way up to the bar while I grabbed a table. I was just about to sit down when I felt a tap on my shoulder. I turned around to find Scott and Danny standing there with drinks in hand.

"What are you two doing here? Aren't you supposed to be working?"

Danny looked at me and said, "Actually we were kind of hoping to run in to you." I asked them to take a seat and explain. Scott started telling me that a few weeks ago he had organized a party at Linekers for tonight. Apparently the footballer Gary Lineker and a few of his footballing mates were going to be here to help promote the family business, and Scott had flown in a couple of extra DJs from the UK to help the night go with a bang. The problem they had was that one of the DJs had managed to get himself arrested last night for being drunk and disorderly, and the local police were refusing to let him go until Monday morning when the courts opened. As you can imagine, this left them with a major problem. Scott didn't want to lose face in front of everyone, especially with Gary Lineker being over here, so they were looking for a replacement who was competent enough to fill in for him, and the first name that popped into their heads was mine.

At this point Nicola returned with the drinks, and I filled her in on the situation. Once I knew Nicola was cool about it, I agreed to help Scott out. We finished our drinks and made our way over to Linekers. The bar was still closed to the public as they were getting ready for the night's entertainment, and the staff were buzzing around everywhere trying to sort things out. Kirby, Fallon, and a few of the others were getting the promotional fliers ready, and Luciana and the rest of the bar staff were busy stocking up the fridges and the bar. Scott went into his office, and Danny made his was up to the DJ booth to show the other DJ where everything was. Nicola asked if there was anything that she could do to help, and Kirby told her that she could help her by giving out the fliers if she wanted too. I gave Nicola a kiss and then joined Danny at the DJ booth to go through the equipment with him.

I glanced over to the entrance and saw Tony walking in followed by the main man himself—Gary Lineker and a few of his friends. They walked up to the bar to get a drink, and then Gary walked around the bar to introduce himself to all the staff, eventually making his way up to me, Danny, and the other DJ, whose name was Andy.

I couldn't quite believe it. Here I was working as a DJ in Spain for the night and shaking hands with the infamous Gary Lineker! Is that mad or what? I didn't really say much to him, as for once I was actually lost for words. He shook my hand and wished us luck and then made his way over to see Scott in his office. The bar opened at about 10.45 p.m., and sure enough, the place was packed in less than half an hour. Danny started the night off playing party tracks from the eighties while I took requests and chatted to the crowd on the mike.

Danny handed over the decks to Andy at about midnight, and we made our way over to the bar for refreshments. Luciana came over to tell us that all the staff were going on to a club later at the expense of Gary Lineker as a way of saying thank you, and she wondered if Nicola and I would like to join them. I told her that we'd love to come and thanked her for inviting us. I was going to ask Luciana which club they were planning on going to, but she was too busy to chat as the other bar staff were being run off their feet, what with all the people in here tonight, and on top of that the new DJ Andy had just about everybody dancing on the tables, singing, and generally going crazy.

At this point Fallon came in and led a group of lads up to the bar. She spotted me straight away and threw her arms around me. She pressed herself against me and planted a big sloppy kiss on my lips.

"Hiya, sexy, are you enjoying yourself?"

"What is there not to enjoy? This place is fantastic. Great music, great lifestyle, and I'm always surrounded by sexy, bubbly people. Like I said, what's not to enjoy?"

"When you say 'sexy people', I hope you're including me in that statement," said Fallon, twirling her hair.

"Of course, that goes without saying," I replied. I asked her how Nicola was getting on, and she told me that she seemed quite a natural when it came to chatting up the lads to get them inside the bar. Fallon asked me how long it was going to be before I went up to play my set. I told her that I was up next, probably in the next half an hour. With that she grabbed my hand and pulled me over to the dance floor.

"Come on! You only live once, so let your hair down and enjoy yourself."

I didn't really have time to object, and before I knew it we were both on the floor, dancing to the tunes that Andy was spinning. Fallon seemed really charged tonight. By that I mean that she had trouble standing still and she couldn't stop talking. A short while later Nicola and Kirby came into the bar and joined us on the dance floor.

"You two look like you're having fun. So what's going on here then?"

"We're just having a laugh—nothing for you to worry your pretty face about!"

Nicola grabbed hold of me and kissed me smack on the lips as if to mark her territory. "It's okay," she said with a smile. "I was only winding you up. It's great here isn't it?"

"Yeah, it's a shame that we're going home in a couple of days."

"All the more reason to make the most of our time left out here then."

I told Nicola that we'd been invited to a club later with the rest of the staff, which brought a big smile to her face. We carried on dancing together until Andy stopped the music to announce Gary Lineker's presence in the bar. Everybody clapped and cheered as he made his way up to the microphone. He thanked everyone for coming and said that for the next ten minutes the drinks were on him. Suffice to say, this brought another cheer from the crowd, followed by a mad rush to the bar.

Andy beckoned me up to the DJ booth to take over from him. I wasn't quite sure how I was going to follow Andy's set, as he was a very good DJ, so I decided to wing it for a bit by playing a few participation games with the audience. I started off by giving half a dozen girls the task of persuading as many lads as possible to give up their underwear to them and said that the winner would be the girl that collected the most. This caused pandemonium in the bar that you wouldn't believe! It was extremely funny, and eventually we had a winner; one of the girls had managed to collect nearly a dozen pairs.

Once I'd finished with the girls, I reversed the roles with the lads having to get as many bras as possible, and as you can imagine, this was equally as amusing. Chants of "Get your tits out for the lads!" rippled through the bar. Like the boys, the girls were eager to comply, baring their breast to all without a care in the world. Everyone seemed to be having a great time, including me. There was a great buzz in here tonight.

I followed the games with an hour of playing music and finished my set to cheers and screams for more. Danny took over from me to finish the night off, and I made my way back over to the girls, who were now propped up against the bar knocking back the drinks like there was no tomorrow. Nicola spotted me coming towards her and flung her arms around me, kissing me again and again.

"I take it you're pleased to see me then, and maybe a little plastered?" I said.

"Yes, a lot plastered actually, and very pleased to see you. You were great, babe." She'd obviously had quite a bit to drink by now, and I was keen to catch up with her and enjoy the rest of the evening with everyone, so I spent the next hour slowly getting pissed and larking about with the girls until the bar eventually closed at about 3 a.m. All the staff were gathered together to be congratulated by Scott and Garry. It had been a total success, and there were free drinks all around.

We stayed in Linekers until about 4 a.m. and then set off towards the 57 Club, which was situated about half a mile along the coast from the port. On the way down to the club, Scott personally thanked me again for helping him out tonight and invited me and Nicola to a pool party that he was having at his villa on Monday afternoon. Of course, I told him that we'd love to come and thanked him for the invitation.

The club seemed quite busy inside, and like the Underground club, we didn't have to pay to get in. It seemed commonplace out here to only charge the tourists and to let the residents in for free. The club was quite a dimly lit place, with upholstered seating and low-level tables scattered about everywhere. There was the usual designated dance area, and, of course, the bar, which had pictures of Cindy Beale from the television series *East Enders* scattered about on the back wall. Scott told me that he believed the owner was dating her or something.

Most of the girls made their way onto the dance floor, whilst the rest of us made a beeline for the bar. We stayed in there partying until they kicked us out at about 8 a.m. I remember leaving the place and walking up some steps into the blinding sunshine. Most people had come prepared and had put their sunglasses on before leaving the club. I couldn't help but giggle to myself, thinking that they had obviously done this many times before. We said our goodbyes and made our way back to the apartment, where we crashed out for the rest of the day, getting up only for something to eat before crashing out again until Monday morning.

The morning came around before we knew it. Nicola was up before me and was busy packing up most of our stuff. I told her to leave it until later as we weren't flying back until 11.30, but she insisted on finishing her task, saying that it was better to do it now than to have to rush around at the last minute.

After getting dressed, we made our way down to the port for some breakfast, and Nicola compiled a list of the presents that we had to take back for our friends. I reminded her that we'd been invited to Scott's pool party which was due to start in a few hours' time, so after eating and doing a bit of last-minute shopping, we made our way back to the apartment to grab our swimming stuff and to drop off the gifts we'd just brought. We then grabbed a cab to Mijas to join Scott and the others at his villa.

By the time we got there, the party was in full swing. Scott had set up a barbeque by the pool, and the music was playing through the patio doors. Nicola spotted the gang from Linekers, and we made our way over to them, hugging and kissing them all. Scott told us to help ourselves to the food and drinks, and we sat down around the pool chatting and jumping in and out of the water. We must have spoken about everything that we had got up to in the short space of time that we'd been out here.

I don't think I can ever remember feeling happier or more at home anywhere in my life than I did at that moment in time, but eventually we had to say our goodbyes as we were due to fly back to England in a few hours' time. It was a strange feeling saying goodbye to all these people, and there were a few tears and a lot of hugs and kisses all around. I guess you could say that we had strong feelings of mixed emotions. On the one hand we felt really happy at having made such great friends, and we'd had a terrific time out here, but on the other hand we were quite understandably upset and sad at having to leave them all behind and go back to our humdrum lives in the UK.

Scott repeated his offer of a job for me if I ever changed my mind, and I thanked him once again and wished him well. We said our last goodbyes and then left to make our way back to collect our bags. Then we went on to the airport, where we met up with the other couple of girls with whom we'd originally come out here. They said their goodbyes to the lads they'd hooked up with out here, and we checked in our bags.

After a long wait, we finally boarded our plane and took off for our flight home to England.

CHAPTER THREE

Setting the Wheels in Motion

I slept for most of the flight home, only waking to feel a cold chill running up my legs and the sound of the pilot's voice being broadcasted across the plane telling us that we were now making our descent into Luton Airport. The plane landed about five minutes later, and we all made our way into the baggage hall to collect our bags, and then out of the departure gate and into the pouring rain. Typical, isn't it? We'd only been back for five minutes and already we were soaked to the bone!

It took us about half an hour to get back and drop off the other girls. We then made our way to Nicola's flat, unloaded our luggage, and went inside, throwing our bags down in the front room. Nicola made a cup of tea to take to bed with us as we were feeling pretty knackered after all that travelling, and it wasn't long before we were both sound asleep in the land of nod.

We spent the next day visiting friends and telling them all about the people we'd met in Spain and going over just about every experience that we'd had out there. It was good to talk about it, as it brought back so many great memories. The only problem was that by the time we'd got back in the evening and relaxed, we found ourselves feeling quite deflated It had now dawned on us that we were finally back in England!

"I feel quite down now," said Nicola.

"Yeah, I know what you mean. I'm missing Spain already."

"Same here. Don't you just wish we could live out there?"

"Well, if that's how you feel, then why don't we move out there? What's to stop us?"

"It's a nice idea but . . .," said Nicola, smiling.

"But what? What is it that you'd be giving up by going?"

"You're serious, aren't you?"

"Of course I'm serious! We could raise some money and set up shop out there. You said yourself that you loved it over there, so why not?"

It was Nicola's turn to be lost for words. She just sat there deep in thought. There was a silent pause of about two or three minutes. Then I broke the silence and told Nicola that I'd be prepared to give up my work in England if she decided she wanted to go. Nicola went to answer me but I stopped her, saying that she should sleep on it first and then let me know her answer when she was good and ready.

I tried for ages to get to sleep that night, tossing and turning until the early hours. If I was lucky, I might have got a few short naps later on. Nicola was the same. We both got up the next day feeling totally exhausted. The worst part of it all was that we were both due back at work that day. I guess in hindsight that we should have rung in the day before and taken the rest of the week off, but I suppose that's what they call sod's law, isn't it?

As you can imagine, I struggled that day at work and found it difficult to concentrate, not just because I was extremely tired but also because all I could think about was the possibility of starting a new life in Spain. It seemed that I'd planted a seed in my own head as much as in Nicola's, but you know what they say. Once you start the ball rolling, it's difficult to stop it. Far easier to jump on the band wagon and enjoy the ride, wherever it may take you.

I didn't mention any more on the subject that week, as I wanted to give us both time to think about it, but by the time Friday night came around, I was itching to talk about it. In fact I was practically arguing with myself to bring the subject up again. I suggested to Nicola that we should go out to the local pub for a drink and for something to eat. Nicola hadn't said any more on the subject since I'd spoke about it earlier in the week, but I couldn't control my thoughts any longer. Before Nicola could take the first bite of her meal, I blurted it out.

"Well, what do you think? Have you made your mind up yet?"

"What do you mean? Made my mind up about what?"

"You know what I mean. Don't toy with me," I said.

"Oh, you're talking about Spain, aren't you?" replied Nicola.

"Of course. What else would I be talking about? I was serious when I asked you."

Nicola paused for a moment before saying, "Yes, I've thought about nothing else, turning it over and over in my mind, but I didn't say any more about it because you hadn't mentioned it since the other night."

"It's funny, I was waiting for you to talk about it first, as I didn't want to pressure you. Well, you still haven't answered my question. What have you decided?"

"Can I eat my meal first before I give you my answer?"

"You bitch! I can't believe you could be so heartless as to make me suffer for another half an hour. You're outrageous!"

Nicola just looked at me, trying her best to keep a straight face, but eventually she burst into laughter. "I'm sorry. I couldn't resist it, babe. You're so impatient, aren't you?" she said, still giggling to herself.

"Please, Nicola, do you want me to get down on one knee and beg you?"

"That's what I like to see—a man at my feet," chuckled Nicola.

With that I got off my chair and dropped to my knees. I took Nicola's hand in mine and began to plead for an answer.

"Get up, you fool. You're embarrassing me."

"Not until I get an answer out of you," I said.

"Okay, okay, just get up. Everybody's looking at us." I stood up, and still holding her hand, I asked her again. "Yes! My answer is yes! Are you happy now?" she replied quite loudly.

I leaned over the table and pulled her towards me and planted a big kiss on those luscious lips of hers and gave her a big hug. To our surprise the whole restaurant erupted into cheers and started clapping. Looking straight at each other, it dawned on us that anyone looking on must have thought that I'd just proposed to Nicola. We both found this very amusing, but we decided not to let on about their error. We just went along with it for a laugh, and as a bonus the manger gave us a large bottle of bubbly on the house to celebrate.

As you can imagine, it turned out to be a very late night. When we finally got home, we ended up staying up for most of the night going over different ideas about which sort of business we'd like to run in Spain. We avoided the obvious choice of setting up a bar at first, as we thought that the competition would be too fierce. After all, there are many bars out there. I suggested that I'd like to run a night club, but we also ruled that out, as we thought that it would probably be out of our price range. Nicola said that she'd like to run a hairdresser's, but what would I do in there? I'm not really the type of guy for blue rinses and flower talking old ladies, so eventually we came back to our original thoughts and settled on a small bar with daytime food and music in the evening.

As far as funding the project, we decided that I would sell my house and Nicola would raise some money from the collateral on her flat and then rent it out through an agency. That way we'd always have something to come back to if everything went tits up! Well, that's Nicola for you, always planning ahead.

Over the next few weeks I put my house up for sale. Nicola applied for a secured loan, and we enquired into what sort of rent we'd get for the flat. It turned out that we'd be able to cover her mortgage and still have a little left over from the rent for ourselves. I'd bought my house from the council just over three years ago for only thirty-five thousand pounds, as I'd been given a sixty per cent discount on account of time served, so to speak. I hadn't been able to sell it up to now, as you have to pay back the discount if you sell it before the three-year period that the council sets you. The full market value of the property had risen considerably over the last few years, and it was now said to be worth around a hundred and twenty grand. This meant that after paying back the bank and legal fees, I stood to gain around eighty thousand pounds towards our project, and with the extra money that Nicola could raise as well, we should have more than enough to pay for the project ahead.

It wasn't long before I received a solid offer on the house, which I accepted, and then we got on with the process of moving my personal possessions into Nicola's flat. It seemed that we were now a *bona fide* couple. Our relationship had developed very quickly, but as I've said before, it felt like it was meant to be. It was certainly strong enough to make me want to move in with Nicola without any obvious reservations whatsoever.

We were told that it would take about six to eight weeks to complete the sale of my house. We didn't see any reason to wait that long to get the ball rolling, so we booked a flight to Spain in a couple of weeks' time so that we could start searching for the bar that would reshape our future. We hadn't told anyone about our plans yet, as we didn't want to tempt fate. After all, nothing was set in stone yet.

The two-week wait seemed to take forever. It's funny, isn't it? Time seems to go so slowly when you're waiting for things to happen. Hence the old saying, 'A watched pot never boils." Eventually the time came around though, and we packed our bags and were once again heading for the airport, this time with a different agenda in mind!

We arrived at Malaga airport at around midday, and as soon as we walked through the departure gates we felt a sense of *déjà vu* as the searing heat hit us once again. All the memories from a few weeks ago came flooding back. It was as if we'd never left. I guess the only way I could explain it would be to say it was like coming home!

We'd booked in to stay at the same hotel as before in front of the London Bar in Fuengirola, as we felt familiar with the area now. One of the first things that we did after settling into the apartment was to go down to the high street to hire a car. The thought of all that walking about in the searing heat of the day searching for bars to lease was enough to convince us that it would be money well spent.

Once we had the car, we drove down to the local police station to register for our national insurance numbers which would allow us to work legally in Spain. For this we had to supply a couple of passport photos and fill in a form using our passports as ID. We were told to return in a couple of weeks' time to pick up the paper work. It was a very simple procedure.

It was about 5 p.m. by the time we left the police station, and most of the shops were now starting to open up after the usual siesta shut-down period. We decided to go on a tour of all the estate agents in the area to see if we could set up a series of viewing appointments and generally to look at lists of all the businesses that were available. Nicola made a list of all the bars that we were interested in, and we left our mobile number for the estate agents to contact us once they'd arranged the viewings. It was about 8 p.m. by the time we'd got back to the apartment, and as you can imagine, we were starting to feel a little tired, so we hit the showers, got changed, and headed back out for some food and refreshments.

We decided to make our way down to the German restaurant called the Ku Dam on the port near to Linekers bar, as we remembered that the food and service down there was excellent. We found a table and then ordered our meals from one of the waiters.

I glanced up at Nicola and thought to myself that she looked so happy and contented just sitting there. In my heart I knew that we were doing the right thing moving out to Spain. Being here felt like we had a purpose to our lives—like it was meant to be! Nicola looked up and caught me staring at her, and I felt a smile creep across my face.

"What are you looking so happy about?" she asked.

"I just can't believe that we're sitting here in the process of starting a new life together."

"Yeah, I know what you mean. It's hard to take it all in."

"It's unbelievable. To think I only met you a few months ago, and now here we are planning our future together abroad. I guess I just can't stop smiling."

We spent the best part of two hours in the restaurant, trying to take in what we were about to do. We both seemed to be on a continual high.

"Well we can't go home too early on our first night back here, so why don't we try to track down Luciana, Tony, and the others at Linekers and make a night of it," said Nicola.

We paid the bill and left the restaurant to walk along the port towards Linekers. Nicola stopped for a second to take in the view, and I pulled her towards me and gave her a long sexy kiss.

"Hmm . . . what was that for?"

"Because I think that you're the most beautiful and sexiest woman in the world and because I love you."

"Ah, be careful! Flattery will get you everywhere," she replied, giggling.

"That's what I was hoping."

We both burst into laughter and carried on towards Linekers. The evening was just starting to go into full swing. What you've got to understand about Spain is that in the daytime there is a different sort of person on the streets; it's more your family and middle-aged type of person bustling around, shopping, sightseeing, and of course lying about on the beach catching the rays from the sun, but in the evening most of these people seem to disappear into their homes and hotel bars, and then the night crowd starts to appear. They are a much younger and more vibrant type of person. By that I don't mean just teenagers; there is also the thirties-to-forties age bracket, but with a much younger and more relaxed attitude towards life.

As we approached Linekers, the first friendly face that we recognized was Tony. He was standing at the entrance of the bar, and his face lit up the moment he saw us. He stretched out a hand to welcome me back and then hugged and kissed Nicola on the cheeks.

"So how have you been? It seems ages since we saw you last," said Tony.

"We've been doing okay. In fact you may be seeing a lot more of us if things work out."

"Oh yeah? Tell me more."

"Not just yet, Tony. You'll have to wait a little longer for that information. So how's Luciana? Is she about?"

"Yeah, she's great, thanks, and she's working behind the bar tonight." With that he walked us up to the bar and beckoned her over. Luciana spotted us with Tony and came running over, screaming that girly noise that the women seem to make out here, and of course Nicola didn't waste too much time getting back into the swing of things and was soon screeching right back at her. We were both smothered in cuddles and kisses. I must admit I still found this quite amusing if not a little embarrassing.

Luciana and Tony both took a break, and we all sat down at a table on the terrace and started chatting. We were all genuinely pleased to see each other again.

"So have you two seen anyone else out here yet?" asked Luciana.

"Not yet. We only arrived here today."

"So what's this you were telling me earlier about seeing a lot more of you then?" asked Tony.

Nicola looked straight at me. I could tell that she was busting at the seams to tell them about our plans. Like every woman, she just loved to gossip!

"Go ahead, Nicola. You can tell them if you want."

"Thanks, babe," she said, blowing me a kiss.

Well there was no stopping her now. It all came out how we were so impressed with the lifestyle and how much we loved the people out here. Tony and Luciana were delighted with the news.

"This calls for a celebration!" they both said.

"Remember we haven't actually found anything yet."

"Not yet, but I'm sure you will," said Tony.

We all toasted to our future success, and Tony then told us that if ever we needed any help in regards to the law or the language out here, then I only had to ask. As I said before, people always seemed willing to go that extra yard for you out here. There was a sense of camaraderie amongst the English that didn't seem to exist back in the UK.

We stayed in Linekers until it closed and then went on to the Underground nightclub until the early hours, where we eventually said our goodbyes and headed back to the hotel to crash out for what we hoped would be a very productive day ahead.

Sure enough, by 10 a.m. the next morning the mobile started ringing, and within the space of an hour of so we'd set up a dozen viewings. Suffice to say, we were very excited. Nicola had staggered the appointments with the estate agents at half-hour intervals. As usual she was very organized. We grabbed a breakfast at Scottie's and then made our way up to our first appointment in Los Boliches, which is on the edge of Fuengirola. To give you an idea of the layout of the area, there is one main road that runs from Malaga down to Torremolinos and Benalmadena and then on to Los Boliches, Fuengirola, and after a few small towns, down to Marbella and on to Gibraltar. This coastline is better known as the Costa del Sol, or to some as the Costa del Crime!

We met the estate agent outside a bar facing the beech in Los Boliches. He sorted the keys out and we went inside. The bar was filled with sports memorabilia, and there were oak tables and chairs everywhere. It was very clean and well presented, and you'd have to say that at just under £30,000 it was definitely a bargain. The only drawback we could see was that it was in Los Boliches, as opposed to being in the heart of Fuengirola where most of the passing trade was. We looked at half a dozen other bars on the outskirts of Fuengirola, but none of them were a patch on the first bar we'd seen.

After taking a break for food and refreshments, we made our way down to the next appointment, which was a bar down on the port in Fuengirola. The bar was in a great location, but unfortunately it only catered for around twenty people. This seemed to be the case for most of the bars in the central area, unless you were prepared to pay silly money for a bigger bar.

It was now 7.30 p.m. and our last appointment wasn't until 10 p.m. This was the only time that the owner was available to open up for us. We had a bit of time to kill, so we went back to our hotel room to freshen up and then onto the London Bar, before making our way up to the last viewing.

We arrived back at the bar, which was located one street back from the sea front. It was on the main high street, which was only a few doors down from the bus station, so the location was great. We walked up to the bar's entrance, where we met the estate agent and the owner a Mr Larry

Greenwood. The bar was located underground beneath some apartments and offices and was surrounded by metal gates and fencing.

We introduced ourselves to the owner, and he unlocked the gates and we descended down some concrete steps that led to the front doors of the club. We went down a short corridor into what could only be described as a huge room with its own dance floor and seating areas and a fully equipped DJ booth. There were mirrors and lights all over the walls and bar front and a very long bar that stretched from the DJ booth right around to the entrance where we first came in. Behind the bar by the entrance was a door that led to a small room and then back out into the entrance corridor, where you could also find the toilets.

What could I say? The place was incredible!

It had the potential capacity of around 200 people and was fully air-conditioned, with blue and red cushioned seating around the dance area. On the negative side, I'd have to say it had a bit of a damp smell as it had obviously stood empty for quite a while. Also, it would have to be run as an evening bar only. But that aside, I'd have to say that we fell in love with it.

Next came the big question . . . the price?

We expected it to be well out of our price range, but to our surprise Larry was only looking for a premium of £45,000 for a four-year repeated lease with all the contents included and a monthly rent of £800. We'd have to set up licenses and take the usual health and safety courses to operate the bar, and we'd have to get a solicitor to draw up the contracts to make it all legal. Since I was a child, one of my dreams had been to have my own club. Don't ask me why. It was just one of those silly ideas that you get in your head when you're young, and here I was standing on the verge of achieving it.

Nicola took Larry's business card, and we told him that we'd call him tomorrow with a final decision. We shook hands and then left and made our way down to Linekers so that we could relax and chat about everything that we'd seen that day. We had so much to take in from the events of the day, but to be perfectly honest with you, in our minds there were only two candidates that fitted the bill. They were the bar in Los Boliches and, of course, the evening bar that we'd just seen. After a lot of discussion between us about the two bars, it seemed quite obvious to us that although we'd lose the food and daytime trade by selecting the night club, it was too good an opportunity to miss. So we decided to take our chances on the late bar. This was quite an exciting moment for us, but at the same time it was a little scary. We decided to call it a night and headed back to our hotel to get a good night's sleep so as to be ready for the day ahead.

At about 9 a.m. the next morning the mobile started ringing. I couldn't be bothered to get up and answer it, so I gave Nicola a nudge.

"Nicola, the phone's ringing. You'd better answer it as it might be important."

Nicola reached over to the bedside cabinet and grabbed the mobile. "Hello," she said.

The volume on the phone was turned up fairly loud, so I could hear the other person on the phone. It was the estate agent. He wanted to know whether or not we'd made any decision on the bars he'd shown us yesterday. Nicola told him that we'd decided to make an offer of £35,000 on the late bar and asked him to get back to us as soon as possible if that was acceptable to him. She thanked him for calling and then hung up the phone, before snuggling back up to me, and then we both dozed back off to sleep.

You know, they say in Spain that you should never expect a quick answer as everything over here is *manana*, which means "tomorrow", but to our surprise we received another phone call a couple of hours later from the estate agent, saying that he'd spoken to Larry and that he'd accepted our offer, providing that we agreed to pay three months' rent up front as soon as we'd signed the contracts, and he also wanted us to put down a deposit of £2,000 this week to secure the offer we'd made. I told the agent that that would be acceptable to us and that we'd be in touch with him as soon as we'd spoken to our solicitor to arrange the necessary paperwork. I thanked the agent for calling and hung up the phone.

We got up and went down to Scottie's for breakfast, before heading into town to see the solicitor to talk about setting up the contracts and any other legalities that we'd have to go through. Our solicitor was an English woman called Rosa. She had lived in Spain all her life, and she knew all the ins and outs of the legal system out here, so we felt quite confident about her.

Rosa told us that we'd have to pay for the license and set up a health and safety inspection from the fire brigade to get the required certificates to be able to operate the bar. This involved getting the required fire extinguishers and fire proofing treatment for any materials in the bar and checking that all entrances and exits were up to scratch. We'd also have to take a health and safety course to be able to work in the bar, and Rosa would have to do the usual searches on the business to make sure that we didn't inherit any past debts. As far as the time limit was concerned, she told us that the whole process should take about ten weeks to complete, which seemed like a reasonable time frame to us.

Rosa also gave us a legal document for Larry to sign once we'd handed the deposit over to him, which would basically make him accountable and would make the sale legally binding. The approximate cost of the solicitor would be around £2,000. Rosa told us that she would get onto it straight away. We thanked her and said our goodbyes.

No sooner had we had left the solicitor's than the mobile rang. It was the agent again, saying that he'd spoken to Larry and that he was eager to go ahead with the deal. I told him that we'd seen our solicitor and that we were happy to meet with Larry that evening to sort out the deposit and to get the ball rolling. It wasn't until I'd hung up the phone that I realized that we hadn't brought enough cash with us. Everything had happened so quickly that we hadn't had time to think things through properly. We managed to resolve the problem by way of credit cards, and although this left us a bit short of spending money, it seemed the only course of action for us to take.

We met Larry later that evening and got him to sign the document that Rosa had given us and handed him the deposit as arranged. After that we made our way down to the London Bar for a drink to celebrate what we had just achieved. We walked up to the bar and ordered our drinks from the barman.

While we were standing there, we overheard the conversation of a couple of lads who were standing next to us at the bar. One of them said to the other that apparently a London couple had just bought the late bar that we'd just secured and were planning to open it up shortly. We were quite shocked at hearing this as we'd only just handed over the deposit and shaken hands with Larry on the deal. News seemed to travel extremely fast out here. I was tempted to say something to them, bearing in mind that I wasn't actually a Londoner. I was an Essex boy and proud of it. However, we decided not to intervene as we didn't want to fuel any gossip, so instead we just sat down and laughed about it. We stayed in the bar for another hour or so just relaxing, before going back to our hotel for a night of debauchery and passion to celebrate.

We got up the next morning realizing that we'd pretty much achieved all that we'd set out to do on this visit, and rather than spend any more time here waiting for things to happen, we decided that it was time for us to return to the UK to tie up any loose ends in preparation for things to come. We rang to arrange a flight home, packed our bags, and headed for the airport. After the usual airport wait, we were on our way home again.

CHAPTER FOUR

The Final Preparations

The next few weeks passed by in a flash. Unlike before when we were waiting to go out to Spain to find something, there didn't seem to be enough time now to get everything done. But surprisingly after a lot of rushing around, everything seemed to fall into place.

The sale on the house finalized okay, and we managed to line up a tenant for Nicola's flat. We transferred the funds over to Rosa our solicitor in Spain, and she completed the paperwork for the lease on the bar. She also managed to sort out a long-term rental on a villa for us. All that was left to do now was to finish packing in preparation for the big move to Spain!

Well, it was now the day of reckoning, and I couldn't begin to describe to you how excited we both were. Nicola was running around like a headless chicken, and I must say I found it quite surreal watching someone else going through the same excitement and anxieties as myself.

We'd decided to drive out to Spain with the help of a good friend of mine called Alan who owned a large Luton-bodied van, which was the perfect size for packing away all our worldly goods. Alan was twenty-six years old, the same age as me. He had worked for the same painting company as I did for the last few years, and we'd become quite good friends. He had short dark hair and, like me, he had quite a sarcastic sense of humour.

Alan and I had agreed to share the driving of the van between us, and Nicola was going to follow us in her car with one of her mates who was called Peta. Peta was twenty-three years old, and, like Nicola, she had long brown hair. Best of all, she came from my neck of the woods in Essex. Nicola had known Peta for a few years now, and from the few times I'd met her, she seemed like a really nice girl.

It was late afternoon on a Wednesday. We'd just finished packing the last of our gear into the vehicles, and we were finally ready to close the door on our past lives and journey into the unknown, so to speak. Nicola shut the front door and climbed into her car. I told her and Peta to follow us, and we set off on our drive to Dover to catch a ferry to France. We'd mapped out a route through France down to the Pyrenees border which separates France from northern Spain. After that we'd have a twelve-hour drive through Spain, passing through Madrid and then on to the coast of southern Spain, before arriving at our destination in Fuengirola.

The drive through France took a lot longer than expected, about twenty-four hours in total. It was a very tiring drive, and in hindsight we probably should have caught a ferry directly to Santander in northern Spain, as it would have been a lot less stressful. The road signs in France were pretty much non-existent, unless you were prepared to use the toll roads which were very expensive. By the time we hit the border, we were all starting to get a little ratty.

We stopped in Santander for a couple of hours to get some refreshments and to generally stretch our legs and wake up for the next stage of the journey. Next we made our way down to Madrid which took a further six hours. Once we'd reached Madrid, we came across a large intersection which must have been at least eight lanes wide, shooting off in all directions. As in France, the road signs were nowhere to be seen, and there was a lot of traffic on the road as there was a football match going on that day with Real Madrid playing at home.

I decided to take a chance on the far right-hand lane, only to find out at the last minute that the sign ahead for the southern coast of Spain was pointing towards the far left-hand lane! This left me with only one option, and without thinking about the girls behind me, I swung the wheel of the van over to the left and cut across the busy lanes of traffic. Nicola and Peta did the same, and amazingly enough we made it across okay through all the tooting and cussing from irate drivers.

At this point Alan burst into laughter and told me to look in my mirror. I glanced in the door mirror to my left and caught sight of Nicola's face. She looked like she'd seen a ghost and was cussing profusely. She could be quite a fiery character, and I was glad at that time that I was sitting next to Alan and not Nicola, as she would have probably belted me one for that suicidal move, not to mention giving me quite an earful as well.

Once we'd made it past Madrid, we carried on towards Granada, a deserted mountainous area with nothing in sight for what seemed like miles. We'd now driven for about nine hours since leaving northern Spain and about thirty-three hours in total since entering France. As you can imagine, we were all getting extremely tired and were desperately in need of a break.

We pulled around the next bend in the road, and to our surprise there was a fairground set up next to a small farm house in the middle of nowhere. It was packed to the rafters with people. It looked like a scene from the twilight zone. We decided to pull over and park up. Everybody staggered out of the vehicles and headed straight for the toilets first, and then we made our way over to the burger stalls for refreshments.

As predicted, I got an earful from Nicola and Peta for my death-defying move in Madrid earlier, but once they'd got it off their chests, we did have quite a giggle about it. We spent another half hour or so walking around the fairground before making our way back to the vehicles.

We were only a few hours away from our destination now, so it seemed only logical to carry on the rest of the way and relax once we got there. The last few hours passed by quickly, and before we knew it we were pulling into Fuengirola high street. It was now about 8 a.m. on Saturday morning. The funny thing was that the second we parked up and got out of the vehicles, the tiredness all seemed to fall away from us as though a weight of stress had been lifted from our shoulders.

"This is it, guys. We're finally here," I said.

"I know. I can't believe it," replied Nicola. Hugging me tightly, she pressed her lips against mine and passionately kissed me.

"Mmm, what was that for? Not that I'm complaining of course."

"That was for luck," she said with a big smile on that beautiful face of hers.

"We don't need luck, sweetheart. We only need each other."

"I love you, Kurt Collins. I feel like the luckiest girl in the world right now."

"You are the luckiest girl in the world, babe. After all, you've got me, haven't you?"

Alan and Peta pulled us apart saying, "Come on, guys. Ease off. We're going to starve to death watching you two love birds canoodling together."

"Okay, let's find a café and get some breakfast, and then we can go and see Rosa to pick up the keys for the villa and bar." We walked along the promenade before eventually finding an English bar that was serving food. It was important to us to eat in a café run by English people, as the Spanish café owners tended to cook everything in olive oil, including the toast! As hard as the Spanish tried, only the English could adequately reproduce an English breakfast.

Once we were fed, we made our way down to Rosa's office to sign the lease contracts on both the bar and the long-term rental on the villa, and then we took possession of the keys to both premises. I thanked Rosa for all her help, and we walked back to the vehicles and made our way up the hill to Mijas, where our villa was situated not far from Scott's villa where we'd attended the pool party previously.

We pulled up onto the drive of the villa, parked up, and entered the front door. Like most of the premises in Spain, it was very spacious with white marble floor tiles, white walls, and pine woodwork. It had a large fitted kitchen, two bathrooms, two bedrooms, and a small garden with a pool.

We didn't really spend too much time exploring our surroundings as we were completely shattered from all the driving we'd done, so we just threw our bags down and crashed out.

I woke up at 6 p.m. feeling a lot better for sleeping, but it was still fairly hot in the villa. Nicola and Peta had already been up for an hour or so. They had been down the local supermarket to get some basic supplies and were now in the garden by the pool. I gave Alan a shout to wake him and then joined the girls in the garden. Once Alan was up, I got him to help me unload the van, and then we all unpacked as much as we could to try and make the villa feel a little more homely. By the time we'd finished, it was quite late and no one really felt like going out, so the girls rustled up some food and we just spent the rest of the night chilling out with some beers by the pool.

Everyone was up and ready to go by 10 a.m. the next morning. It wasn't worth leaving any earlier, as Spain is like a ghost town before this time. We all jumped in Nicola's car and drove the short distance from Mijas to Fuengirola. The only good thing about getting into town at this time is that it's generally the only time that you can find parking in the day down by the port, which is the central point of the town.

After grabbing a bite to eat, our first port of call was at the police station to get our national insurance papers. Then we were on to the town hall, where we had to sign some papers to give us official permission to open up the bar to the public, subject to our meeting the fire and safety requirements. The next stop was the electricity board to register the bills in my name. Here we came across our first problem, as once I'd signed for the bills, I was informed that an engineer would have to come down to remove the electricity meter and replace it with a new one. They told us that this was standard practice in Spain. Unfortunately, it was going to cost us £500.

I've got to say that this was my first experience of what I can only call the exploitation of the English—better known as being ripped off!

The electricity board set up a date to change the meter in one week's time, and they told me that it would be okay to carry on using the electricity in the meantime. We then went on to the fire department and arranged for a representative to come down to the bar later that day to let us know what was required to get the necessary health and safety certificate. It was becoming quite obvious to us that after buying a bar in Spain, you should take into account the amount of hidden costs that you will incur to enable you to legally open up here. We had been warned about this to a degree by Rosa our solicitor, so luckily we had set aside a couple of grand for this purpose. None the less, it still came as a surprise to us.

Anyway, we'd done all that we could for now on the legal front, so we decided that it was time to go and have a proper look at the bar that we'd just acquired and assess what was needed inside the bar to get it ready to be opened. We made our way up to the entrance gates of the bar. The old sign still hanging above the gates read "The Penguin Bar". That name definitely had to be changed!

I unlocked the large padlock and removed the chain that held the gates together, and we made our way down the steps to the front double entrance doors. I opened the doors and we entered the darkened corridor. Alan found a small cupboard in the wall which contained the electric meter and turned the power on. As we walked left through the door into the main bar area, a strong smell of damp hit us. This was common in the underground bars in Spain, especially as it had been closed down for some time.

It was an incredible feeling walking into the bar for the first time knowing that it was all ours. After a general walk around, we all sat down at the main table, which was situated by the entrance to the bar area. We decided to call this the captain's table.

Nicola and Peta had made a list of the bar equipment and stock that we needed, while Alan and I listed the technical equipment that was required for TV, sound, and lighting. On the technical side of things we needed to bring in some new speakers, record decks, televisions, and lighting, and we also needed to set up a satellite link to receive the Sky TV channels. In addition to Nicola's bar stock list, we would also need a couple of extra glass-front fridges and a glass washer. We only had a couple of hundred mixed glasses, so we would probably need a few boxes of them too, and of course we'd have to ring the breweries to install various lager pumps.

The other thing that we discovered was that there was a large ice-making machine in the office at the end of the bar. We weren't sure if it worked or not, as it had obviously not been used in some time. When we opened the lid of the ice machine, a strong smell of stagnant water hit us, not to mention the various insects swimming around inside it. We couldn't test the machine at that time, as there was no plug on the power lead and the office was full of old boxes and rubbish filling most of the floor and shelving areas.

The ladies' and gents' toilets were probably in the best condition of all the areas in the bar. They were marble-tiled from floor to ceiling, and the fixtures and fittings were all in good working order.

The first thing we decided to do was to have a general clean up and wash everything down with disinfectant. Nicola and Peta attacked the bar and toilets, while Alan and I worked on the main seating areas and dance floor.

This task took us several hours. Whilst cleaning the seats at the back of the club, I discovered some long red curtains that were covering a set of double doors that turned out to be the exit doors. I opened these doors to let some fresh air into the bar. We also switched on the air conditioning to try and clear the smell of damp from the air.

At about 4 p.m. the buzzer to the bar went off, and I went outside to open the gate and let the fire and safety engineer inside. Luckily for me, he spoke fluent English. We walked around together and he took notes on what was required. He told me that I would need to have all the carpets and upholstery sprayed with a fire proofing. He could arrange for this to be done at a cost of £300. On top of this, we would need to replace all of the fire extinguishers at a further cost of £250. In the toilets we would need to fit electric hand dryers, and we also need an electrical safety certificate for the bar. For this we would need to find a local certified electrician. Before leaving, he arranged to do the fire proofing and to fit the extinguishers in four days' time and told me that if I'd managed to sort out the electrical requirements by that time, then he would have no problem in issuing us the safety certificate that we required.

The bar was looking much cleaner now, and it was fast approaching early evening, so we decided to call it a day and get something to eat. We closed up the bar and walked down to the port area and came across an establishment called the Yorkshire Rose, where we grabbed a table and sat down to eat.

"So what are you going to have?" asked Nicola.

"Well, I think that after all that hard work I deserve a steak."

"Mmm, sounds good, but I think I'll have the roast," replied Nicola.

Alan and Peta also went for the roast. I told them that the food was on me, as they'd all worked pretty hard today. The waiter came over and we ordered our meals and drinks. It was obvious to me and Nicola that Peta had taken quite a shine to Alan. We felt that they would make a perfect couple, so we went out of our way to encourage this to happen. Once we'd finished our meals, we ordered several more rounds of drinks and just chatted about the next steps that we'd have to take to get the bar operational.

"Okay, back to business. We need to find an electrician and someone to supply the stock for the bar and some glasses. I think the best way forward would be to get the local paper to see who's advertising in it," suggested Nicola.

"Great idea, and as far as the technical equipment is concerned, it would probably be best if we got most of what we require from the UK."

Alan agreed to drive back to the England to get what I needed. After all, he did have to take the van back anyway. Once he'd acquired the equipment, he would arrange to fly back with it, and we would then meet him at the airport to pick him up. Peta had agreed to go with him to keep him company on the long drive back, although this time he was intending only to drive to Santander and then get a ferry straight to the UK.

"Okay, that's the business side of things sorted out, so in the meantime I think we should go out and celebrate over a few drinks."

I paid the bill and we made our way down to Linekers for a well-earned session. So far we hadn't run into any familiar faces, but we knew that that would change once we'd entered Linekers, as this was the first place that the English started their night's entertainment.

"I'm really looking forward to seeing everyone again," said Nicola.

"Yeah, me too. It seems ages ago since we last spoke to them."

As we walked down towards the port bars, the usual flier staff was out in force, dishing out the two-for-one drinks tickets to try to get you into whatever bar they were promoting. We walked past all of them and made our way up to Linekers terrace, where Alan, Peta, and Nicola sat down at a table while I made my way to the bar. The first familiar face I came across was of course big Tony, who was working on the door and keeping an eye out for trouble makers. He spotted me straight away and welcomed me with open arms.

"Hey, Kurt, it's great to see you again."

"Thanks, Tony, it's great to see you too. So where's Luciana tonight then?"

"She's just popped out with Kirby for an hour or so, but I'm sure she'll be delighted to see that you're back. I take it Nicola's with you."

"Yeah, she's sitting on the terrace with a couple of friends of ours called Alan and Peta."

"Well, while you get the drinks in, I think I'll go and say hello then."

"Okay, cool. Can I get you a drink while I'm at the bar?"

"Sure, I'll have a whisky, please."

Tony headed off towards the table and left me to order the drinks. Whilst standing at the bar, I felt a tap on my shoulder and I turned around to find Danny the resident DJ I'd met before standing behind me.

"Hiya, Kurt, I wondered when we'd see you again. You two caused quite a stir the last time you were out here."

"Really! Why's that then?"

"Well nobody could stop talking about you for weeks after you'd left. You were quite a hit."

"Yeah, we did have a blast, didn't we?"

"I'll say! You two were like a breath of fresh air around here."

"Careful! Too many compliments might go to my head," I replied. We both laughed and shook hands.

"So what's been happening since we've been gone? Any gossip that I should know about?"

"Not much really. It's been getting busier by the day here as we head up towards the summer season."

"Yeah, I noticed that there are quite a few more people here now."

"Yes there are, and it will get a lot busier than this before long, I can tell you."

"So how is everyone then? We've only just got back, so we haven't really seen anyone yet."

"Everyone's great, thanks. Fallon's gone back to Sweden for a couple of weeks to see her family. Oh, and Kirby's split up with Ricky, so we've been keeping an eye on her to try and keep her spirits up."

It was a shame to hear about Kirby and Ricky, but I guess relationships out here are probably difficult to sustain.

"So tell me, Kurt, I'm dying to know. Are you back to stay or what?"

"Yes is the answer to your question. We've just finalized the lease on a music bar, and we're back to get it ready to open in a few weeks' time."

"Wow! That's fantastic news. I hope you'll let me play in this new bar of yours once it's open."

"Of course I will. That goes without saying. You're a very good DJ."

"Well, this calls for a celebration then. You take the drinks back to the table, and I'll order a couple of bottles of champagne and join you in a bit, okay?"

"Thanks, Danny, that's really nice of you."

I made my way back to the table and dished the drinks out. Tony had pulled up a chair and was deep in conversation with everyone. Danny followed shortly with the bottles of bubbly. We chatted for ages about what we'd got up to when we were here last and about the possibilities of the future. Tony and Danny offered to help out as much as possible, and Tony also recommended a local electrician for me and gave me the number of the drinks supplier that Linekers used in Los Boliches, which was great news, as it killed two birds with one stone.

Scott the manager of Linekers was the next familiar face to join us. He gave Nicola a big hug and a kiss, shook my hand, and welcomed us both back. The drinks kept coming for quite a while, and then we heard the familiar girly shrieks starting up as Luciana and Kirby walked onto the terrace. Nicola jumped out of her seat, screaming quickly, followed by Peta. It was like listening to a mating call in the jungle or something. There was hugging and kissing and screaming all around. God knows what the punters sitting around us must have thought. I looked over to Alan to see a totally bemused look on his face.

"Don't worry about it, Alan. This happens a lot out here. You'll get used to it," I said, laughing.

"Fuck me! I wondered what the hell was happening."

"Yeah, I guessed that." We both burst into laughter and sat back down. The table was starting to fill up now, so I ordered a few more bottles of champagne, and we all got noisily pissed over the space of a few hours. Before we knew it, the bar was closing, as it was now two o'clock in the morning.

Over the course of the evening, Nicola had found out that Kirby's boyfriend had gone back to England to study in college, and they'd agreed that it would be best if they just called it a day. Kirby had taken it quite badly and was trying her best to put on a brave face. Nicola had taken quite a shine to Kirby, and she told her that rather than let her go home alone, she could stay with us for a bit if she wanted too. Kirby burst into tears at this act of kindness from Nicola and gave her a hug, thanking her repeatedly.

"So it's settled then. You'll stay with us until you get back on your feet, okay?" said Nicola to Kirby.

"Okay, thanks, I really appreciate this, but are you sure you're okay with that, Kurt?" asked Kirby.

"Hey, it will be a pleasure having you there, okay? You're more than welcome."

Kirby's eyes welled up and she thanked me with a big kiss on the cheek. We said our goodnights to Tony, Luciana, and Danny and made our way up to the taxi rank and caught a cab back to the villa to crash out. We left the car parked up by the port, as we were obviously in no position to drive home that night.

Sunday morning arrived with the usual burst of heat, which inevitably woke me up in a pool of sweat and with a considerable headache. I threw back the sheets and staggered the short distance to the en-suite bathroom and jumped straight into the shower. I stepped out ten minutes later feeling a little more refreshed but still carrying this thumping headache, so after drying myself off, I wrapped a towel around my waist and made my way into the kitchen to find some headache pills and of course to stick the kettle on and threw a few slices of bread into the toaster.

Nicola was next to appear. She had a similar headache, and like me, she went straight for the paracetamols.

"Oh, my head hurts," she whined.

"Yeah, I know exactly how you feel, babe. I've got a funny feeling everyone's going to be suffering this morning."

Nicola gave me a hug from behind and kissed the back of my neck before reaching forward and pinching one of the slices of toast I'd just buttered for myself. She ran off giggling into the bedroom.

Kirby was next to wander into the kitchen wearing a pair of Nicola's pyjamas.

"Morning, sweetheart. Are we feeling a little fragile today as well?"

"Oh, morning, Kurt," she replied, kissing me on the cheek. "Oh is that for me," she said, grabbing a piece of toast.

"Oi! Hands off! That's mine."

"I knew you wouldn't mind, as you're such a little darling," she giggled.

I smacked her pert little arse and told her not to make a habit of it, but she just smiled and ran from the room, toast in hand.

Nicola had put Kirby up on the couch for the night, and as I couldn't see Peta anywhere, it seemed obvious that she'd jumped in the sack with Alan. Well, I can't say that I didn't see that coming! I finished making the tea for the three of us, and after giving Kirby her cup, I made my way back into the bedroom to finish off the last slice of toast before anyone else got their greedy little hands on it.

We had quite a lot to do today, what with sorting out the bar stock, getting hold of the electrician, and finishing off the cleaning, not to mention that Alan and Peta would be leaving us to go back to England to pick up the rest of the equipment, which would leave us a couple of bodies short.

Nicola and I finished getting dressed and then joined Kirby in the front room. I left Nicola to persuade Kirby to help us out at the bar today while I went off to give Alan and Peta a shout to wake them up. Alan acknowledged me with a groan. I told them both to get up and then left them to it and re-joined the girls, who were now lying out by the pool. The three of us lay there until Alan and Peta joined us.

"Morning, guys. I take it you two had a little extra fun last night then?"

They just looked at each other blushing and smiling and said, "Just a little."

"Really? From the noise you two were making last night, I'd say quite a lot," said Kirby. Alan and Peta both looked extremely embarrassed now.

"Yeah, poor little Kirby was left all on her own, bless her," said Nicola sarcastically.

"Yeah, I know. It's not fair. If I wasn't so pissed up, I'd have jumped in with you and Kurt for a bit of tomfoolery."

"Mmm, we'd have liked that!" replied Nicola.

"Hey! Pack it in you two. You're getting me all excited now," I said.

"Yeah, pack it in Kirby. It's too early to get Kurt excited," replied Nicola.

"Hey, don't pick on me. You encouraged me to tease him." Nicola and Kirby both fell about laughing.

"Okay, enough of the wind ups. Alan and Peta have got a long drive ahead of them," I said, "and the three of us have got a lot of work to do, so I suggest we all get going."

I gave Alan a couple of grand in cash for the equipment and a spare set of keys to the villa for when they returned, and we said our goodbyes and headed back into Fuengirola. We arrived in town at midday, and after parking up we headed down to Scottie's on the port front for a bite to eat. Nicola ordered the food while I made a couple of phone calls.

First I called the electrician to arrange for him to pop down to the club later that day and second a guy called Pablo who owned the liquor store in Los Boliches about a mile or so up the coastline. I read out a list of everything that we required, including several boxes of glasses. He assured me that he'd be able to drop a delivery down to us later that day. He also said that he had a friend who might be able to help us out with the glass washer and fridges and that he'd give him a call for us as well. I thanked him, hung up the phone, and made my way back to join the girls who were now tucking into their food.

I sat down at the table, and Jimmy the bar owner brought out my meal and an ice-cold beer. Jimmy shook my hand and welcomed me back and then asked me if I'd managed to bring back any football shirts for his bar. As I've said previously, the walls of his bar were adorned with football shirts from all over Europe. I told him that as it happened, I'd brought an old 1970s Arsenal top for his collection but as yet I hadn't unpacked it, so I said I'd bring it down to him as soon as I possibly could.

Once we'd finished eating, we walked up to our bar and went inside. There was still a faint smell of damp in the air, but it was much better now and noticeably cleaner than before.

This was the first time Kirby had seen the inside of the bar, and she was very impressed. Nicola took her on a grand tour while I sat down at the captain's table to go through the paperwork to try and find out what I'd have to do to change the name of the bar. It turned out that once I'd got written permission from the landlord, all I had to do was to fill in a form at the town hall and register the new name with them to make it legal.

The only other thing that we had left to do at the moment was to clean the multitude of mirrors that were stuck over the walls of the bar. So once the girls had finished their little tour, we set about doing just that. This took a couple of hours to do, and after completing the task, we all sat down and cracked open a few bottles of wicked that we'd brought back from Scottie's.

We'd also brought a small portable stereo so that we'd have some background music in the bar while we were down here. We managed to tune it to a local radio station that was playing the latest UK chart music. A track came on the radio by a group called Babybird called "You're Gorgeous", and somewhere between the chatting and drinking we all started singing along. The girls got up bottles in hand and dragged me over to the dance floor. We were having quite a laugh when the buzzer went off, scaring the shit out of us, as it was very loud. Nicola and Kirby burst into fits of laughter after having both screamed at the shock of hearing the buzzer go off. I was obviously going to have to do something about that!

I left the girls and went outside to see who was there. I found a couple of Spanish guys waiting outside the gates with a lot of crates and boxes. It turned out to be Pablo the drinks supplier and one of his sidekicks. For a change, someone in Spain had actually turned up on time! I opened the gates and helped Pablo and his lad bring in all the boxes, and I can tell you there were quite a few of them.

The bill came to £1,800. This included 400 assorted glasses. I settled up with Pablo by credit card, and he gave me his business card for future orders. He also told me that he'd taken the liberty of contacting several brewery reps for me and that they would be dropping by to speak to me about fitting some new lager pumps. As far as the bar equipment was concerned, his friend had told him that he would come down and see me in an hour or so.

I thanked him for his help and then saw him to the door, before returning to the bar to check out the merchandise. By the time I'd got back inside, the girls were already into the boxes. I asked them to get behind the bar while I passed the boxes up to them so that we could unpack them and place the contents into position straight away. We started with the glasses, followed by the top-shelf spirits, and worked our way down to the optics, soft drinks, and beers, most of which were placed in the fridges. Unfortunately, we ran out of fridge space, so we just racked up all the crates and boxes that were left over at the end of the bar.

We took a short break after sorting out the stock and sat back down to catch our breath. We hadn't been sitting for more than five minutes before the buzzer went off again. It was turning out to be a very hectic day.

At the gate was standing a guy called Paul. He told me that Pablo had sent him down to see me about some bar equipment that I'd required. Paul led me to his van, where he had loaded several glass-front fridges and a glass washer. The equipment was second hand but in remarkable condition. I agreed to take two of the fridges and, of course, the glass washer for £450 on the condition that I could see them working first. We carried the pieces of equipment down the stairs to the bar and installed them. Once I was satisfied that they were okay, I paid Paul and saw him out to the door while the girls finished off unpacking the crates into the fridges.

Time was getting on now, and I still hadn't heard from the electrician, so I decided that it was time to call it a day. The bar looked fantastic now. I've got to say the girls had done a great job, and I had no hesitation in letting them know how I felt.

"Well, it's now coming up to 6 p.m., and I think we've achieved a hell of a lot today. To show my appreciation I'm going to take you both out shopping as a treat."

"Yes! That's what I love about you, Kurt. You always know how to do the right thing," shrieked Nicola.

"Thanks, Kurt. Apart from the obvious, I'm beginning to see what Nicola finds so attractive in you."

"Don't sound so surprised, Kirby. I'm not just a pretty face, you know."

"Well, I won't deny you're a good-looking guy, Kurt, but I meant what I said. Honesty and morals are rare qualities in people, and you do seem to have them in abundance."

Nicola and Kirby were very excited about the shopping trip, so after locking up the bar, I made a phone call to the electrician and arranged for him to come down tomorrow instead. Then we made our way down to the port to catch a cab to the town of Benalmadena. It was about five miles up the coastline towards Malaga, and like Marbella it was a port town with lots of boats moored in the harbour. It was very much a Spanish residential town, and it was definitely a lot more upmarket than Fuengirola in its shops, bars, and general appearance, with most of the activity centred around the harbour area. I told the girls that they could choose a complete outfit each, which seemed to light up their pretty eyes.

As I've said before, when I go shopping for clothes I tend to make a quick decision on what I like, but Nicola and Kirby typified everything about what it was like to go shopping with the girls! They were as bad as each other. It was like taking a couple of kids into the sweet shop and telling them to help themselves. First of all they went searching for footwear. Nicola eventually picked out a pair of white stiletto shoes, and Kirby chose a pair of knee-high black lace-up boots.

After this we started working our way through the clothes shops, and again this seemed to take forever with the two of them in and out of the changing rooms like yo-yos trying on different outfits. Nicola eventually settled for a short white tight-fitting lacy dress, while Kirby picked out a short black suede dress with a built-in petticoat that fluffed the skirt part out. I must admit the two of them looked pretty stunning, and they made me feel a little underdressed, so I decided to pick a suit off of the rack at one of the designer outlets.

As we were all dolled up now, it seemed only right to make a night of it on the town. We made our way towards the harbour front bars and took a table at a restaurant to have an evening meal. The food was delicious, a little more expensive than usual, but it was well worth it. Once we'd finished eating, we made our way along the busy harbour front. I felt pretty special all suited up with a pretty brunette on each arm. We carried on walking along the front until we came across a large music bar on the corner. It had a huge terrace with high standing tables and, from what we could see, a very high-class clientele, and there was a couple of burly doormen to ensure the dress code was respected. We decided that this was the bar for us, and as we were obviously dressed up to the nines now, we had no problem getting in whatsoever.

Once inside, we were shown to a table straight away. It turned out that there was a group lined up to play later that night, so were in for quite a treat. A hostess came over and took our orders, and then I excused myself, as I needed to take a leak. When I returned, the hostess was deep in conversation with the girls, and as I sat down she came over to me and asked if she could shake my hand and kiss me on the cheek. Not thinking anything of it, I stood up, shook her hand, and greeted her in the usual Spanish manner. Her face immediately blushed up bright red, and she thanked me again and ran off giggling with a huge smile on her face.

"Okay, what are you two up to?" I inquired.

"Nothing," they both replied innocently.

"Yeah, right! Now I know you're up to something."

"Honestly, we haven't stitched you up. I promise you," Nicola said, laughing.

"I know you've done something. Why was that girl so pleased to meet me? Tell me the truth or we're leaving!"

"Okay, okay, you're such a spoilsport. If you must know, she thought you looked a little like Ali Campbell from UB40. So we told her that's who you were."

"Oh, thanks! Well, I hope they don't ask me to sing one of his songs."

"Don't worry, we told her that you had a sore throat so that you wouldn't have to."

"Well thank fuck for that," I said, feeling relieved. After I'd taken in their little prank, I must admit that I did see the funny side of it.

We spent the night in the bar taking in the band and generally having a great time. At the end of the night I went up to settle the bill, but the owner would have none of it. He just kept insisting that it was a pleasure having us in his bar. All he wanted was for me to pose for a picture with him and his staff, still thinking that I was Ali Campbell. Well, it seemed a shame to disappoint him and tell him that he was mistaken, so I obliged. I was immediately surrounded by a bevy of Spanish beauties and the owner, while his friend took our picture. Nicola and Kirby just looked on, struggling to contain their laughter and enjoying every second of it.

We left the bar with all the staff kissing and waving us goodbye. People looking on must have wondered what the hell was going on, as it was starting to attract quite a lot of attention. We waited until we'd got around the corner and out of sight of the bar before the three of us burst into laughter.

It had turned out to be a great night, and best of all, Kirby was starting to come out of her shell a lot more now after the disappointment of her relationship break-up. We caught a cab back to the villa in Mijas, and after reminiscing about the night's activities over a few more drinks, Kirby thanked us both and said goodnight before retiring to Alan's room for a good night's sleep.

Nicola then took my hand and then led me to the bedroom, closed the door behind her, and began to undress me, stripping me down to my boxers before pushing me on the bed. She slipped out of her dress to reveal some very sexy undergarments and climbed on top of me, kissing me on the lips and draping her gorgeous long brown hair over my chest and shoulders.

"Oh wow! You look incredibly sexy tonight," I said.

"I wanted to surprise you. That was a really nice thing that you did today, buying Kirby and me the outfits and the night out. It really cheered her up. I really like Kirby, and I had a fantastic time too."

"That's okay. It seemed like the right thing to do, and I enjoyed myself too."

"I love you, Kurt."

"I love you too, sweetie pie, especially looking like that."

Nicola whispered in my ear. "Am I turning you on?" she asked.

"Fuck, yeah! I'm so turned on right now I think I'm going to burst."

"Well, I'd better do something about that then," she said, working her way down my body. Following that statement, she gave me some of the best sex I'd ever had in my life. It was a great end to a great day!

We got up the next morning to the smell of a cooked breakfast. This was Kirby's way of saying thank you for last night. She told us that nobody had ever done anything like that for her before without wanting something in return. With tears in their eyes, I could see that both Kirby and Nicola were about to start crying, so I stepped in and told Kirby that it was worth it just to see the smile on her face and that it was great to see Nicola so happy too! Anyway, I told them that now wasn't the time to get teary-eyed, as we still had a few more things left to do in the bar today, so I needed them both to be strong and ready for action for the day ahead.

Nicola ordered a taxi, as her car was still parked up in town, and while waiting for it we finished off getting ready. Once it arrived we left the villa, and the cab made its way down Mijas hill into Fuengirola.

Since returning to Spain we'd been using telephone boxes to contact people, as we'd cancelled our mobile contracts in England before we'd left. This was causing a lot of inconvenience to us, so my first port of call was to the mobile phone shop in town to pick up a couple of new mobiles. We couldn't get contract phones, as we'd not been living out here long enough, so we plumped for the pay-as-you-go phones instead.

My next move was to set up a bank account, so I left the girls to look around town while I went into the Banco Santander, which is arguably the biggest bank in Spain. This took about half an hour to sort out, and once I'd finished I met back up with the girls at a café in town for a coffee.

Nicola had managed to pick up a local paper called *The Sur In English* and had found an advert inside from a company that set up satellite systems, so I gave them a call and arranged for a rep to come down and see us later that day.

Whilst we were sitting in the café, I gave Alan a call to see how he was getting on. He told me that he'd just arrived back in the UK. He'd caught a ferry from northern Spain, thus avoiding the long drive through France and as he'd slept on the ferry, he would try to pick up the equipment that we needed later that afternoon once he got back home. I gave him my new mobile number and asked him to call me as soon as he had any news.

After hanging up the phone, I immediately rang Rosa and asked her to contact Larry in regards to changing the name of the bar. Rosa told me that she'd call him straight away and as soon as she'd spoken to him, she'd call me straight back. She also told me that we'd been booked in for our health and hygiene tests at the local doctor's tomorrow morning and that she had a couple of hygiene test books that we would need to pick up today.

Once I'd finished making the calls, we left the café. Nicola and Kirby made their way up to Rosa's, while I headed down to the bar. As I approached the gates I noticed someone waiting outside. It turned out to be one of the brewery reps. I invited him inside, and we sat down to discuss what products that he could offer me. In the end I agreed to have two gold-plated Estrella pumps that came with a cooling system that chilled the lager right up to the pumps, thus producing ice-cold beer every time. I signed the paperwork, and he told me that his engineers would be down to install the pumps in two days' time. I thanked him for coming down to see me, shook his hand, and then saw him out.

I left the gates open, as I knew that Nicola and Kirby would be returning shortly from their trip to Rosa's, and then I made my way back inside and headed for the office, as this was the last area to sort out.

The first thing that I did was to bag up all the rubbish that was scattered about the floor. This allowed me to see what else was in the room. Once I'd done this, only four boxes were left on the floor. I opened them up and sifted through them, but all I found was a few old spotlights and several packets of bulbs, so I bagged up the rest of the contents and the boxes and took them outside to dump them in the bins provided by the caretaker Raymond, whom I'd not met yet.

As I dumped the last of the rubbish from the office floor, Nicola and Kirby arrived back carrying a load of paperwork. Nicola had picked up the hygiene books from Rosa for us to study. She'd told her that under Spanish law, anyone who was going to work behind a bar had to have one of these health and hygiene certificates. Rosa had also given her some forms for me to fill in so that I could change the name of the bar.

As we walked back into the bar, the electrician turned up, so I asked the girls to finish off bagging up the last of the stuff from the shelves in the office while I went through the fire department's requirements with him. He informed me that he had several hand dryers in his van and that he could carry out the work straight away if I wanted him to. We agreed a price, and he made his way back to the van to get his tools and the dryers.

The girls were now well into the task of clearing the last few shelves in the office, so I went to help Nicola carry out the bags of rubbish. All of a sudden Kirby let out a piercing scream that made us both jump, as it came totally out of the blue. Both Nicola and I quickly rushed back in to see what had happened. She pointed to the top shelf and told us that it was crawling with bugs, and she refused to go back into the office until I'd got rid of them.

I laughed at hearing this and told her that it couldn't be that bad. I walked into the office and gingerly lifted the last couple of boxes from the shelf to find a couple of very large black cockroaches with long twitching tentacles hiding behind them. I must admit that they did send a shiver down my spine, but for macho's sake I reframed from showing any fear. Nicola handed me an old steak hammer that she'd found behind the bar, and I used it to club them to death. The problem was that as soon as I did this, several more appeared from a small hole in the wall at the back of the shelf. It seemed that there was a whole family of them, so I just kept on whacking them until they were all dead, and then I swept their crushed corpses into one of the bags with the last of the rubbish to leave a nice clean empty room—apart from the ice machine, of course.

By this time the electrician was well into his tasks, so we decided to take a break and sit down with a drink while he went about his business. We were all feeling a little peckish now, so the girls volunteered to go down to the Burger King in town to get a take-away while I stayed in the bar with the electrician. I asked him to look at the ice-making machine while he was there, and I went into the office to empty the stagnant water from the drip tray of the machine and refilled it with fresh water so that it would be ready to use once he'd sorted it out.

The next person to arrive at the bar was the rep from the satellite firm that we'd rung earlier. He shook my hand and sat down with me to ask what it was that I wanted. I told him that I required several connections behind the length of the bar so that I could mount some TVs on the wall. He told me that he could connect up to the existing satellite dish that supplied the whole building and that this would take the engineers a few hours to complete. The problem was that he couldn't send them down for a couple of days, as they were fairly busy at the moment. I told him that that would be okay and then filled in his forms and shook his hand, and then he left.

Shortly after this the girls returned with the food, and we sat down to eat whilst filling in the name change forms that Rosa had given Nicola earlier. The only thing that we had to do now was to come up with a new name for the bar. This proved to be a lot more difficult than we'd anticipated, and it took quite some time before we eventually settled on calling it the Stage Door. After all, if I hadn't been on stage on that fateful night in London in the talent contest, then I would never have met Nicola, and consequently I wouldn't be here right now. So it seemed an appropriate name to choose!

The electrician finished his work in the bar at about 5.30 p.m., which included fixing the ice machine, and he issued us the electrical certificate that we required for the fire department rep. He also informed us that we needed to use Spanish TVs in the bar, as they worked on a different system out here. I thanked him for his advice and paid him for the work he'd done.

Finally, we left the bar, as there was nothing else for us to do down here now until Wednesday when the fire department, brewery, and satellite engineers were due to return. We locked up the gates and walked up to Los Boliches to drop the paperwork in to Rosa so that she could get on with the process of changing the name of the bar. From there we made our way back into town to pick up the car and then drove back to the villa to spend the rest of the evening studying the hygiene books for the test in the morning.

We awoke the next day at about 10 a.m., and I rustled up some breakfast whilst the girls got ready. We then sat down to eat and to discuss the day ahead.

"As soon as we've finished eating, we're going to have to make a move, as we've got this test to sit at 11.30 a.m.," I told Nicola.

"Sure, no problem. Oh, and by the way, I've got a confession to make."

"What's that then?" I asked.

"I've arranged for Kirby to take the test as well."

"Why's that then?" I asked Nicola.

"Well, yesterday I asked Kirby if she'd like to have a job behind the bar with me, and she said she'd love to. I hope you don't mind."

"No, I don't mind, but you should have asked me first so that I knew what was going on. You know I don't like to be kept in the dark!"

"Sorry, sweetheart. I didn't mean to keep it from you, but after what had happened with the cockroach incident yesterday, I completely forgot to tell you. Sorry."

"Okay, apology accepted. I guess we should start thinking about what staff we are going to need, but in the future I'd prefer it if you consulted me on important decisions like employing staff before you say yes to people. In the meantime, all that's left to say is . . . welcome on board, Kirby!"

"Thanks, Kurt, I won't let you down, I promise," she said, hugging me.

After eating, the three of us made our way down to the doctor's in Fuengirola to sit the test. It was quite a simple test really. We just sat in a small room with six other people around a large table and had to fill in a questionnaire about fridge temperatures and boiling points, etc. We weren't even monitored, so everyone helped each other out to make sure we all passed the test. After about twenty minutes a woman came back into the room and went through our answers before congratulating us all on having passed the test. Then she handed out the health and hygiene certificates that we required.

We left the doctors and headed into town to buy some Spanish TVs and DVD players for the bar. After going into several shops, we ended up acquiring four thirty-inch flat-screen TVs and a couple of DVD players, which came to £1,800. We should have paid a lot more than that, but that's the beauty of being in Spain: you can always barter for price with the shopkeepers out here.

We loaded the equipment into Nicola's car and after dropping it down to the bar, we made our way back to the villa to unpack the rest of our stuff and then spent a relaxing evening in for a change.

At about 9 p.m. I received a call from Alan telling me that he'd managed to get all the equipment that I'd needed and that he and Peta were booked on the early morning flight back to Spain and would be arriving at Malaga airport at 8 a.m. sharp. I told him that I'd be there to meet him and then hung up the phone and told the girls what Alan had said and suggested that it would probably be wise if we all got an early night. They both agreed, and after an hour of so we turned in for the night. The next day came around quickly. Before I knew it, I was welcoming Alan and Peta back as they walked through the arrival gates at the airport.

I'd already dropped Nicola and Kirby off at the bar before coming to the airport so that I'd have enough room in the car for both of them and all the equipment and also because I was expecting several visitors at the bar that day. We packed all the stuff into the car and made our way back into Fuengirola and parked up outside the bar, before carrying the equipment down the steps and into the bar. Once inside, we found that there were several people inside milling around, as well as Nicola and Kirby.

The engineer from the fire department was currently spraying the materials with a fire-proofing compound, whilst a couple of his lads were fitting the new fire extinguishers. Behind the bar was a brewery technician fitting the Estrella pumps, and the satellite firm was mounting the TVs on the walls in preparation for the satellite link-up. Nicola and Kirby were just trying to keep out of the way by the captain's table.

"Wow! It seems pretty busy in here," I said to Nicola.

"Oh, I'm so glad you're back. It's been like Piccadilly Circus in here this morning. Everyone turned up at the same time!"

Nicola and Kirby both welcomed Alan and Peta back into the fold, and I left the girls to chat while we carried the DJ equipment behind the bar and down to the DJ booth. The booth was connected to the end of the bar and had raised glass panels around it to stop the public reaching in. On the back wall behind the booth were a dozen wooden boxes that had been built to house all of the twelve-inch vinyl records, and underneath the booth were all the slots to house the equipment and a top shelf to sit the decks on.

I helped Alan unpack the new equipment and then left him to it, as the fire engineer had now finished his tasks and required me to sign for the completed work. After this he supplied me with the last legal certificate that I required to open the bar.

The next thing that I had to do was to speak to the brewery engineer who had also finished fitting and installing the lager pumps, which were now dripping with the condensation droplets from where they were being chilled to the pumps. I now had lager on tap, and of course I had to be the first one to pull a pint. Unfortunately, as I'd never pulled a pint before, I ended up with more froth than lager. This brought fits of laughter from the girls and, I'm ashamed to say, the brewery engineer as well! After that embarrassing moment, I signed for the installation and set up an order number for future keg sales and then bid them goodbye.

The only other thing left to complete, apart from Alan installing the music equipment, was the satellite guys who were now tuning the satellite box in to the Sky TV network for me. Once I was satisfied with the installation and the TVs were up and running, they got me to sign for the work, and then they also left us to it.

It was now beginning to look and feel like a working bar.

I left the TVs on the MTV music channel and went back behind the booth to see how Alan was getting on. The girls were getting a little bored now, as there wasn't really anything for them to do, so I asked them to go back to the villa to pick up my record boxes and bring them back down to the bar so that we could put them in place behind the DJ booth. While they were gone Alan and I finished off installing the equipment and then hung a new set of speakers and various high-tech disco lights over the dance floor.

By the time the girls returned, I was testing out the decks, and we had the lighting up and running, reflecting off the large mirror ball that hung over the dance floor. It was a pretty impressive sight, and by the look on their faces, it definitely wowed them. We all helped carry the record boxes into the club, as they were quite heavy, and once we'd finished placing them into position, we just stood back and marvelled at what we'd just achieved. In a short space of time we'd turned a damp empty bar into something very special. It was a proud moment for me, and I can honestly say that I could feel a lump in my throat as I welled up with pride. The bar was finally finished.

We sat down at the captain's table and cracked open a few bottles of bubbly, and as we laughed and chatted amongst ourselves, the mobile rang. It was Rosa on the other end of the line ringing to say that she had our license and she'd now finalized the name change to the bar, so from this moment on we were now officially known as the Stage Door.

Well that was something worth celebrating, and with tears in my eyes I hugged Nicola and gave her the biggest heartfelt kiss that I'd ever given her. This was indeed a very exhilarating and proud moment for both of us.

During the next week and a half, we had a new sign put up outside the bar, had the electric meter changed, and set up a ton of promotional material for the opening night which was set for the first week in June.

CHAPTER FIVE

Initiating the Dream

It was approaching May 25, and with only one week to go before the opening night, things were starting to get a little tense. Although the bar and all the legalities were in order, we still hadn't managed to sort out the rest of the staff yet. Tony and Luciana had arranged a surprise party tonight at Linekers for Fallon, who was due to return from Sweden at 7.30 p.m. With most of the British locals having being invited, this seemed like the perfect opportunity for me to kill two birds with one stone.

We spent most of the day just lying about by the pool with a few drinks until about 6.15 p.m., when we drove down to Fuengirola and all piled out of Nicola's car to make our way down to Linekers for the party. Kirby was the only one that wasn't with us, as she was at the airport waiting to greet Fallon as she came through the arrival gates. Kirby had been given strict instructions to get Fallon straight into a cab, to take her back to Los Boliches to drop off her bags, and then to bring her straight down to Linekers where we'd all be waiting for her. I also told her to call me as soon as she landed and again as they were leaving Fallon's apartment.

As we approached Linekers terrace, we noticed that it was completely empty and the windows to the bar had been blacked out so that you couldn't see who was inside. We could hear chatter coming through the entrance of the bar, and as we walked inside my mobile went off. It was Kirby telling me that Fallon's flight had landed a little earlier than expected and that they were now getting into a cab to head back to Los Boliches. This meant that we had about half an hour before they'd arrive at the bar.

I hung up the phone and we walked inside. It turned out to be full of people, some of whom I knew and some I didn't. Tony and Luciana greeted us in the usual way, and we told them that they had about thirty minutes before Fallon arrived. After greeting everyone that we knew, I left Nicola, Luciana, and Peta catting together and made my way up to the bar with the lads to order some drinks.

While I was waiting, I took the opportunity to chat to Tony about making a few phone calls to see if he could help me find a couple of good reliable doormen. He told me that he would see what he could do. I then took Danny to one side to ask him if he would be interested in becoming my resident DJ, and I was happy to hear him say that he had no hesitation whatsoever in saying yes to me.

As we made our way back to the girls, the mobile rang again. It was Kirby to let me know that they were just arriving at Fallon's apartment and would be at Linekers in about another ten minutes. The news that Fallon would be arriving soon brought a flurry of activity in the bar, and everyone took their places in readiness for her arrival. Luciana went outside to keep watch while everyone else crouched down on the floor, and before long Luciana came running back into the bar to tell us that they were now here.

A hush fell about the room as we waited for Kirby and Fallon to walk in. We could hear them approaching, saying how quiet it was in the bar tonight, and as Fallon walked in through the entrance, everybody jumped up, letting off party poppers and screaming "Surprise!"

Fallon jumped out of her skin, obviously not expecting the welcome that she'd just received. Danny fired up the music, and then the usual chorus of screaming girls started up and the party began. A large table had been reserved inside the bar for close friends of Fallon, and after everyone had finished welcoming her back, I took hold of her arm and walked her back to it.

The party was in full swing now. Danny was playing tunes over the loudspeakers, and everyone was either dancing or throwing alcohol down their necks at an alarming rate and generally having a great time. Fallon asked me to sit down with her to fill her in on all the gossip that she'd missed out on.

"So tell me, Kurt, when did you get back?"

"Oh, I don't know. I guess it must have been a few weeks now."

"Kirby tells me that you've finished setting up the bar now and that she's been staying with you and Nicola."

"Yeah, that's true. When we got back she seemed quite down on account of the fact that she'd split up with her boyfriend, so Nicola asked her to stay with us just until she got her head straight."

"Yeah, I noticed that Kirby and Nicola seemed to have formed a strong connection. She spoke of nothing else on the drive down here."

"To be honest with you, Fallon, I hadn't really noticed. But thinking about it now, I suppose your right. They do seem to make one another happy. Why? Does that bother you then? After all, she is one of your best friends."

"No! Well, maybe just a little. At one time we were closer than you know. Still, I guess you'll just have to help me get over it then, won't you, Kurt?" giggled Fallon.

"I'm sure I can think of something to cheer you up," I replied.

"Promises, promises!" Fallon said with a flirty look in her eyes.

"You've got a dirty mind, Fallon. Do you know that?"

"I know, but that's what you love about me, isn't it?"

"Anyway, getting back to the gossip. As far as the bar is concerned, the answer to your question is yes. It's ready to go. We open next week, so I trust you'll be there. All the advertising has gone out in the local papers and on the British radio stations, not to mention the hundreds of fliers that have been given out already."

"Wow, you have been busy in my absence, haven't you? Oh, and I wouldn't miss out on the opening for the entire world," she said with conviction.

"Glad to hear it. So how come you've been away for so long? I was told that you'd only be visiting your family for two weeks."

"Well, originally that was the plan, but my grandmother passed away while I was out there, so my parents asked me to stay for the funeral."

"Oh, I'm really sorry to hear that. It must have been awful for you," I said, hugging her.

"Well, it was a difficult time for me, as I had to be strong for my parents who were extremely upset, as you can imagine. At least I got to say goodbye before she died, but I'm okay now, and I really appreciate your concern," she said, returning the hug and kissing me on the forehead.

"Well, enough of that talk. The main thing is you're back amongst friends now, so let's celebrate with a toast to your return."

"To my return, to promises fulfilled, and to your success, Kurt," said Fallon as she chinked her glass against mine.

We chatted for a while longer until Tony came over and introduced me to a couple of friends of his. They were called Steve and Andy. They were both over six foot tall, and like Tony, they were built like brick shit houses. He told me that, as luck would have it, they'd only just arrived in Fuengirola this week and were both looking for work. It turned out that Steve and Andy used to work with Tony in London for a security firm that protected, amongst others, several of the top English boxers and promoters. They were in Spain to try and make a new life for themselves, as they were fed up with living in England and getting nowhere fast.

Fallon realized that we were about to talk business, so she excused herself, kissed me on the cheek, and said that she'd leave us to chat for a while. I thanked her and told her to go join the others and enjoy herself.

I shook Steve and Andy by the hand and asked them to take a seat so that we could chat. I started by telling them that I'd only be looking to pay about £35 a night, as this was the going rate for doormen out here. To be quite honest with you, I didn't think they'd accept that amount of money given their working history, but to my surprise they went for it straight away. We all shook hands on the deal, and I told them that they could start work next week on the opening night. This was great news for me, as I now had most of the staff that I required, which was a big headache off my mind.

We carried on chatting for a while until Nicola came over and sat on my lap, begging me to get up and dance with her. So after introducing Nicola to the new doormen, I made my excuses to them and followed her to the dance floor to join the rest of the crew, who were already up and strutting their stuff.

It turned out to be a good night. At the end of the evening once most of the punters had left, several of us stayed on for a locked-in drinking session with the staff. I got to know Steve and Andy a little better over the next hour or so. People tend to look at bouncers with a certain amount of fear and trepidation because of their hard-man reputation, and although there is some substance in that, underneath all that bravado they are just like anyone else, friendly and very approachable.

We finally left Linekers at about 4 a.m., but as we were all still in good spirits, I invited all those who wanted to come back with us to the Stage Door to finish the night off. Quite a few of the staff came with us, including Danny, Tony, Luciana, Fallon, Kirby, and of course my two new doormen. Alan and Peta decided that they'd had enough and jumped into a cab to head back to the villa for a bit of fooling around, no doubt.

We started walking the short distance from Linekers to the Stage Door. The streets were still quite busy with people. Although most of the evening bars had now closed, the Underground was still in full swing, as were several other clubs in the vicinity. There were a few Spanish clubs open, but they never really attracted the same sort of crowds as the English clubs. It was becoming quite obvious to me that apart from a select few, the Spanish and English didn't really mix. They just tolerated each other, but that was as far as it went.

We walked past the Underground and headed up past the bowling alley at the end of the road, which also had a club underneath it. As we passed the bowling alley, a group of drunken lads came out and started having a go at a couple of girls who were passing by. Naturally, I stepped in and asked them to leave the girls alone. They immediately took offence and turned on me with a tirade of abuse. Before I had a chance to react, Steve and Andy jumped in front of me and whacked two of them to the ground. They then turned on the others, who took one look at them and decided to run away as fast as they could.

Steve and Andy then turned their attentions back to the two lads on the floor, but before they could finish them off, I jumped in between them to stop them causing any serious damage and asked them to back off, as I didn't think it was necessary to do anything else to them. I wasn't really sure how they would react to my request, but to my relief they backed off from the lads, and after making them apologize to the two girls, they sent them on their way.

I thanked the lads for their help, and we all carried on to the entrance of the Stage Door and went inside. The first thing I did after turning the lights on was to fire up the Sky TV and stick on a music channel. Nicola and Kirby jumped behind the bar and started pouring the drinks, while I gave Steve and Andy a quick tour of the bar that they would be working in. There were probably about twenty people in the bar who had come back with us from Linekers, which was just about enough to create an atmosphere. As soon as the drinks were poured, most of the girls made their way onto the dance floor, while I sat down with Steve and Andy to go through what I expected from them once they'd started working for me.

Nicola had stayed behind the bar serving the drinks, and after I'd finished talking business with the lads, I went back there to join her. We stayed down the Stage Door until about 7.30 a.m. and then turfed everyone out, as the offices above would soon be opening up and would no doubt complain about the noise from below. After locking up and saying our goodbyes, Nicola, Kirby, Luciana, Tony, and I made our way down to the port to see if we could find anyone open for breakfast. We approached Scottie's, only to find the shutters pulled down. All around us the other bars were also closed.

"I don't believe it! I really fancied a breakfast to finish the night off, and the nearest decent breakfast bar is in Los Boliches."

"Well, we've walked this far, so I guess another ten minutes isn't going to make that much difference, is it?" asked Nicola.

"Well, if we're all going to walk up to Los Boliches, then the least I can do is invite everyone into mine, and I'll cook breakfast. After all the trouble you lot went to with my party, it's the least I can do," said Fallon.

"Okay, cool! That settles it then, but the question is how good are you in the kitchen?"

"I can assure you that I'm a very good cook, Kurt," said Fallon. She then whispered in my ear, "For your information, Kurt, I'm as good in the kitchen as I am in the bedroom!"

"Well, in that case what are we waiting for? Let's start walking," I whispered back to her.

It took about fifteen minutes of hard walking to get to Fallon's place, which, fortunately for us, was situated on the ground floor of a relatively new apartment block that faced the beach in Los Boliches. Fallon opened her front door, and we entered into a small hallway with several doors in it. One of the doors led straight into a large front room which had a kitchen attached to the end of it and a large set of patio doors that led out onto a private terrace that faced the communal gardens and pool area.

Fallon put on some music and opened up the patio doors to let in some fresh air and told us to make ourselves comfortable while she cooked up some food for us. It was far too hot to be inside even at this hour of the day, so we decided to go out onto the terrace while Kirby, who was familiar with Fallon's place, fixed some drinks. It wasn't long before the food started arriving, and we all sat down to eat what could only be described as a very well-cooked breakfast indeed!

"Oh, my god! I'm shocked. That was beautiful. I'm completely stuffed. My compliments to the chef," I said, tipping my baseball cap towards Fallon.

"Yeah, me too. I really enjoyed that. It was well worth the wait," said Nicola.

"Good, I'm glad to hear it. So, marks out of ten then, Kurt?"

"Well, without a doubt it's ten out of ten from me."

"Thanks. I don't wish to sing my own praises, but I did tell you so," said Fallon, laughing.

We sat around chatting for a good twenty minutes or so after eating to let our food go down before Fallon stood up and started clearing the table. I couldn't let her do it on her own, so I offered to help, being the gentleman I like to think I am. She gratefully accepted.

Nicola and the others decided to go and grab a sun lounger by the pool and relax for a bit, while I made my way inside to help wash up. Once we'd brought everything into the kitchen, Fallon asked me if I'd mind starting without her, as she was feeling a little tired and wanted to get changed and to freshen up a bit.

"Sure, no problem," I said.

"Thanks, you're such a sweetie. Oh, and by the way, I meant what I said about the bedroom. My door's always open to you." Fallon hugged me and kissed me on the lips.

"Hey! Behave yourself. Nicola's just outside."

"She's sunbathing by the pool, and to be quite honest with you, I don't care if she is just outside," she said, smiling.

I told her to stop being naughty, smacked her on the arse, and sent her on her way. It must have taken me all of ten minutes to wash and tidy everything up, as she was quite a messy cook.

By this time I was starting to feel a little dizzy and fuzzy in the head. I guess I must have had more alcohol last night than I'd realized. It was just about then that Fallon reappeared in the kitchen, looking remarkably more refreshed and much livelier than she had been before. She had also got changed into a loosely fitting white blouse that was wrapped around her perfectly formed breasts and then tied up in a knot at the front. Around her waist she was sporting a red and black tartan miniskirt that may as well have been a belt for all the material it contained. Not that I was complaining. Quite the opposite in fact! Looking at Fallon dressed like that was making me feel very horny at this moment in time, and to finish things off, she had on a set of furry white ski boots, and her long blonde Swedish hair was tied up in pony tails.

Believe me when I tell you this, she looked like sex on a stick . . . every man's fantasy!

"Wow, look at you! You look fantastic—far too sexy and alert for this time in the morning."

Fallon glanced down for a split second and then lifted her head. Tilting it slightly to the right, she looked me straight in the eye. Half-smiling, she gently bit down on her lower lip and nervously giggled.

"So tell me, Fallon! What's your secret?"

"What do you mean?"

"I mean, ten minutes ago you looked worn out and dead to the world after a heavy night out, and in the short space of time that you took to freshen up, you've transformed into an alert-looking sex kitten. You'd better give me some of whatever it is you're on," I said jokingly.

"Well, I've got a little confession to make" said Fallon, biting a little harder on her lip.

"Why? What have you done?"

"Well, I didn't say anything before to you, as I wasn't sure about your views on social drugs, although I know that you don't mind having a joint now and then."

"Yes, that's true, but a joint doesn't make you upbeat and alert in ten minutes flat, does it?"

"No, you're absolutely right of course, but as you can see, Charlie does . . ."

"What do you mean by Charlie? Oh right! You mean cocaine, of course. How stupid of me! I should have realized."

"Why's that? Have you tried it before then?"

"No, but many of my friends have used it. Personally, it's not something that I've ever really wanted to try."

Fallon walked towards me. Raising her hand, she gently trailed her index finger over my bottom lip.

"Why don't you try some now? I promise you'll like it."

I shook my head at Fallon, repeating to her that it really wasn't something that I was interested in, but she was persistent in her requests and obviously flirting heavily with me. For a second or two it crossed my mind that she might have slipped something into my drink a little earlier, as that would have explained why I felt so dizzy at the moment. But then

I thought that I was probably just being paranoid, so I decided not to ask her about it. Fallon's persistence was fast becoming overwhelming, so in the end I agreed to try some just as a way of backing her off.

On hearing this, her face lit up with delight, and she stepped back, reached into her blouse, and pulled out a small plastic wrap containing the Charlie. She pulled open the top of the wrap, which had been melted shut, and poured out a pile of white powder onto the kitchen counter and then opened the cutlery draw and took out a small piece of what looked like a Macdonald's straw and a credit card, which she used to cut the powder into two lines.

"Okay, I'll go first just to show you that there's nothing to it." Fallon put the straw to one of her nostrils, while covering the other with a finger from her other hand. She bent over, sniffed the line through the straw, and then stood up with a very satisfied look on her face.

"See, there's nothing to it. Go on then. Now you try it." Taking the straw from her, I bent over and sniffed up the second line. It immediately made me cough as it hit the back of my throat. This started Fallon laughing.

"Don't worry about me. I'm only choking to death over here."

"Ah, poor baby. What you need is some more of the same medicine."

"What! Now you are taking the fucking piss!"

"Trust me, it's the best thing that you can do after the shock of the first line. But this time you should take it shotgun style!"

"That sounds dangerous, so I think I'll pass."

"Please take it. I've only got enough for one more line each and then it's gone."

"Okay, but this is the last one that I'm taking."

"Thanks! You won't regret it, I promise."

"So how does this shotgun style work then?"

"Well, I put a line of Charlie in a note and roll it up into a pipe. Then you just tip your head back and I'll gently blow it through the pipe up your nose. It's as easy as that, and once I'm done, you can return the favour and do me," said Fallon.

Believe me, you don't know how much I'd like to do you right now, I thought to myself. This Charlie stuff certainly made me feel very sexual, which I've got to say felt great. Fallon poured some more coke into a note and asked me to tilt my head back. She then pushed her makeshift pipe up one of my nostrils and gently blew the powder up my nose.

"Fuck me!" I said, stumbling backwards with the shock of what had just happened.

"Are you okay?" she said in fits of laughter.

"Fucking hell! My eyes are watering, my throat and tongue have gone numb, and I feel as dizzy as fuck!" I said. Fallon just stood there with her hand over her mouth chuckling to herself.

Once we'd both regained our composure, I repeated the pipe-blowing exercise on her, and to my delight her reaction was similar to mine, which in turn made me laugh. I let her recover and then suggested that maybe we should re-join the others by the pool.

"No! You can't! Not just yet," she said, grabbing my arm.

"Why not?"

"Well, there's one more thing I need to give you. Stay here and close your eyes. I'll be right back," she said. She pecked me on the cheek and then promptly left the room.

I stood in the kitchen with my eyes closed and my back up against the worktop feeling pretty strange. On the one hand I felt quite dizzy and a little queasy, but on the other hand I could feel the adrenaline rushing through me, lifting my body from the tiredness of the night before. It was an incredible rush, and it wasn't long before I could hear Fallon's footsteps re-entering the kitchen.

"Have you still got your eyes closed?"

"Yes, just like you asked."

"I've just checked up on the others, and they all seem to be quite happily dozing by the pool. Okay, it's time to hold your hands out—and no peeking!"

I did as she requested, wondering what it was that she was up to. It didn't take too long before I realized that Fallon's firm breasts were now in my hands. Half-startled and half-shocked, I opened my eyes. Fallon grabbed hold of my hands to stop me pulling them away. Her blouse was now hanging open, revealing her breasts in all their glory. She moved towards me and pressed her semi-naked body against mine and kissed me passionately on the lips.

In my mind I knew that what she was doing was wrong and I should have stopped her straight away, but I was so incredibly turned on by her actions that I couldn't help myself. It was like I'd lost control of all my senses and reasoning abilities. I was totally overtaken by the situation.

Fallon's lips parted from mine, and with a look of pure desire on her face, she put an arm around my shoulder, pulled herself up onto me, and wrapped her legs around me. She then slid her other hand down between her legs and into my jogging shorts. I gasped as she took hold of me, and before I knew it, she'd guided me inside her. This sent shudders through me that I couldn't even begin to explain!

There was little that I could do to resist her now and within moments of this happening we were frantically banging each other like a pack of wild animals, only stopping briefly to catch our breath before starting again.

Kissing her frantically, I could literally taste the sweat from the both of us on my tongue, and then with an overwhelming sense of desire I looked straight at her, ran my fingers down her now sweat-soaked back, and cupped her arse in my hands. She looked back at me, dropped her arms down around my waist, leaned back, and then proceeded to fuck me as hard and as fast as she could, until we eventually both climaxed together in an explosion of sound and hormones.

It took several minutes before either of us could even speak to each other, let alone move. I just stood there with Fallon still wrapped around me, unable to even lift her off me. We were both physically exhausted!

In those few minutes of passionate embrace, I realized why people took Charlie socially, as the sexual sensations that it brought were second to nothing that I'd ever experienced before. The obvious downfall was that it most definitely clouds your judgment!

Fallon regained her composure and climbed down off me. She glanced up at me with a look of total satisfaction on her face like the cat that had just got the cream, and she slowly kissed me once more.

"Mmm, now that was what I call intense!" said Fallon.

"Fuck yeah! That was incredible, but we shouldn't have done it."

"I didn't hear you complaining at the time," said Fallon, trailing her finger tips over my lips.

"Fallon, I was so turned on that I couldn't have stopped you if I'd tried."

"I knew you wouldn't disappoint me," she said, smiling.

"You can't say anything to Nicola. Promise me!"

She assured me that she wasn't a kiss-and-tell type of girl, so I didn't need to worry, as she wasn't going to say anything to Nicola or anyone else for that matter, and with that she kissed me and then left the kitchen to freshen up once more.

It took a few minutes more before it properly dawned on me what I'd just allowed to happen. I couldn't believe how fucking stupid I was to get drawn in and carried away like that! I guess I was just lucky that we hadn't got caught. I tided myself up and splashed some water on my face before going back into the front room where Fallon was now waiting for me. She once again assured me that she wouldn't say anything and that it would be our little secret.

We re-joined the others who were still dozing on the sun beds outside. Quite frankly, I'm surprised that they didn't hear us, what with all the noise that we must have made.

I still felt a little fuzzy in the head—not surprisingly really after all the alcohol, drugs, and rampant sex I'd just had, although I would have to say that having sex did take the edge off the effects of the cocaine. Releasing all that sexual tension definitely had the effect of bringing you back down to earth with a bang.

I decided to lie down by the pool for a bit myself before waking up Nicola, as she was now obviously starting to burn in the sun. The others soon followed suit, and we had one more drink before gathering our things to leave. In a flurry of kisses, we were out the door and on our way home. I felt that it would be best to avoid Fallon over the next few days to let the dust settle, so to speak, as I didn't want to jeopardize my relationship with Nicola, what with the Stage Door opening next week. At this moment in time I had far too much to lose for the price of temptation.

No, the best course of action for the rest of the week would be to give as much time to Nicola as possible and maybe encourage her friendship with Kirby to grow a little more so as to take the spotlight away from me. Apart from my obvious guilty conscience, this would be the last bit of free time we'd have for a while.

We didn't go anywhere in particular; we just lazed around by the pool and had a couple of nights out in the Mijas village bars. Alan and Peta hired a car to go exploring the nearby towns for a few days, which left me, Nicola, and Kirby, who was still staying with us for the moment at least. She still had her apartment, but she was now in two minds whether or not to keep it. Alan had been offered a villa of his own just down the road from us and was on the verge of deciding whether or not to take it once the current tenants moved out. Nicola told me that she'd spoken to Kirby, and between them they'd decided that, subject to my approval and Alan's decision, Kirby could move into Alan's room permanently and give up her apartment to save on cost.

Kirby was quite a cute bubbly girl and really seemed to make Nicola happy. In fact, they'd become inseparable of late, and I must admit I quite liked having her around, so I agreed to her request. A smile lit up across Nicola's face. She was noticeably pleased with my decision and straight away dragged me out to the pool with her to tell Kirby the good news. Well, at least I'd managed to do something right this week, I thought to myself. Kirby was obviously pleased with my decision, and the two of them spent the rest of the day pampering me, which I gratefully accepted.

The next few days went by fairly quickly in much the same way, and before we knew it, we'd reached the day before the opening night.

It was 11 a.m., and the sun was starting to stream through the cracks in the blinds. Nicola was lying on her stomach with her right arm trailing over my bare chest, still sleeping. She looked as stunning as ever with her long brown hair covering her freckled back. I would have been sleeping too but for a knock on the bedroom door.

"Come in," I said.

The bedroom door slowly opened, and Kirby entered carrying a tray of teacups.

"I couldn't sleep, so I got up and made tea, and I'm cooking us all breakfast."

"Fucking hell! We are privileged."

"Oi, you, don't be cheeky or I won't make it."

"No, no, don't do that. I'm starving."

"Okay, you wake Nicola up while I finish off cooking, and I'll join you in a second," said Kirby.

I pulled Nicola's hair away from her face and kissed her on the cheek to gently wake her up. Nicola stirred and eventually sat up. I told her Kirby was on her way with the breakfast, so she slipped on a nightdress, as we always slept naked, what with the heat out here. A few minutes later Kirby returned with the food and sat down on the bed with us to eat and chat about the day ahead.

"This is the life, eating breakfast in bed with two sexy girls still in their nightdresses!"

"Hey, behave yourself or the pair of us will turn you over and smack that bare arse off yours," said Nicola.

"Now you're teasing me, but carry on. I like it."

Nicola and Kirby just looked at each other and burst into laughter.

"Okay, enough fooling around. What's on the agenda today then?" asked Nicola.

"Well, I guess we should go down to the Stage Door and run through our final checks to make sure everything's ready and working for tomorrow."

It was about three o'clock by the time we got down to the Stage Door. There was a little cleaning up to do, as we'd left it in a bit of a state from the other night, so while the girls got on with that, I went around checking all the equipment and lighting. Once I was satisfied that everything was okay, I sat down to make my phone calls to the rest of the staff just to make sure that there'd be no hiccups, and I arranged to meet them all at the London Bar the following night.

All of this took a couple of hours to accomplish. Once we'd finished, we locked up and went into town, as we still had to check with the printers to see if the last of the fliers were ready to pick up. Everything seemed in order there, and as we had very little else to do, we decided to walk down toward Linekers to get some dinner.

As we approached the port, we noticed that they'd set up a row of market stalls along the promenade full of bargains, which as everybody knows is like a red rag to a bull for a woman. As a consequence we spent the next two hours walking up and down window-shopping trinket stalls!

Luckily, at about seven o'clock it was just starting to rain, so we cut short our bargain hunting and made our way into the nearest restaurant. It was the first time we'd experienced rain out here, and although it wasn't raining heavily, it was still quite constant. Unfortunately, we'd come out in our usual summer wear. It was still raining when we left the restaurant a couple of hours later, so rather than getting soaking wet going from bar to bar, we decided to call it a day and made our way up the hill to Mijas to the comfort of our villa.

Once inside we dried each other off, had one more drink, and then went to bed, leaving Kirby curled up fast asleep on the couch.

At about 4 a.m. we were both woken up by a very loud bang. It was the sound of thunder outside. It wasn't raining anymore, but it had now turned into a pretty nasty electrical storm. The next thing we knew, the thunder banged again and Kirby burst into the room in tears, telling us how frightened she was of the storm. This was followed by another loud bang, which made Kirby jump onto the bed and grab hold of Nicola. I told Kirby that she could stay in here with us tonight. This seemed to calm her down a touch, and she climbed into bed between us and cuddled up to Nicola. I eventually drifted back off to sleep.

I woke up the next morning to find Kirby snuggled up tight to me with Nicola cuddled up tight to her. The storm had stopped and the usual rays of light were now back, piercing through the blinds once more. I was dying for a pee, so I gently lifted Kirby's arm from around my waist, trying hard not to wake her. I slipped out of the bed and quietly walked towards the bathroom door, stopping en route only to pick up my jeans, as I wasn't wearing anything at the time.

"Nice arse!" said Kirby in a sleepy voice.

"Oi! You're supposed to be asleep."

"Sorry, but you woke me getting up."

"Okay, but cover your eyes. You're not supposed to be looking."

"Yeah, cover your eyes, Kirby. Although she's absolutely right—you do have a nice arse," piped up Nicola, who, it seemed, was now also awake.

"What! And miss my chance to see you naked? No way!" giggled Kirby.

"You girls are worse than us blokes," I said.

I reached the bathroom door and closed it behind me. After showering, I pulled on my jeans and re-entered the bedroom to find Nicola and Kirby giggling together about Kirby catching me sneaking across the room naked. Nicola didn't seem to have a problem with that—in fact, quite the opposite. She found my embarrassment very amusing.

They told me that the storm had carried on and kept them awake for another couple of hours until they'd eventually fell asleep.

"Shit! If only I'd managed to stay awake for a little longer, we could have joined in with the banging and had a threesome to pass the time."

"Yes, it's a shame. That's what we were hoping too. Unfortunately, it was not to be, so we had to make do without you," said Nicola smiling.

"Ooh, you're such a teasing bitch. Now I'm going to have a hard-on all day just thinking about it."

After a little more teasing and flirting, I got up and left the girls to shower and get dressed while I relaxed by the pool. We laid in the garden until the sun went down, jumping in and out of the water every now and again just to cool down.

Well it's was finally here. The opening night!

We'd arranged to open the Stage Door at 1 a.m., but before that I'd given strict instructions for everyone to meet up in the London Bar at around 10 p.m. just to go through everyone's roles and to reassure myself that none of the staff would let me down. We walked into the London Bar just after 10 o'clock, and I was happy to see Steve, Andy, and a couple of the local flier girls sitting around the table chatting together. There was still no sign of Danny who was supposed to be opening with me, which was a little worrying, but it was still early yet.

"Hiya, guys! No sign of Danny yet then?"

"No, not yet, but don't worry. He's playing a set down at Linekers until 11 p.m."

"Oh, right. Well, can I get anyone a drink then while I'm at the bar?"

"It's okay. I've just got them in. Just look for Keeley behind the bar. You can't miss her. She's the redhead with the big tits," laughed Steve.

I walked up to the bar, which was just starting to get busy now, and caught sight of Keeley straight away. Well, you couldn't really miss her! Even in the drab grey uniform that they had to wear she stood out by a country mile. She was a full bodied redhead with a smile that would light up the darkest of nights, and Steve was right. She definitely had a pair of tits to die for. In fact, I must have been staring for too long, as she started waving at me to attract my attention.

"Like what you see, do you?" she said sarcastically. I laughed to myself feeling a touch embarrassed.

"Yeah, sorry about that, but seeing as you're asking, I'd have to say yes. They look superb and very appealing to me, as do you."

"Well, thank you. I suppose I should take that as a compliment."

"Sorry about that. Let's start again. I'm Kurt, owner of the Stage Door that's opening up tonight. No need to tell me your name as it's written on your breast . . . I mean your chest . . . sorry, I mean your name badge," I said, laughing.

"Well, I'm very pleased to meet you, Kurt" she said in a very posh London accent.

"Likewise!" I leaned over and kissed her on the cheek. "I believe Steve got some drinks in for me?"

Keeley served me and then asked me if it was okay to have a private word with me later. She was new in town and was still looking for some more work to help pay her way out here. I told her that I was a little busy at the moment, but if she wanted to drop by the club tonight, then I'd be happy to talk to her then. She smiled at me and kissed her middle finger and then touched me on the lips with it.

"Thanks, you're a darling—and a very sexy one at that" said Keeley.

"No promises, mind."

"Hey, nothing's definite in life, but you know what they say. 'Don't ask, don't get.' And I've never been a shy girl"

"No, you certainly don't strike me as being shy. In fact, I'd imagine that you're quite the little handful once you get going. Still maybe I'll see you later, Keeley."

I gathered up the drinks and then re-joined the other at the table. Nicola and Kirby were deep in conversation with the pair of flier girls, sorting out the two-for-one introductory drinks tickets for them to give out. They'd decided to go out with them for the first hour or so just to help them out for a while.

Everyone seemed in great spirits, cracking jokes and messing around. I had a good feeling about tonight.

Ten minutes later a waiter tapped me on the shoulder and asked me if I could go up and talk to the resident DJ, who was called Jewels. I excused myself from the group and told Nicola that I'd be back in a while. I walked across the bar to where Jewels was playing and introduced myself to him. He told me that Keeley had said that I was in the bar tonight, which he was glad of as he'd wanted to talk to me for some time.

"It seems that I'm quite popular tonight, especially with people I've never met before."

"Yeah, I'm sorry about that. I meant to introduce myself to you last week, but I haven't seen you about for a while."

"Okay, well I'm here now, so what can I do for you?"

"Well, I work for one of the local British radio stations that you're advertising on."

"Oh, right. Well that explains how you know me."

"Well, I was wondering whether or not it would be possible to get a spot playing in your new club?"

I told him that I'd already promised the resident spot to Danny, but if he wanted to he could pop down and have a try out on the decks for an hour or so to see if Danny and I liked him or not. He thanked me and shook my hand, and I turned around to walk back to the table, only to find Fallon standing behind me looking as sexy as ever. She was standing with a couple of girls I hadn't met before.

"Hiya, gorgeous. Long time, no see," said Fallon. She took me a bit by surprise, as I hadn't expected her to be standing there. "So why have you been avoiding me then?"

"Well, to be honest with you, I thought it was the best course of action. Not that I've got any problem with you, sweetheart. It's just that . . . well . . . we shouldn't have done what we did the other morning."

"Let me guess. You were worried about me spilling the beans. I told you I wasn't like that. You should have more faith in me."

"Well, I was naturally concerned. People say many things in the heat of the moment and generally don't keep their promises for whatever reason. As I said, what we did was wrong and unfair on Nicola."

"What? Shag each other, you mean?"

"Well, yes, what else would I be talking about? Look, I just got carried away in the heat of the moment, what with all the alcohol and drugs that I'd had. I just thought that I'd step back so as not to alert suspicion or put temptation in either of our paths."

"That's okay. I'm only teasing you, Kurt, and by the way, I really enjoyed our encounter last week. You're a very sexy guy."

"Fallon, you're such a naughty Swede, but you should know that it won't be happening again."

Fallon just smiled at me, saying, "Okay, we'll see. Time will tell."

"So aren't you going to introduce me to your friends then?" I asked her.

"Oh, sorry, Kurt. How rude am I. this is Rachael from America. She's over here with her parents for a couple of weeks on holiday. I met her last night at Linekers. And this is Kimberly. She's an old friend of mine from Sweden. We grew up together. She only arrived in town this morning, and she's going to be staying with me for the summer."

Rachael didn't seem too interested in meeting me, so I just greeted her in the usual way with a hug and a peck on the cheek. She was about five foot six inches tall with blonde hair and was quite pretty, but she spoiled it because she had that "I love me. Who do you love?" attitude about her, as though she felt she was above everyone else.

But Kimberly was different. She looked me straight in the eye and told me how delighted she was to meet me. I could feel a definite connection between us, so playing on that, I took her hand and kissed it as if she was a princess, telling her that it was always a pleasure to meet another enchanting Swede.

This obviously hit the spot. She immediately looked down and blushed. I looked at Fallon, and we both laughed at her embarrassment. Kimberly regained her composure and lifted her head and said, "It's true what Fallon said about you then, Kurt." I looked straight at Fallon as if to ask what had she been telling her. "Don't worry. She hasn't told me anything juicy yet! Although, god knows I've tried, and judging by your expressions she's definitely hiding something," laughed Kimberly. "No, what I meant was that she said that you were the perfect gentleman and that you were very attractive. And she was right."

"Did she also tell you that I'm very attached to my girlfriend Nicola?"

"Oh, we Swedes don't worry about little things like that," she said, looking very mischievous.

"Well, it's a pleasure to meet you anyway, and I hope we'll see each other again soon."

"Oh, you can bank on that, preferably between the sheets," she said, smiling.

"Stop teasing him, Kimberly. I'm sorry she's such a flirt," said Fallon.

"You two are as bad as each other," I replied, laughing. I gave her the customary double kiss, and she made her way up to the bar with Rachael and Fallon.

Kimberly was obviously much more approachable than Rachael. She was slightly taller, with the trademark blonde hair, a very cute face, and a great body—just like Fallon. I would have to say that she would probably be a lot of fun to be around and perhaps a little naughty and tempting in a flirtatious sort of way—again like Fallon. But after what had happened between me and Fallon, it definitely would not be to wise to get too friendly with her. I fancied she would be trouble with a capital T, and given the right circumstances and with Fallon's help, she would probably be able to manipulate me between the sheets, as she'd put it. So it was obvious to me that I needed to be on my highest guard with these two.

I walked back to re-join the others at the table, which was now beginning to fill up as Tony, Luciana, and Danny had just arrived with several of their friends. I sat back down with Nicola to see what she was up to. She said she was working out where to give out the fliers with Kirby and the other girls and that she was going to have to love me and leave me in about ten minutes, as it was now just after 11 p.m. and time was knocking. Besides, if she stayed in here much longer, she'd be too pissed to work, as two more drinks had arrived since I'd left the table. I looked down and, sure enough, there were two more pints sitting in front of me. I'd been in here for about an hour now and I hadn't spent a penny. This was definitely the life, but Nicola was right. I'd have to ease up on the drinking if I was going to get through the night!

The next ten minutes passed by very quickly. True to her word, Nicola got up with the girls, gave me a big hug, and then left the bar, telling me to behave myself and not to get to drunk. She also told me that she would meet me back at the Stage Door at about 12.30 a.m., and then she was gone.

Once Nicola had left, I took the time to speak to Danny. "Hey, Danny, sorry I haven't spoken to you properly yet. How are you tonight?"

"I'm great, thanks, and don't worry. I can see how busy you are. I'm quite looking forward to tonight. It's very exciting to be playing on the virgin night of a new club."

"Hey, if you think you're excited and nervous, how do you think I feel?"

"Yeah, fuck, I bet!" he said, laughing. "Anyway can I get you a drink?"

"To be quite honest with you, I've still got over a pint left here."

"Well, I'll get you a brandy then. You've got to toast to the opening night with me or else it could bring you bad luck."

"Well, we wouldn't want that, would we? So I guess I'll have that brandy then," I replied.

Danny got up to get the drinks, and Fallon joined me at the table, sitting down next to me. She'd overheard my conversation with Danny about the drinks and leaned over to me and whispered in my ear.

"You know what's best to keep you sober, don't you?"

"No, and if you're going to suggest a shag in the toilets, then I think I'll give it a miss, thanks."

"No, silly, although the thought's quite tempting. What I actually meant was that you should have a line of coke."

"And look where that got me last time!"

"Yes, but as much as I'd like to rub skin with you again, what I really meant was that it's not just an aphrodisiac. It also nullifies the effects of alcohol. Honestly, it will stop you feeling drunk."

"I don't know if I should."

"It's up to you, but the way you're going through those drinks, you'll be drunk before you get there, and that won't go down too well with the lovely Nicola, will it?"

"No, I guess you're right. Okay, you win. Pass it over here then."

"Kimberly's got it. She's just about to go to the little girls' room, so if you go with her you can share what's left. It's okay. She's sound"

I got up with Kimberly and she took my hand and led me to the toilets. After a quick peek through the door to make sure it was empty, she dragged me inside with her, and we went into one of the cubicles and locked the door behind us.

Well, this was a strange situation to find myself in—locked in a cubicle of the girls' toilets with a busty Swede I hardly knew. If Nicola caught me in here now it would certainly take some explaining, I thought to myself!

Kimberly wiped the cistern lid clean. It looked like we weren't the only ones sniffing lines in here. She then poured the remainder of Fallon's powder out and racked up two big fat lines. Next she took hold of the silver chain around her neck which was hanging down her cleavage and pulled it out of her blouse. On the end of the chain was a small hollow silver pipe, which she used to sniff up one of the lines, causing her face to flush up.

"Oh, fuck me. That's good shit!" she cried out.

She then unclipped the pipe and passed it over to me, saying, "I'm told Fallon broke your virginity last week."

"Hey, I lost my virginity years ago," I replied.

"No, what I meant was the coke. Fallon told me it was your first time. I bet that was an experience for you."

"Yeah, you could say that. So tell me honestly, what else has she been telling you?"

"Nothing. In fact, she's been really tight-lipped and closed-mouthed about you, which is quite unlike her. That makes me very curious. She's obviously holding a torch for you, and I can sort of see why," she said, running her tongue over her teeth.

"Well, I think you're just seeing things that aren't there," I said, smiling.

I thought I'd leave the conversation there before I revealed too much. I took the opportunity to take my line, which yet again made me cough as the powder hit the back of my throat. This time it wasn't as much of a shock to me as the last time, as I was more familiar with the taste and knew what to expect. It wasn't long before it made my tongue and my gums go numb, which explained why Kimberly had been licking her teeth earlier, and it didn't take long before I too felt the rush of it.

"Wow, fucking hell! That's strong stuff," I said, like I was a professional user now.

"Yeah, strong but fucking lovely," she replied.

"I guess we'd better get back before people start wondering where we are."

"Okay, but before we do, there's one more thing that Fallon did tell me."

"And what was that then?"

"It's okay. Don't panic. It's nothing bad. On the contrary, she said that you were a great kisser. So if you want me to let you out of here, then you'll have to buy your way out with a kiss to prove it."

"Kimberly! I've got a girlfriend."

"Hey, I just want a kiss. That's all. I promise I'll let you go afterwards."

"Okay, but one kiss only and then we go, all right?"

"Okay, cross my heart and hope to die," she said.

Kimberly put her arms around me, pulled me in close to her, and proceeded to press her lips against mine. I seem to be getting myself into these situations far too often, I thought to myself, but I thought that as long as I was here in this position, then I might as well give it my all.

I put my arms around her waist, placing one hand on the small of her back, and slipped the other hand inside the band of her skirt and pulled her body tight against mine. Passionately kissing her, I pushed my tongue deep inside her mouth, causing her to gasp and just for a second taking her breath away.

"Mmm, Fallon was right," she said as our lips parted.

With the taste of cherry lipstick in my mouth, I gently bit down on my lower lip. I told her that she was a great kisser too but that it was time that we got back to the others. She agreed and then released me from her grip and unlocked the cubicle door. We left the ladies' room past a bevy of girls who were now in the toilets busy pampering themselves in front of the mirrors provided, and then we re-joined the others.

I sat down next to Fallon and thanked her for the stuff with a discrete kiss on the lips. She just smiled at me, placing one hand on my upper thigh under the table and whispered in my ear, "No problem. Anything for you, sweetheart."

At that moment Steve and Andy turned around just in the nick of time to say that it was time to go. This was perfect timing, as Fallon's hand position had moved up between my legs and was having an obvious reaction. Saved by the bell, you might say!

One thing was for sure. I'd have to keep my wits about me with this couple of minxes. I'd already succumbed to my sexual weakness once before with Fallon, and her friend Kimberly didn't seem a lot different to her. It seemed that the more people that knew you out here, the more people that would tempt you with their forbidden fruit, irrespective of who you were with, and it was very hard to resist. Fortunately, Fallon had so far been true to her word and not kissed and told on me, which would have no doubt destroyed my relationship with Nicola.

Being the red blooded male that I am, I still find one side of me wishing that I was single right now, but on the other hand I really cared a lot for Nicola and wanted it to work out between us. She was undoubtedly the best thing that had happened in my life up to this point. Still, it was a nice dilemma to find myself in.

We entered the Stage Door at about 12.20 a.m. Danny decided to do the first set on the decks, which would free me up to keep an eye on things in the initial stages to make sure everything ran smoothly. It took us about twenty minutes to set everything up so that we were ready to go, which left us another twenty minutes or so before we opened up.

Nicola and Kirby arrived back five minutes later, and we all gathered around the captain's table for a final toast before taking up our positions for the opening night. Steve and I were on the door. We'd set a five-pound entrance fee, although I'd decided not to charge the English residents to get in, as that would guarantee a certain amount of people in the bar.

I could hear people outside the doors, as Nicola had opened the gates at the top of the stairs when she'd returned and I'd also turned on the external signage to help attract people.

It's funny what goes through your head just before you open up for the first time. I found myself imagining all sorts of scenarios, from having an empty club to being packed to the rafters. Still, I guess the only way that I was going to find out was to open the doors, so I asked Danny to fire up the lighting and music, and we opened up.

To my delight I was pleased to see a queue of people stretching up the steps past the gate and around the corner. Sure enough, one after the other they poured in through the doors, filling the club very quickly. Before long they were three deep at the bar.

Nicola beckoned me over to help her and Kirby out, so I jumped behind the bar for a while, just until we got it down to a reasonable level where the girls could cope. An hour passed by before I got out of there, and by then the steady flow of customers had been reduced to a trickle, but the good news was that we were now pretty full.

Steve stayed on the door while Andy circulated around the club. Danny was doing a great job on the decks, but he had been playing for some time now, so I went behind the bar and walked down to the DJ booth to make sure he was okay.

"How's it going, Danny?"

"Hey, Kurt, I'm having a great time. This crowd is terrific."

"Well, in that case I'll leave you to it for a while longer. If you need a drink, just give one of the girls a shout, okay?"

He nodded towards me and then took the mike and shouted out to the crowd for requests. This brought several girls shuffling off the dance floor towards him. It was funny to see. The die-hard clubbers won't even stop dancing when they're getting a drink at the bar, let alone requesting a song from the DJ.

It was getting pretty hot in the bar now, what with all these people in here, so I went out into the hallway and turned the air conditioning on. I decided that while I was near the entrance doors, I might as well pop outside for a smoke and some fresh air. I'd not been outside very long when I heard a Geordie accent coming from the top of the stairs congratulating me on the opening night. When I turned around, I saw that it was Scott, the manager from Linekers with a group of friends. One of them was the lovely barmaid that I'd met in the London Bar earlier. Scott and his party walked down the concrete steps to greet me.

"Hi, Scott, it's good to see a fellow manager down here," I said, shaking his hand.

"Hey, Kurt, how's tricks?"

"Good, thanks. We're very busy tonight, which I can tell you is quite a relief."

"Glad to hear it. I couldn't resist coming down here on the opening night."

I opened the door for him and told Steve that there would be no charge for this group. Scott and his party thanked me and then made their way into the club, apart from Keeley that is. She'd hung back from the rest of the group so that we could have that chat that I'd promised her earlier.

I greeted her in the usual way with a hug and a kiss as her perfume wafted up my nose. I'm no expert on perfumes, but I could tell that she was wearing Chanel No. 5. I knew this because it was also Nicola's favourite perfume and I was quite fond of it. She'd obviously been home to get changed since I'd last seen her. She looked a lot different now out of her barmaid's outfit. She was now sporting a black pin-striped miniskirt with heavily patterned black stockings and stilettos. She also had on a black open-fronted top that revealed a red lacy bra underneath it, which was holding in those fabulous breasts of hers. She was a very attractive girl who would stand out in any crowd and was definitely a lot more upmarket than most of the girls around here. She also had a very approachable nature about her. I suppose many guys might have found her a little imposing, which is understandable.

I on the other hand just loved confident people. I found it to be a compelling trait in a woman, and I loved the challenge that this type of personality brought. I've been out with a few girls in my time, and the pretty ones would always tell me that most guys wouldn't even approach them for fear of rejection. Seeing Keeley in front of me now, I sort of understood why they'd feel that way.

"Well, I've got to say, Keeley, you look fantastic—good enough to eat, one might say."

"Well, thank you, Kurt. I might take you up on that one day," she said, chuckling to herself.

"So what is it I can do for you, Keeley, apart from the obvious, that is?"

"Well, to be honest with you, I'm looking for some more work. I've just moved out here, and I need a little more money to pay my way."

"Well, I can't promise you anything, but I'll have a chat with Nicola and see what she thinks."

"Thanks. I'm only her for a short time, so I want to make the most of it."

"So what brings you out here then?"

"Well, I've just finished college, and I thought I'd take a break before starting my new career."

"And what would that be?"

"Well, now that I've turned nineteen, I'm going to be going into glamour modelling. My friends a page-three girl, and she's just got me a photo shoot with the *Sun* newspaper, so things are looking quite promising."

"Wow, only nineteen and with a body like that! I'm sure they'll snap you up."

"I like you, Kurt. You're quite the little charmer, aren't you?"

"Hey, I assure you there's nothing little about me."

We both laughed and I took her arm in mine and escorted her into the bar. We walked over towards Nicola, and I introduced Keeley to her. She took one look at her and seemed to take an immediate dislike to Keeley. She greeted her coldly and then dismissed out of hand any possibility of her working here with us. She was very dismissive of practically every word that came out of Keeley's mouth.

In the end she just gave up trying to talk to Nicola and turned to me, saying, "What's the point? She doesn't even like me!"

"I'm sorry. She isn't normally like this."

Out of sight of Nicola she squeezed my hand as if to thank me for trying, and after receiving her drink, she made her way over to re-join Scott's group who were now sitting with all the Linekers staff.

I felt quite embarrassed for Keeley and immediately turned on Nicola!

"What the fuck was that all about?"

"You know full well what that was all about!" Nicola seemed to be quite annoyed. It was quite obvious that something had upset her.

"Look, I really don't know what's got into you, but one thing I do know was that she didn't deserve that."

"You walk in here, arm in arm with that stuck-up slut, and ask me to give her a job!" she said, pointing aggressively at me.

"Whoa! What the fuck has got into you, Nicola?"

"She was all over you like a fucking rash. If you think I'm going to work with that bitch, then you're very much mistaken."

Before I could answer, Andy tapped me on the shoulder to tell me that Danny was requesting a break.

"We'll talk about this later," I said sharply to Nicola.

I turned away from her before she had a chance to reply and made my way over to the DJ booth. When I got there, it turned out that he wasn't quite ready to finish his set yet.

"What's going on, Danny?"

"Sorry, but I couldn't help noticing the argument between you and Nicola, so I thought I'd better step in and save you both."

"Thanks. I suppose it's not really the time and place for a row. I just don't know what's got into her. It was like she'd been possessed. I didn't recognize her."

"Well, it's not really that hard to work out if you think about it."

"What do you mean?"

"Well, it's fairly obvious to me that Keeley really likes you, and she's quite a stunner to look at. Nicola was blatantly jealous."

"But Nicola sees me with a lot of girls, and she's never reacted like that before!"

"True, but to be fair, your Nicola's quite a stunner too. Most of the girls that you chat to, although attractive, are not quite on her level. But Keeley definitely is! That, my friend, makes her a threat!"

"So tell me, Danny, when did you become such an expert on women then?" I asked him, laughing.

"Hey, I've been out here for so long now that I've seen it happen over and over, but believe me, I'm no expert," he replied.

"Okay, thanks for saving me and for the advice. Wrap up your set now. I need something to do to take my mind off of it."

Danny finished off his session and then announced on the mike that I was taking over, which brought a big cheer from the crowd. I kicked off my set with the new "Magic Carpet Ride" track by the Mighty Dub Katz, which sent everyone shuffling onto the dance floor. Danny had done a great job warming up the crowd, which made it much easier for me to get them all in a party mood with tracks like "The Original I Love You Baby" and "It's Gotta Be Big" by Tory Amos. This lifted everyone, which in turn lifted me.

I carried on playing until about 5 a.m. when Danny took over to play the last hour out, as we were only licensed to open until 6 a.m. Once Danny had taken over, I made my way back behind the bar towards Nicola, who now had Luciana as well as Kirby assisting her. Luciana gave me a hug as I passed by her, and I eventually reached Nicola, who was chatting to Kirby by the office door. I asked Kirby to give us a minute, took Nicola into the office, and closed the door behind me.

"Look, I'm sorry that I went off at you earlier, but I'm not having her working in here with me," she said.

"I don't know what you've got against her, but if that's how you feel, then that's fine with me. Just don't embarrass me like that again, please."

"I didn't mean to embarrass you, but that bitch . . ."

"Hey, enough of the bitch stuff! You don't even know her."

"I don't need or even want to know her. I've met here type before."

"Sweetheart, she was just looking for some work."

"She was looking for more than that!"

"Okay, stop right there. I won't offer her a job, all right? Now can we forget it, or are you planning to keep this up all fucking night?" I shouted.

Nicola went silent on me. She looked straight at me, and then her eyes welled up and she started to cry. It was the first real row that we'd had, and seeing her so upset made me feel guilty for shouting. I felt so sorry for her too. I didn't like seeing my princess cry, so I pulled the hair away from her face, wiped the tears from her eyes, and gave her a big cuddle to reassure her that I loved her.

"Hey, there's no need for that. I didn't mean to upset you, sweetheart. Stop crying now or you'll stain that pretty face of yours."

"I'm sorry, okay? I don't want to argue with you," she said, still sobbing.

I kissed her forehead, stroked her beautiful brown hair, and repeatedly told her how stupid the situation was, until she finally regained her composure and that gorgeous smile of Nicola's crept back to her face. I finished drying her eyes and we went back into the bar together full of smiles and kisses, which didn't go unnoticed by the customers and staff alike.

Danny wound the night down on the decks. He finally finished at around 6 a.m. by thanking everyone for turning up and encouraging them to come again.

I'm pleased to say that it was a very satisfying and successful opening night. All my worries about having an empty club had been dispelled. I still wasn't entirely sure how much money we'd made, but judging by the amount of empty bottles we'd generated, it was obvious that we'd done quite well. To celebrate we decided to have a lock-in for the staff and a few selected friends. Suffice to say, Keeley wasn't one of them!

I must admit I was eager to find out what the final takings were, but you know what they say. You never count your money while you're sitting at the table! I did get Nicola to bag up the money while I served a round of drinks to the people who stayed behind. Apart from the staff, the usual crew had stayed including Luciana, Tony, Fallon, Kimberly, and a few of the Linekers staff. I suppose there must have been about a dozen of us in total, and apart from the few that were sitting at the bar, the rest of us had gathered around the captain's table for a toast and to chat about the night's events.

Fallon and Kimberly sat down either side of me, while Kirby and Nicola were deep in conversation at the bar. After toasting the evening, Fallon asked me if it would be okay to rack up a few lines on the table; she said that pretty much everyone in here takes it. I told her that until I'd cleared it with Nicola, she'd have to use the toilets, as I wasn't sure how she'd react.

While everyone nipped off to the loos, I took the opportunity to turn off the music equipment and switched the TVs on to the music channels so that we had some background sounds. I also took the opportunity to take the last of the rubbish out and to lock up the gates and the outside doors. Just as I was about to re-enter the bar, I heard a Spanish voice behind me at the top of the stairs.

"Kurt! Kurt!"

I turned around to see a small skinny-looking man standing at the other side of the gates. He was dressed in a scruffy sort of attire. He was wearing a crumpled pair of corduroy trousers with a pair of old brown shoes and an old stripped collared shirt with dishevelled hair.

"Kurt, the music last night!"

"Hang on a minute! Who the hell are you?" I asked.

"Oh, I'm sorry. My name is Raymond. I'm the caretaker for these buildings."

"Okay, so what can I do for you, Raymond the caretaker?"

"Well the music last night!"

"What about it?"

"I've had complaints from the flats above the shops"

"Okay, no problem, Raymond. I'll keep it down next time." Before he could say any more, I disappeared back into the club and locked the doors behind me. The last thing I needed right now was some scruffy whining little spic to bring the mood down!

I re-entered the main bar area to find that all the girls, including Nicola, had now gone into the ladies' leaving Steve, Tony, and Danny still sitting around the table. I must admit I was a little concerned about Nicola's reaction to seeing the other girls sniffing coke!

Whilst they were in the loo, Tony pulled out a big bag of Charlie and asked if it would be okay to do some on the table now that the doors were locked. I agreed, as long as he was quick. It seemed to be par for the course out here to use cocaine as a social drug, and it was fast dawning on me that it wasn't so much a case of who was using it but more a case of who wasn't. It was becoming obvious to me that the latter were the few as opposed to the many.

A few minutes later the girls returned, giggling and laughing amongst themselves. Nicola came over to me hand in hand with Kirby, and they both sat down either side of me, kissing and cuddling up to me.

"Okay, what's got into you both?"

"Well, you know that we've had a great night?" said Nicola.

"And you know that following a great night, we should do something to celebrate," said Kirby.

"Okay, but as much as I'm enjoying the pair of you pawing at me, it's fairly obvious that you both want something from me."

"Yes, we do," they said together.

"So tell me girls, what's it going to cost me?"

"Well, all the other girls, including us, have been sniffing coke in the toilets, and to be honest with you, we fancied getting some for ourselves. What do you think? Can we have some?"

"Nicola! I'm shocked. I thought you were a good girl and a novice to the drug scene. I can understand Kirby being into it, as she's lived out here for some time, but not you!"

"Just because I hadn't smoked pot before doesn't mean I'm a novice to everything else. You shouldn't assume you know everything about me!"

"So it seems."

"If you let me have some coke, it would go a long way to make up for upsetting me earlier."

"Well, first I would never intentionally upset my princess. I love you too much for that. I'm sorry that that situation happened earlier. I should have been more thoughtful. I honestly didn't see it coming."

"I'm sorry too. So . . . what's your answer then?"

"I'm not sure if you should," I said, winding them up.

"Please, please!" I got it in both ears.

They both carried on pleading with me, planting kisses on me and generally annoying me, until I finally caved into their requests.

"Thanks, babe, you won't regret it," said Nicola.

"That's a promise," said Kirby.

For once it seemed that I was the novice, although I wasn't about to let Nicola know that. It doesn't do much for your ego to find out that your misses is not so innocent after all. It made me wonder what else she hadn't told me. Still, I don't suppose anybody really knows anybody when it comes down to it!

"Okay, so how much do you need?" I asked Nicola.

"Well it's about £50 a gram, so a couple of hundred should do it"

"Fucking hell! This coke stuff seems to be quite an expensive habit."

"Please, honey bunny, I'll make it worth your while."

"Careful! I might hold you to that," I giggled.

I told Nicola to take it out of the night's takings, and both Nicola and Kirby planted a kiss on me saying, "Thanks, gorgeous" or words to that effect. Then they went off to the toilets with Luciana to sort it out.

I stood up and made my way over to the bar to refresh everybody's drinks and then joined Fallon, Kimberly, and Danny who were all sitting at the bar chatting. I was starting to buzz a bit from the line Tony had given me earlier. As a result, I was deep in conversation when Nicola approached me from behind and tapped me on the arm to discreetly pass me a wrap of coke, telling me to go and have a line for myself, which I duly did before returning to re-join the others at the bar.

Nicola and Kirby were now behind the bar, so I sat back down next to Fallon and placed my hand discreetly on her knee, slowly sliding it up to her inner thigh muscle so as to get her attention, which instantly had the desired effect. She stared straight at me with a look of surprise and desire in her eyes.

"Here's a little something for you," I whispered to her, passing her the wrap of Charlie.

"You shouldn't tease me like that, Kurt. I thought you wanted something else."

"It was the first thing that I could think of to get your attention. Besides, I like to tease," I said, giggling.

"Well, you've certainly done that, and you don't have to give me this either."

"I want to give it to you. Let's just say it's from me to you with lust," I joked.

As I went to remove my hand she grabbed it and pressed it hard between her legs. "Be careful, Kurt," she said. "I like to tease too, and unlike you, I don't have any restrictions. There's an old saying in Sweden. Roughly translated, it means, 'You shouldn't stoke the fire unless you want it to burn.'"

"Fallon, pack it in. Nicola or Kirby might see us."

"Kirby won't see us; she's got other agendas in mind."

"Oh yeah. And what would they be?"

"You really can't see it, can you?"

"See what?"

"Well, remember I said before that Kirby and I were much closer than you realized?"

"What the fuck are you on about, Fallon?"

"I'll spell it out for you, Kurt. Girl-on-girl action. Kirby and I were an item. She dates girls as well as guys, and it looks like Nicola does too. It seems she's not so snow-white after all, eh?"

Fallon released my hand and thanked me for the stuff and then made her way off in the direction of the loos with Kimberly. I sat and thought about what Fallon had just said, but I just couldn't believe that Nicola was like that. She'd never really let on as much to me. They did sort of flirt with each other quite a lot, but then girls always seem to do that anyway. Besides which, it could be a little jealousy from Fallon after sort of losing a girlfriend to Nicola. She may just be trying to stir the pot a little or just be fucking with my head, so I think I'll leave that one alone for a while at least.

At this point Luciana joined me at the bar, and I took the opportunity to have a quiet word with her about trying to get Keeley some work in Linekers. She told me that she'd try her best and promised me not to mention it to Nicola. This sort of fulfilled my promise to help Keeley out if I could.

The only people I hadn't seen here tonight were Alan and Peta. They'd been exploring the southern coastline, but I had hoped that they would pop in on the opening night. I decided that if I hadn't heard from them by this afternoon, then I'd give them a call. In the meantime, it was getting on a bit, and as we still had Saturday night to get through, I decided to call it a night and encouraged everyone to drink up.

We said our goodbyes, locked up, and then jumped into a cab and headed home to the villa. The girls entered the villa first arm in arm, whispering and giggling with each other. We were all in very high spirits and no doubt a little drunk and still buzzing from the gear we'd had earlier.

This move to Spain was turning out to be far better than I'd expected, although I've got to say that I was finding out that there was a lot more to Nicola than meets the eye. I poured some drinks and walked into the front room, where I found Nicola leaning over Kirby stroking her hair. Kirby was now out cold on the couch. The night's events had obviously proven too much for her, so I picked her up and took her into our room and put her to bed. Nicola wanted to keep her with us to keep an eye on her.

The thought of what Fallon had said to me earlier immediately crossed my mind as I tucked her in, but I dismissed it as paranoia. I kissed her on the forehead and went back into the front room with Nicola.

"Okay?" said Nicola.

"Yes, everything's fine."

"Why don't you strip off and lay down on the couch for me and let me give you a relaxing massage?"

"Mmm. What's brought this on then, not that I'm complaining of course?"

"Well, I seem to remember saying that I'd make it worth your while earlier, so that's what I'm going to do. Is that okay with you?" said Nicola in a very sexy tone of voice.

"Fuck, yeah! That's more than okay with me."

"Good, then strip off and pass me some oil," she said as she slipped out of her dress.

I can't tell you how sensual it felt being massaged, especially after taking all that coke and alcohol. My skin felt red hot and was tingling all over as was Nicola's. She was also experiencing the erotic sensations that the cocaine brings.

The massage was followed by some rampant sex, which ended with us both lying in a tangled heap on the floor. It was fantastic—great sex. Once we'd regained our composure, we made our way into the bedroom to check on Kirby, and then ended the day with us crashing out in each other's arms.

CHAPTER SIX

Teething Trouble

It was now Saturday afternoon. As usual, I was the first to go into the bathroom as the girls were still sleeping. I turned the shower on and stepped inside. I love showering first thing in the morning. It's so refreshing. Once finished, I dried myself off and then opened the door to find Nicola standing there.

"Morning, gorgeous," she said, and she followed it up with a kiss.

"Hey, princess, it's actually afternoon now, but it's great to see you anyway."

I gave her a hug and then left her to it while I went into the kitchen to rustle up some food. Kirby was still out cold, lying face down in the bed, although I fancied that the noise of Nicola's hairdryer would soon wake up sleeping beauty. Sure enough, by the time I returned to the bedroom with the food, both girls were up, sitting in their bikinis in front of the mirror, brushing each other's hair, and applying their makeup.

"I take it you two beautiful creatures are going to be lying out by the pool for the rest of the day then?"

"Yes, how did you guess? You're so clever, Kurt," said Kirby.

"Ooh, we are in a sarky mood today, aren't we?"

"Sorry, Kurt, I couldn't resist it. Now pass that breakfast over here. It smells terrific."

"Looks like she gave you some of your own medicine," said Nicola, laughing.

We ate the food and then spent the next few hours dozing by the pool just catching the sun's rays until the phone rang. It was Alan calling to let me know that he and Peta would be arriving back into Fuengirola in a couple of hours' time and he wanted us to meet them at the London Bar, as they had an announcement to make. Intrigued by this, I agreed to his request, and we all got dressed and made our way into town.

We still had an hour to kill, so we decided to go shopping. As we walked along the high street, we passed a pet shop window which stopped Nicola dead in her tracks. I turned around to see what it was that she was looking at, and through the window sitting in a small wire cage was the cutest Siamese kitten, looking very distressed and hopping around on three paws. We went inside the shop, and on a closer inspection it was obvious to me that apart from the obvious dehydration, the kitten was suffering from a broken paw. Being the animal lover that I am, I turned to the shopkeeper and gave him a piece of my mind! He was quite taken aback by my outburst, and in the end after a heated exchange he offered me the cat at a knock-down price of fifty pounds. He even threw in a cat box and basket! Suffice to say, Nicola was over the moon with her new kitten and couldn't thank me enough. She decided to call the cat Charlie as she said that it cost the price of a gram.

By the time we arrived in the London Bar, Alan and Peta were already waiting for us, and it wasn't long before we found out their intentions. They told us that as much as they'd enjoyed their time in Spain, they were actually now missing England and were eager to return to build a new life together in the UK. They considered it less of a risk, as they both had good jobs to go back to. Alan told us that they had both considered staying out here but that their minds were now made up.

I can't say that I wasn't disappointed by their announcement, but I guess that sometimes you just have to respect the decisions that people make, even if you don't agree with them. They'd also decided that they didn't see the point in delaying the inevitable, so they'd already booked their flights home for tomorrow morning.

As you can imagine the mood was now tainted with sadness, and the tears soon started flowing. There wasn't much that I could say or do but to wish them well and to ask them to keep in touch. I suggested that they should at least come down to the Stage Door this evening, as it would be their last night out here, which they happily agreed to.

Nicola and Kirby then took Peta on a last-minute shopping trip so that they could say their own private goodbyes, leaving me and Alan in the bar. I filled him in on last night's events, and we spent the next half hour chatting until a familiar face walked in.

It was Keeley coming in to do her shift behind the bar. She caught sight of us and made a beeline straight towards me.

"Hiya, sweetheart, it's good to see your pretty face in here, although I much preferred you in the outfit you were wearing last night—very sexy!"

"It's good to see you too, Kurt. In fact, I'm glad I've ran into you without Nicola."

"Oh, and why's that then?"

"So that I can do this." Keeley put her arms around my shoulders and kissed me smack on the lips.

"What was that for?" I asked, looking puzzled.

"That was for talking to Luciana last night. Thanks to you, she put in a good word for me, and I was offered three nights a week working in Linekers"

"That's great news! I'm glad to have been of service."

"I won't forget it, Kurt. You've helped me out big time, I can't thank you enough."

"Hey, it was nothing. If a guy can't help a damsel in distress now and then, the world would be a very sad place indeed and certainly not one that I'd like to live in."

Keeley paused for a moment in silence and just looked straight at me. With her arms still trailed over my shoulders, she kissed me once again and said, "Nicola's a very lucky girl. If you were mine I'd never let you go. Oh well, I guess I'd better get back behind the bar before I say something I shouldn't."

"Okay, that's probably for the best. Preferably before Nicola returns and catches you in this position with me!"

I gave her one last hug, and she went off to do her shift behind the bar. I sat back down at the table with Alan, and he immediately wanted to know all about Keeley.

"Wow, she was fucking gorgeous and all over you, I might add! So spill the beans. What the fuck have you been up to?"

"Yes I know she's gorgeous, but it's not what you think. I haven't shagged her."

"Why the hell not? She's obviously into you in a big way, and that's on a plate for you if you want it."

"You seem to be forgetting Nicola in this equation. They've already had one set-to. Last night in fact! Somehow I don't think it would take too long to spread on the grapevine that I was banging the page-three bird from the London Bar, would it?"

"What! You mean she's a page-three girl as well? Fuck me, you lucky bastard. You've certainly landed on your feet, haven't you?"

"Actually, she's not quite a page-three girl yet. She's just been booked in for a photo shoot."

"Hey, that's good enough for me," said Alan, laughing and shaking his head.

"Drink up! We're supposed to meet the girls in town, and then I'm going to take you and Peta out to eat. My treat, and no arguments, okay?"

We finished our drinks and then after I said goodbye to Keeley, we left the bar. After meeting up with the girls, we found a restaurant, and the waiter quickly showed us to a table. The girls were laden down with shopping bags, and we joked about how they were going to get them all on the plane. Unbeknown to Alan and Peta, I'd had a word with the waiter on the way in, and much to the delight of everyone he brought over a tray of sparklers fizzing away in champagne glasses and, of course, a large bottle of bubbly in ice.

We thanked them both for all their help and wished them all the best for the future before devouring the delicious food that had been placed in front of us. Eventually we left the restaurant and caught a couple of cabs back to the villa to relax for a while before getting ready once again for the night ahead.

As usual we met the staff as arranged and then went on to open up to yet another full house. While I was chatting to Alan at the bar, a group of lads next to us ordered a round of drinks, and once they had been served, they each proceeded to drop a walnut into their drink. Following this, they held their glasses high and toasted to the great walnut in the sky. Alan and I just looked at each other and started laughing.

"What the fuck was that all about?" said Alan, looking totally bemused.

"Beats me! This place sure is full of weirdoes tonight, but if they keep ordering drinks, then that's fine by me," I replied, laughing.

"Ain't that the truth?" said Alan.

"I bet you wish you were staying now, don't you?"

"No, you can keep the weirdoes. I'm going back to sanity," said Alan.

Alan and Peta enjoyed themselves immensely on what was to be their final night in Spain for some time. In the morning I helped them pack, and after getting a cab into town to pick up the car, we took them both to the airport for a very emotional goodbye.

It was now Sunday afternoon. We had no work tonight, as we'd agreed to only open up on Thursday, Friday, and Saturday nights, as these would be the best nights to capture the most customers. Besides which, you've got to rest sometimes, haven't you? We'd decided to use the time off to see and experience as much of the lifestyle as we could, and that is exactly what we did!

For the next three weeks things went completely to plan. We filled the bar from Thursday to Saturday without any problems, and we made quite a few friends along the way. It was now approaching July, and we'd gone from strength to strength. It seemed that nothing could go wrong for us.

Wednesday morning came around once again and we started gearing up for another busy weekend. Nicola and Kirby were hard at it restocking the bar while I went through my electrical checks on the music system. I was halfway through my checklist when the mobile rang. It was Tony's voice on the other end of the mobile telling me that Danny had been involved in an accident and had been rushed to Marbella hospital. He and Luciana were on their way there now.

"Oh, my god!" I said out loud.

"What? What is it? What's happened?" said Nicola, sounding very worried.

"Danny's been involved in a car accident, and he's on route to the hospital."

"Is he okay?"

"I don't know, but it doesn't sound good."

Nicola and Kirby both started crying. I tried to console them, but to be honest with you, I felt close to tears myself. I told Tony that we'd meet him at the hospital and then hung up the phone, and we jumped into the car and headed up there.

We arrived at the hospital reception about forty-five minutes later to find Tony and Luciana waiting patiently for news.

"What's going on? How's Danny?" I asked impatiently.

"The doctor thinks he's ruptured his spleen amongst other things. And he will have to stay in hospital for some time!"

"Oh shit! Can we see him?"

"The doctor said it would be a while before he could see anyone, but we were more than welcome to wait if we wanted to."

"Of course we'll wait. That goes without saying," I said. The girls were in tears, and I must admit that I had a lump in my throat too.

We waited several hours before they let us see Danny. It was extremely distressing to see such a close friend lying there wired up to all sorts of machines with tubes hanging out of him. He was heavily sedated and barely conscious, which was probably for the best. We stayed with him for the best part of an hour before the nurses asked us to leave. We were told that he needed to rest but that we were welcome to visit again tomorrow.

We drove back to Fuengirola to drop off Tony and Luciana at Linekers, as they had to work later. None of us felt like going home yet, so we joined them for a drink to discuss what had just happened. Naturally we were all feeling pretty upset at this moment in time.

I felt it was down to me to try to lift their spirits and get them thinking positively, even though I clearly felt as bad as them. I'd built up a strong friendship with Danny since I'd been out here, and he was going to be sorely missed. After toasting to Danny's speedy recovery, I put on a happy face and turned the conversation to the problem at hand.

"It was a terrible thing that happened to Danny today, and our thoughts are with him, but we still have a business to run, and we're now a man down. I know it sounds callous, but it will help no one, including Danny, if we let this setback destroy us now. It's not what Danny would have wanted."

"That's true. So how can we help?" asked Tony.

I told him to ask around to see if he could find us a temporary replacement for Danny for tomorrow night and suggested that we all pull together to get over this difficult time. After all, the show must go on.

Tony went off to make some phone calls and came back about ten minutes later to tell me that there was a DJ called Simon who had a lot of experience working in the clubs out here last year. The only problem was that he was what you might call a loveable rogue. He'd had a few run-ins with the law involving drugs and other petty crimes.

"What do you mean, other petty crimes? He sounds like a shark."

"Oh, nothing much. Just a bit of shoplifting, burglary, drunkenness, and selling pot. Oh, and he's been barred from just about every bar around here. On the good side, he hasn't ever been charged for anything, just cautioned several times," laughed Tony.

"Oh, that's okay then," I said sarcastically.

"I hear what you're saying, but he's actually a very good DJ."

I've got to admit I wasn't too keen on the sound of this guy, so I asked Tony what he thought I should do.

"Well he's the only decent DJ that's about at the moment, and it would get you out of a hole for now. It doesn't have to be long-term, and I suppose everyone deserves another chance, although god knows, he's had his fair share of them. Besides which, if you keep an eye on him, I'm sure he'll give it his all."

"Okay, we'll give him a trial for now. Tell him I'll meet him here tonight at ten o'clock, and we'll see how it goes from there." I thanked Tony for his help, and we left for home to freshen up and to get a bite to eat before returning later that evening to meet up with Simon.

We arrived back at Linekers at just after 10 p.m. and met up with Tony. He took us over to a table at the back of the bar where there was a young guy sitting between two brunettes. When he saw us approaching, he realized who I was and stood up straight away and stuck out a hand to greet me.

He was about five foot six tall with short dark hair, and he had that London cockiness about him—what I would call a rough diamond with quite a good fashion sense. He spoke very quickly as if he was struggling to get his words out, almost like an excited schoolboy.

My initial reaction was to be a little cautious, given what I'd originally been told about him. To me he seemed a little over eager to sell himself, but he had a definite charm about him, and I sort of liked him straight away. I agreed to give him a chance, although I let him know that I was fully aware of his history, and I told him that I wouldn't tolerate any mischief from him. I left him with no illusions that this was most definitely a trial period only!

Simon seemed extremely grateful for the opportunity, repeatedly telling me that he wouldn't let me down. I told him to meet us in the London Bar tomorrow night at about 11.30 p.m., where I'd introduce him to the others, after which we said goodnight and left for home.

We were up fairly early the next day. Nicola had a few things to do in town, so I dropped her and Kirby off and then drove up to the hospital to see how Danny was fairing. I arrived at around midday and went straight in to see him. He was still wired up to the machines but looked a lot better and was much more coherent.

"Hey, Danny boy, how's it going?"

"Not so good."

"Well, it could have been worse. At least you're still with us."

"True, but I don't think I'll be working in the club for a while."

"Hey, don't worry about that. What's important to me is that you get better. Your job will still be waiting for you whenever you're ready for it, okay?"

"Thanks, Kurt. That means a lot to me. So what are you going to do about tonight then?"

"Well, I've sorted out temporary cover for you for now. He's had some problems in the past, but I'm told he knows his stuff. His name is Simon. Tony introduced him to me."

Danny told me that he was indeed a good DJ and a very popular one at that. He also told me that he was a bit of a blagger and full of bullshit, which had got him into trouble several times over the last couple of years, not to mention his run-ins with the law. It seemed that Simon had managed to alienate himself from most of the local bars, mainly because his reputation preceded him. That aside, Danny quite liked him and thought that he would be good for business. I thanked Danny for his honesty and then left him in peace, before heading back to Fuengirola to rendezvous with the girls to give them a lift home to get ready for the evening.

We arrived back in town and headed for the Ku Dam restaurant on the port for dinner. Once fed, we walked up to the London Bar for a drink before anyone else got there. It was still pretty early, so the bar wasn't quite full yet. Nicola grabbed a table while I made my way up to the bar. It took me a little while to get there, as it seemed that everyone in there wanted to chat or shake my hand. The funny thing was that I didn't really know most of them, but out of politeness I greeted them back. I couldn't help thinking to myself that this notoriety business was beginning to be a right pain in the arse!

I finally reached the bar to be served straight away by Keeley, much to the dismay of those who had been waiting for a while. Keeley asked after Danny, and I told her that he was doing okay considering what he'd been through. News of Danny's accident had spread like wildfire amongst the locals. Nothing stays quiet out here for long, I guess. I thanked Keeley for her concern and told her that I'd give Danny her best. Then I made my way back to the table through the customers to re-join the others.

It's funny, we'd suddenly found a lot of new friends or people who just wanted to be around us. Some of them were okay, but others bore a resemblance to what I could only call leeches! I wasn't quite comfortable with all the so-called hangers on, but Nicola on the other hand was in her element. She just lapped up all the attention that was bestowed on her. Before I had the chance to sit down, one of the doormen tapped me on the shoulder and asked me to sort out a commotion that was occurring at the door.

It turned out to be my new DJ Simon. He was trying unsuccessfully to gain entry to the bar. The bouncers had been given strict instructions not to let him in because of his past history. I felt sorry for him in a strange sort of way, and I guess I also felt a sense of responsibility, so I found the owner and managed to persuade him to let Simon in as a favour to me. The owner reluctantly agreed with my request on the condition that he could only enter the bar when I was in here with him. Any other time the ban stood. He was sort of putting him on probation, so to speak. I thanked him for his concession and escorted Simon over to our table, making it perfectly clear to him that I'd gone out on a limb for him, so he'd better not let me down.

I introduced Simon to Nicola and Kirby and to Steve and Andy, who had also just joined us. Simon tried his charm on Nicola to try to impress her, knowing that she was my girlfriend. This was a bad move, as she immediately shot him down in flames with some cutting remark about him being a little boy in a man's world or something. This had the effect of temporarily shutting him up. I had to laugh, as the first time I met Nicola she did the same to me.

We stayed in the bar for a few hours before getting up to leave. As we made our way out of the bar, Keeley tapped me on the shoulder to tell me that her page-three buddies were in town tonight and they were going around the bars promoting Rothmans cigarettes. She asked me if it would be okay if they popped into my bar to stand at the door to promote their products to my customers as they arrived.

"Hang on. Let me get this straight. You want to know if a bunch of page-three glamour models can stand at the door of my club giving away free products. Let me think. Hell, yeah!" I said with glee.

"Thanks, Kurt. You're a star," said Keeley, kissing me on the cheek.

"No problem, but do me a favour. Keep away from Nicola if you come down, okay?"

"Of course I will. That goes without saying," she assured me.

I told her that I'd see her later and then left to catch up with the others. Once inside, I showed Simon the music equipment so that he could familiarize himself with it and generally helped everyone get organized so that we were ready. Sure enough, by the time the doors opened, the queue of people had begun to arrive. So we let them in, charging the tourists but letting the residents in for free.

It wasn't long before Keeley arrived at the gates with a few of her friends, carrying several boxes containing the cigarettes and some Rothmans ashtrays and a few ice buckets for the bar. Keeley introduced me to the girls, one of whom was called Melinda Messenger. She was quite petite and very pretty with blonde hair, although I'd have to say that she looked like she'd put her makeup on with a shovel! The thing is, the girls out here are all very well-tanned and generally dressed to kill without being buried in makeup—more natural looking, you might say. This made Melinda, although she was very attractive, look a little plain to me. But still, she was a page-three girl, fact which would undoubtedly bring in the trade, so I greeted her with the customary double kiss and a hug. This job certainly had its perks!

I thanked Keeley for bringing the girls down, and she gave me a big hug and kissed me on the lips. She liked to do this as a way of trying to enchant me or something. I just played along with her, but never in front of Nicola of course. She'd hit the roof if she saw me doing that. The way I saw it, it was just a bit of playful fun.

The girls stayed on the door for about an hour or so before moving on to their next venue, leaving me the remaining cartons of cigarettes to give away or not!

Inside the DJ booth Simon was coping well, and as Danny had said, the punters seemed to like him. So for the moment at least the immediate crisis seemed to have been averted. I took over the decks from Simon after a couple of hours and dedicated my set to Danny, much to the approval of the crowd.

Looking over towards the bar, I could clearly see Nicola and Kirby working their little socks off. Nicola loved being behind the bar dealing with the customers. She had a way with people which could only be described as gifted. The customers adored her, and the funny thing was that she didn't take any shit from any of them!

Simon took over for the last hour while I stood at the door with Steve seeing everybody out. We locked up at 6 a.m. on the dot, as I didn't want to have to deal with Raymond the scruffy caretaker moaning at me for whatever. In the few times I'd seen him, he'd done nothing but moan about the noise levels and the closing times.

As usual the staff and a few friends stayed behind for a late drink. There were never any arguments during the lock-in session, just a group of friends winding down after a hard night's work. Simon joined us at the captain's table with his new girlfriend Zoe, whom he'd just met tonight. She looked a little like one of those new-age travellers and was a little on the thin side—almost bulimic, you might say. She didn't talk too much; she just clung on to Simon like a leach, chain smoking one after the other.

Nicola and Simon were still bickering, as if to try and score points off one another. They were developing a sort of love-hate relationship, but not in a malicious way. In fact, it was quite amusing most of the time. Simon, though, was no match for Nicola and generally ended up being the butt of most of the sarcasm and jokes because of it. Tony sat with Steve and Andy chatting to them. You could tell that they went back a long way by the stories that they'd tell about the times when they worked in the UK. I seemed to be surrounded by a great bunch of characters and lots of pretty girls—Zoe aside, that is!

Fallon and Kimberly were practically joined at the hip now. I had a lot of time for the pair of them, especially Fallon, given our brief history. Both of them were very well liked. There had, of course, been the usual flirting between myself and the Swedes, and I'd gotten to know Kimberly a lot better now. As I'd earlier suspected, she was just like Fallon, always trying it on. She was a terrible tease towards me, but luckily, like Fallon, she was also pretty discreet about it. Nicola and Kirby were also now inseparable. They couldn't have been any closer if they'd tried. This seemed to complete Nicola and made her very happy, which was good enough for me.

We all left the Stage Door at about 8 a.m. and made our way down to Scottie's for breakfast; this was fast becoming a ritual. It's funny, no matter how much alcohol or Charlie you took, you could always fit in a fried breakfast.

It was now Friday afternoon. I had to go down to the printer's to pick up some promotional material for the bar. I left the girls at the villa and made my way into town. As I passed by one of the cafes in town, I bumped into Simon and Zoe, who were sitting on the café's terrace having something to eat. Simon called me over and convinced me to join them. He wanted to sound me out on the possibility of his bulimic girlfriend doing some promotional work for me. Personally, I think he just wanted to keep her out of the way so that he could chat up anything in a skirt while he was working.

There was something about Zoe that I didn't like. I've always prided myself on the fact that I was a pretty good judge of character, and my gut feeling about her wasn't good. In my mind, negative people are a cancer. They spread their negative vibes very quickly, sowing seeds of doubt, and before long they infect everyone around them. I couldn't choose Simon's partners for him, but I could limit the contamination by keeping her as far away as possible from everyone else, so I agreed to his request without hesitation and then left them to it.

I arrived back at the villa to find Nicola and Kirby lying out by the pool, and I decided to join them, although, unlike them, I just dozed off in the shade so as not to get burnt by the intense heat of the sun. Sometime later I awoke to a call from Nicola, who was already up and dressed with Kirby.

"Hey, sexy, it's time to get up."

"What time is it? Why didn't you wake me sooner?" I asked.

"Well, you seemed so peaceful there that I didn't want to disturb you. Besides, it takes us girls a lot longer to get ready than you. It's eight o'clock now, so time's getting on."

"Okay, I'm getting up, and by the way, you look ravishing tonight."

"Always the charmer, Kurt. That's why I love you so much," she said, pulling me up.

I made my way into the bathroom and glanced in the mirror. I was quite burnt by the sun even though I'd been in the shade. It just goes to show that you've got to be so careful out here, especially if you're fair-skinned like me. After showering, I pulled on my jeans and a t-shirt, and we left to make our way into town. As we parked up, we bumped into Steve and Andy, who were on their way up to have an Indian meal. They invited us to join them, and we followed them into the restaurant.

Now I've got to say that I'm a typical English guy with simple taste buds. I like nothing better than cod and chips, egg and beans, pork chops, and British beef. I don't mind some Chinese food as long as it isn't too spicy. To be perfectly honest with you, I'd never eaten a curry before, let alone an Indian meal, so the prospect of eating one now was a little daunting to me. But what the hell, you only live once, and as they say, "When in Rome . . ."

We sat down at a table and ordered our food. I had a mild korma, and the girls went for the chicken curry. Steve and Andy went for the hottest meal that they could order. How people can eat food like that amazes me. The thought of burning a layer of skin off of the inside of my mouth really didn't appeal to me, and how the hell could you enjoy the taste afterwards anyway? I'd only eaten about half of the meal, which I'd have to say I really didn't enjoy, when Steve dropped the latest bombshell in my lap.

"Kurt, we've got something to tell you, and you're not going to like it."

"Why? What's up?"

"Well, something's come up, and we've got to leave for England tomorrow."

"Oh, that's just great! What's the problem? What's happened?"

"Look, we're really sorry. We were really enjoying our time out here and never intended to leave so soon, but we've got no choice."

"What about tomorrow night's shift? Saturday's our busiest night!"

"Look, it's a long story. The truth is we took something from somebody. That's why we were out here in the first place. Unfortunately, these are not the sort of people that you want to mess with, and it turns out that they've found us. We've got no choice but to go back and sort things out. I'm sorry," said Steve.

"Okay, I suppose that I should be grateful that you're at least staying for tonight. Hopefully, you'll be able to sort things out soon."

"Yeah, hopefully," they both replied unconvincingly. This was obviously a serious situation that the boys had got themselves into, and although I felt sorry for them, I had to think about the dilemma that I was now in.

We reached the London Bar at about 10 p.m. to find Simon and Zoe waiting outside. Inside we joined Tony and Luciana at the bar.

"Hey, Tony, how are you doing?" I asked him.

"Better than you by all accounts. I hear the boys are off home to sort out a bit of business."

"Yeah, bummer, eh?"

"Well, don't panic. I've already taken the liberty of ringing around for you."

"And?"

"And I've managed to find someone to help out. He's an Essex lad called Peter. He used to bounce the doors out here for quite some time, but he now works in the time-share business."

"So is he any good?"

"Yes. As I said, he worked the doors out here and ran his own bar in a place called Calahonda, which is not far from here on the road to Marbella. Unfortunately, it all went tits-up last year for him, but he's still well known and well respected in these parts."

"That's great news. You're a life-saver, Tony. I owe you big time."

We stayed in the London Bar until it was time to open up again. To be perfectly honest with you, I don't think that I could have stayed in there much longer anyway, as Nicola and Simon were still digging at each other. Actually, it was quite comical to watch them most of the time, but there was only so much that I could take! Before we left, I took the opportunity to speak to their resident DJ, Jewels. I knew that he was eager to play in the club, and I agreed to give him his spot tonight.

Once we'd got everything ready to go in the Stage Door, we opened up, leaving Simon on the decks while I took a night off from being a DJ to work the door with Steve for a change. Tony had arranged for Peter, the new bouncer, to pop in and see me later.

Working the door was always a lot of fun. It gave you a sort of power over people. The guys entering the bar would always try to talk to you like they'd known you forever, even if they'd never met you before, and they were generally devastated if you refused them entry for any reason. The girls on the other hand were a totally different kettle of fish altogether! Most of the local girls were fine, although there were the exceptions. But the tourists were something else. If they weren't trying to kiss you, they were putting their hands all over you—and I do mean all over you! They would often grab your hand and thrust it into their tops or down their knickers. They just didn't care. They were practically feral, like wild animals. More often than not, they would pop their tits out, especially if there was a group of them, and they had the crudest mouths that I've ever heard. I lost count of the number of times one or more of them asked me back to theirs for a shag. One girl even wanted to bang me up against the doors there and then while her mates watched. It didn't matter to them that I had a partner inside. In fact, I'd often tell them that, but to no avail. They simply had no morals at all.

Don't get me wrong. I loved all the attention I was getting from these sexy girls. It was very flattering, and I'm certainly no saint, but I did try my best to stay true to Nicola, and I definitely wouldn't want to hurt her for some morals-free little slapper who had just fallen into my lap. The truth was that I could have had a dozen girls a night if I wanted to. This place was a wicked bed of temptation for a single guy, let alone for someone who was in a relationship, and I've got to say that at times it was extremely difficult to resist.

I'm sure Nicola was having similar experiences with the guys, and I could only hope that she was strong enough to resist them. This place was certainly going to be a test for the both of us.

Once the bulk of the customers had entered the bar, I left Steve on his own and made my way inside to check on Nicola and the staff. Between them, Simon and Jewels were doing a great job on the decks. The girls were coping well behind the bar, and the only problem I had was the fact that I was running out of whisky and the suppliers were now closed, so I decided to drive down to the Underground to see if I could borrow some from Cirrus the owner.

My car was parked right outside, so I jumped straight into it and headed down to the port. As I approached the lights, they turned red on me. It was early in the morning, and I couldn't see any traffic on the roads, so I impatiently drove straight through them and turned right towards the Underground. The next thing I heard was the wail of sirens. Sod's law, eh? There had been an unmarked police car parked up on the side of the road. I stopped the car, and one of the officers walked up to my window.

"*Conducer de cadanet por favour,*" he kept saying to me.

I think it meant "Produce your driving license, please." I'd been learning a little Spanish since I'd been out here, and I understand him perfectly well, but I made out that I was just a tourist, saying, "*No compredo. Tourista, tourista!*" in the hope that they would let me go.

Luckily, it worked and they ushered me on my way, as neither of them spoke any English. This was commonplace with most of the police out here. After that experience, I continued on my way very slowly. I parked up and went into the Underground to talk to Cirrus about my predicament. One of the doormen led me to the back of the club where Cirrus was sitting with some friends. The doorman introduced me, and Cirrus stood up to greet me. I had met him once before when I was with Luciana, but I didn't know him that well, as I'd not spent much time in here, but he seemed to know who I was. He asked after Nicola and enquired how well the Stage Door was doing. I told him we were slowly building the club up and that we were running out of whisky and wondered whether he could help out.

Without hesitation he agreed, wished us well, and called a doorman over to sort out some bottles for us. I thanked him and waited by the bar. The smell of Channel No. 5 turned my head, and standing behind me was Keeley. She was wearing a pair of ankle boots, a sequined silver bra, and a pair of white hot pants with stockings underneath them. Oh my god, I thought to myself. She couldn't be any sexier if she tried!

"Hiya, gorgeous, you look terrific," I said to her.

"Aren't you going to buy me a drink then?" She replied in a soft voice.

"Of course I'll get you a drink, sweetheart. So do you often creep up on people then?"

"I was going to make you jump, but you sensed I was there before I could scare you."

"That's not very nice, is it? Besides, there's nothing scary about you. Quite the opposite in fact."

"Why, thank you, Kurt. I find you irresistible too!" she said, trailing her fingers across my chest.

"So tell me, if I'm so irresistible, then how come you're down here and not in my bar?"

"That's because down there I have to keep my distance."

"You could talk to me at the door."

"Yes, but that's not enough for me. You see, I'm a very greedy girl," she said slowly, kissing me on the lips.

"Mmm, you're a very naughty girl and a very attractive one at that. You could have any guy you wanted out here, so why waste your time and efforts on me? After all, I'm already taken."

"Most blokes just look at me as a trophy or as eye candy on their arm, whereas you're different. You're exactly the type of guy I go for. You're confident, handsome, funny, sensitive, and definitely driven, and not being available is exactly the point. We all want something we can't have, don't we?"

"I'm very flattered, but as I said, I'm taken."

"And therein lies the challenge," she said, licking her lips.

"Well, on that note I think I'd better go while I still have the willpower to do so."

All the time Keeley had been talking to me, she had been slowly dancing to the music, grinding her hips up against me, and naturally this had got my blood pumping, which Keeley couldn't have failed to notice. I told her again that I had to go or otherwise Nicola would be wondering where I'd got to, but she kissed me again and pressed her hand up against the bulge in my jeans, and for a moment I got carried away and kissed her back before pulling away from her saying, "Look, I've really got to go, Keeley, and you're far too much of a temptation for me to be around right now. So you have a great night, and maybe I'll see you later, okay?"

"Okay, baby, but you don't know what you're missing. Maybe next time, okay?" she said, blowing me a kiss.

The doorman returned with the boxes of whisky for me, and I left the club and made my way back to the Stage Door. I'd have to consider that a lucky escape. Keeley was intoxicating, and if I'd stayed in there much longer, she'd have been taking me home to have her wicked way with me. Given the friction between her and Nicola, I didn't think that that would be a very good idea!

Nicola was pleased to see me return with the whisky, as they were now down to the last bottle. I got myself a drink and walked back to the entrance to join Steve. He was talking to a stocky guy who was about five foot ten with short dark hair. Steve introduced me to him.

"This is Peter Rogers, your new doorman."

I stuck out my hand and greeted him. He was very upbeat and had an air of confidence about him. We sat down and spoke to each other for quite a while, eventually agreeing the wages and working hours. I had a good feeling about him, and as we sat there I couldn't help noticing that quite a few people were acknowledging him. He was obviously well respected by the locals.

We stayed open until the usual time before closing up, and after a late drink we had the ritual breakfast before going back to the villa to crash.

Kirby was already up making tea when I entered the kitchen in the morning, so I got her to throw some bread in the toaster for me. I'd got up early myself today, as I wanted to visit Danny while the day was still young. I let Kirby know that I wouldn't be back for a while and asked her to tell Nicola where I'd gone, as she was still sleeping. Then I left to make the drive to Marbella Hospital. It wasn't long before I was talking to Danny again.

"You're looking a lot brighter today."

"Thanks. I feel a lot better, especially as they've now removed some of these tubes and wires."

"Glad to hear it. Last night went off okay, and you were right. Simon was really good. I also used Jewels from the London Bar. We packed the house again."

"Okay, okay, don't rub it in. I hate being laid up in here when I could be out partying with you guys."

"Poor old Danny! It won't be long before they have you hobbling around again. Oh, and Keeley sends her love. I saw her in the Underground last night."

"You wanna be careful with that one. Given half a chance, she'd have you between the sheets in a flash," Danny said, smiling.

"You don't know the half of it."

"Why? What's happened? And what were you doing in the Underground last night?"

"Well, we were running out of whisky, so I went down to see Cirrus to ask if I could borrow some. While I was waiting for the whisky, Keeley crept up behind me and sort of pinned me against the bar."

"Mmm, you lucky bastard! What I wouldn't give for her to do that to me," he joked.

"Yeah, she's quite tasty, isn't she?"

"Yes she is, but she's also very dangerous to yours and Nicola's future. So think carefully before you act. That's my advice anyway."

I stayed with Danny for another hour or so, filling him in on my doorman troubles amongst other things. He seemed a lot better in himself today, and hopefully it wouldn't be too long before he was up and about, even if it was on crutches. I left the hospital and made my way back to Fuengirola, as I had to see Rosa my solicitor to sort out my accounts. I never was much good with paperwork.

On leaving Rosa's office I received a phone call from Nicola to tell me that they had caught a cab into town to meet up with Fallon and Kimberly and were going to spend the afternoon on the beach. I still had a few things to do in town, so I told her that I'd come and find them when I was done.

I was feeling a little peckish, so I drove down to the port, parked up, and made my way into the local Burger King. I've got to say, the food they serve in the Burger Kings out here actually looks like the pictures on the advertising boards. By that I mean that they were so fresh and clean—much better than the Burger Kings in the UK. Everything was cooked fresh and not just reheated. What can I say? Delicious! Once I'd finished eating, I walked along the beach and found the girls on the sun loungers provided.

"Afternoon, ladies. I brought some cold drinks for everyone, so help yourselves."

"Oh, great! I'm dying for a drink," said Kimberly and Fallon, sitting up.

I stripped down to my shorts and joined the girls for a while before getting up to have a swim in the sea to cool down, as I was starting to burn. Kirby, Kimberly, and Fallon soon joined me with a beach ball that they'd picked up on the way down here. Nicola as usual stayed on the beach sunbathing. As I've said before, she didn't really like going in the sea.

All the girls were topless, as were most of the women on the beach. It seemed very surreal to me playing volleyball with three semi-naked beauties in the sea while my girlfriend sunbathed on the beach not ten yards from me. Could you honestly see that happening in the UK? I don't think so!

We messed around in the water for quite a while before joining Nicola on the beach. She was now turning very brown.

"I'm so jealous that you can tan like that," I said, rubbing some crème into Nicola's sizzling hot back.

"Yeah, I know. It's hard work being a goddess," replied Nicola, giggling.

"So how's Danny?" asked Fallon.

"He looks a lot better today. They've unplugged him from most of the equipment now, and he's awake and talking. You should go up and visit him. He'd like that."

"I'd love to, but I don't drive and cabs are expensive," said Fallon.

"Kurt's planning on going up there again soon, so he could give you a lift if you like. You don't mind, do you, honey bunny?" asked Nicola.

"No, of course I don't mind."

"Thanks, honey bunny," said Fallon and Kimberly sarcastically. The girls fell about laughing on hearing Nicola's nickname for me.

"Nice one, Nicola. Thanks," I said, squirming with embarrassment.

"Sorry, it slipped out," she said, giggling into her hands.

"Okay, well, it's time we made a move anyway, as I'm burning up in this heat and we need to get ready for tonight."

We packed up our stuff, walked back to the car, and said goodbye to the Swedes before heading back to the villa.

I was a bit anxious about tonight. I had the new doorman starting and, of course, we were still running a temporary DJ, what with Danny still being in hospital. Hopefully, though, it would all run smoothly. So far we'd had no real trouble in the bar, which is how I'd like it to stay!

We met as usual in the London Bar, and true to his word, Peter arrived on time, bringing along a group of his friends and his girlfriend Melanie. She was a very pretty girl with long brown curly hair, and like most of the girls out here, she had a figure to die for. It turned out that she was also a singer who performed up and down the coastline in various cabaret bars and clubs, and you could tell that she obviously doted on Peter.

One of Peter's friends was a Geordie lad called Andy. Geordie told us that he used to be an amateur boxer and had won several trophies in his time. I asked him why he hadn't turned professional, but he wouldn't give me a straight answer. He just got very vague about the subject whenever I brought it up. He seemed fairly well-mannered and, like Peter, he seemed quite popular with everyone in the bar.

I introduced Nicola and the rest of the staff who were present to him. Unfortunately, Simon was nowhere to be seen. I waited around until midnight for him, but much to my dismay, there was still no sign of him.

Time was knocking now, so we gave up on him and left the bar to walk the short distance to the Stage Door. I hung back from the rest of the group to talk to my new bouncer Peter while Nicola and the others went on ahead. Nicola and Kirby reached the end of the road before everyone else, and there they were joined by a guy who was crossing the road at the same time. I couldn't quite make out who it was, but I could hear a raised-voice conversation going on. Geordie Andy got to Nicola first, and the next thing I saw was punches being thrown. At this point I ran towards them with Peter, but by the time we got there, the mystery lad had run off.

"Are you okay? What happened?" I asked Nicola. "What happened?" I demanded to know.

"It's okay. It was just Simon," said Nicola.

"I'll kill him," I replied angrily.

"It wasn't his fault, Kurt. He was just making his excuses for being late, and when I told him not to bother, he raised his voice to plead with me," said Nicola.

"It was probably my fault actually. I thought he was having a go at Nicola, so I waded in with a few punches, and he ran off," said Geordie Andy, apologizing.

"It's okay, Geordie, and thanks for protecting her. I appreciate that. The problem is you've just beaten up my DJ, albeit with good intentions."

Peter and Geordie went on with Nicola to set up the bar, while I ran off in the direction of Simon to try to catch up with him. I didn't have to travel too far. He was cowering in a doorway a few streets down.

"Kurt, Kurt! I didn't do anything wrong. I promise."

"If I find out from Nicola that you were out of line in any way, I'll personally beat the shit out of you myself. Do you understand?" I shouted at him.

"Please, Kurt, you have to believe me, I would never intentionally upset Nicola. We argue all the time, but she enjoys it. We have a good relationship. She'll tell you that herself," he pleaded.

"You shouldn't have raised your voice to her. Geordie thought you were attacking her."

"I didn't know who he was, so I told him to mind his own business, and he just went nuts."

"Well, maybe this will teach you a lesson then. Next time keep your mouth shut, and if you have any work-related issues then, you come to me, not Nicola, okay? Now stop fucking around and get yourself back to work."

Simon stopped blubbering and stood up. "There's no way I'm going back in there with him. He's a lunatic!"

"Look, don't worry about Geordie. I'll talk to him, okay? In the meantime you can start by apologizing to Nicola, getting back behind the decks, and by keeping your fucking mouth shut."

"Okay, but promise me you'll square it with Geordie straight away."

"Yes, okay. Now come on, let's go."

Simon followed me back to the bar where he immediately said sorry to Nicola and then did as he was told and went back behind the decks, which is where he stayed all night.

I pulled Geordie and Peter to one side and asked them to go easy on Simon, which they agreed to do, although they both made it perfectly clear that they thought that he was a loud-mouth little prick who had got what he deserved. Geordie was actually a really nice guy, but once he had a few drinks, he tended to start shadow boxing on the spot as if he was about to go into the ring or something. He didn't mean any harm by it, but most people tended to give him a wide birth once he'd started. Even his close friends backed off a little. In his defence, he was sort of aware of what he was doing, as you could see him getting frustrated with himself the more he did it, until he eventually made his excuses and left.

The night went off without any more problems, and judging by how upbeat Peter was at the end of it, I'd say he definitely enjoyed his first night. Simon left fairly quickly at the end of the night, and after a couple of drinks we soon followed.

I was glad to get the working week out of the way, as it had been a difficult time for us to say the least. It seemed that I was now an agony aunt to the staff as well. Still, I suppose it comes with the territory, although it wasn't quite what I'd expected.

I slept through most of the next day, only getting up to eat before crashing out again until eleven o'clock on Monday morning. I found Nicola already up, so I got dressed and went into the front room, where I discovered Nicola and Kirby in what could only be described as a passionate embrace, kissing each other.

"What the fuck's going on?" I asked. I'd startled both of them, and they released each other straight away.

"Nothing's going on, Kurt. We were just messing around, honestly," said Kirby nervously.

"What do you mean nothing's going on? I saw you both!" I said, raising my voice.

"We were only mucking about, honey bunny," pleaded Nicola.

"Don't honey bunny me, sweetheart. And don't take me for a mug either. That wasn't messing about!" I replied, pushing Nicola away.

"Please don't push me away. I love you," she said, turning on the waterworks.

"Look we were only fooling around, Kurt. It's what girls do."

"Don't lie to me, Kirby! I know you're into girls as well as guys. I've been told, okay?"

"We just kissed, Kurt. Nothing else! We didn't mean any harm, I promise."

"What? Didn't mean any harm? Fuck this! I'm out of here. I need to get my head around this," I said, storming out of the door.

Nicola ran out of the villa after me, begging me to come back inside so that we could sort it out, but I'd got myself into such a rage that I just jumped in the car and drove off.

How could she do this to me, I thought to myself. I was only in the other room for fuck's sake! All sorts of things were going through my mind. What else had they been up to? She'd shared our bed a couple of times when she was scared of the lightning and when she was poorly! Did they get up to anything then? Fallon was right about Kirby. I should have listened to her.

My mind was getting ahead of itself and I needed to clear my head, so I drove into town to grab a drink in the London Bar. I ordered a double brandy and just sat at the bar in a state of shock mulling things over in my mind. How could I have been so stupid? I practically pushed them together. It's funny really. Sometimes you can see things unfold right before your eyes, but it still shocks you even though you saw it coming—if that makes any sense.

"Hey, Kurt, penny for your thoughts." I turned around to find Keeley standing there.

"Hiya, sweetheart," I replied.

"What's up? You look like you've lost a pound and found a penny. What's wrong?"

"It's personal, Keeley. I don't want to talk about it."

"Hey, that's not like you. Something's happened, hasn't it? It's Danny, isn't it? Is he okay?"

"No, it's not Danny. Don't worry. It's just something that happened between me and Nicola. That's all."

"You've had a row, haven't you?"

"You could say that," I said sharply.

"Hey, don't take it out on me. It wasn't my fault, was it?"

"No, and I'm sorry. I didn't mean to snap at you. Forgive me," I said, hugging her.

"Okay, I'll forgive you this time, but only if you help me pack."

"What do you mean 'pack'? Where are you going?"

"Well, you can tell me what's wrong with you and Nicola while you're helping me pack, and in return I'll tell you where I'm going, okay? Come on, what have you got to lose?"

"Yeah, what the hell? Fuck it! Why not?" I said.

We left the bar together and I drove Keeley to her apartment on the edge of town. I parked up and we went inside. It was quite a modern apartment with a large front room. I sat down and Keeley fixed the drinks before joining me on the couch.

"Before you tell me what's wrong, you'd better have one of these. It will help you relax," she said, pouring a large amount of cocaine onto the coffee table.

"No thanks, I don't really feel like it right now."

"That's the point! You're so wound up and you really need to relax, so take some please . . . for me," she said.

"Okay, fine. Why the hell not?" I replied.

We sat there chatting and sniffing coke for quite some time, and as I relaxed I told her what had happened between Nicola and Kirby. In return, she told me that she was going back to England in the morning, as the *Sun* newspaper was doing the photo shoot and an interview with her this week, which is why she needed to pack.

"You know, you could use this to your advantage and have threesomes every night. Most guys would jump at the chance," she said, laughing.

"Don't get me wrong. Kirby's a pretty girl, and I'd be a liar if I said that I hadn't fantasized about it before. But what happened this morning felt like a betrayal."

"Ah, poor baby, you're all wound up and tense." Keeley sat astride of me and slowly started rubbing my shoulders.

"What are you doing?" I said.

"God, you're so tense. You need to lie back and relax while Keeley helps you unwind."

I was going to argue with her, but I have to admit that what she was doing felt so good. And she was right. I did need to relax. On top of that, my body was positively buzzing from all the gear we'd just had.

Keeley pulled my t-shirt off and unbuttoned her blouse. She started kissing me and blowing in my ears. I could feel her breasts brushing up against my chest as she leaned over to kiss me, which sent shivers through my body, and I reached up to cup her beautiful firm breasts. Her skin was soft to the touch like silk. I couldn't resist kissing her full on the lips. After that point my hormones took over, and I let her pull me to my feet to lead me into the bedroom, where we both indulged in our carnal desires.

"Wow! I knew you'd be a great fuck," she said, catching her breath.

"Hey, you didn't do so badly yourself," I replied, laughing.

"Why, thank you, Kurt," she said, giggling. "So what are you going to do about Nicola and Kirby then?"

"I don't know, but I'm hardly the one to talk, seeing as I'm lying here in bed with you."

"I think you should forgive her. After all, it could turn out to be a lot of fun."

"It's not funny, but I suppose you're right—although I think I'll make her sweat for a while to teach her a lesson."

"Why don't you stay here for the night? That way you can take me to the airport in the morning and then go back to make it up with Nicola afterwards. You could always say you stayed in a hotel for the night."

"Clever girl! You're not just a pretty face then after all, are you?" I said with a kiss.

I spent the night with Keeley making love to her once more in the morning before driving her to the airport to catch her flight back to the UK. I thought a lot about what I was going to say to Nicola on the drive back to the villa. This was the first time that we'd been apart since we'd moved out here, and it would be hypocritical of me to take to the high ground, as I been unfaithful to her twice already, albeit in mitigating circumstances. I parked the car outside and started walking towards the front door, but before I got there it opened and Nicola burst through it and ran towards me.

"I'm sorry. I'm sorry," she just kept saying. "Please tell me you're back to stay. I really missed you last night," she sobbed.

Nicola was practically hysterical, crying her little heart out. Seeing her like that made me feel awful. How could I possibly be mad at her? After all, I was the one that had just climbed out of another girl's bed.

"Hey, it's okay, princess. It's all going to be okay," I said, holding her tightly. "Don't worry, sweetheart. I'm not going anywhere, okay?"

"Okay, you promise?" she said, uncontrollably sobbing in my arms.

"I promise. Now c'mon, let's go inside and we'll talk it over."

Nicola just nodded and looked straight at me, half-smiling through her tears. I walked her inside and closed the door behind me. Inside I found Kirby sitting nervously on the couch.

"I'm really sorry, Kurt. I never intended to hurt you. You've been really good to me in the past. I've already packed my stuff, so I'll get out of your way so that you can sort things out with Nicola."

"Kirby, sit down! You don't have to go anywhere. In fact, I personally don't want you to go. I like having you around, and let's face it, you make Nicola very happy. The truth is, I probably overreacted anyway. It's just that I don't like being deceived, that's all. If Nicola wants to experiment with her sexuality, then that's okay with me as long as it's done in the open with no sneaking about. You know I'm much more open-minded than you give me credit for. That goes for you too, princess."

"Okay," they both said together.

"Now I think the pair of you should come over here and give me a big hug, and hopefully you'll both forgive me for being such a twat!"

"Are you sure it won't cause a problem between us? I couldn't bear to lose you again," said Nicola.

"Yes, I'm sure, princess. I thought a lot about it last night."

"Thanks, Kurt. I really love you, and maybe the three of us could have a little fun now and then. I'm sure Kirby wouldn't be opposed to the idea, would you?" said Nicola.

"Definitely not. The pleasure would be all mine," replied Kirby, smiling.

"Well, maybe not all yours," I replied.

They both did what I suggested, and we hugged each other for ages. There was a strong feeling of happiness back in the villa, which I for one was very pleased about. They say the best part of breaking up is in the making up, and they're absolutely right. Things settled down over the next couple of days, and as a result of what I'd said to them we seemed to grow a lot closer for it.

Chapter Seven

Unexpected Pressure

Thursday and Friday passed by without incident, and before we knew it we were getting ready to open up for another Saturday night. We opened the doors, and as usual it didn't take long to fill up. Everything went well until about 3 a.m. when a commotion kicked off at the back of the club. There was a large group of people sitting at one of the tables, and they'd started arguing amongst themselves.

Peter made his way over there to sort it out, but before he could get there, one of the guys had grabbed a fire extinguisher and let it off, spraying the girl sitting next to him in white powder. Within minutes the powder had spread throughout the bar, with the help of the air conditioning no doubt. This created a panic, as it took your breath away, and everyone began running for the exits.

Peter quickly opened the back doors, while I helped get everyone out of the front entrance. While I was doing this, Nicola took it upon herself to march over to the guy who let off the fire extinguisher. She proceeded to shout at him, telling him that what he did was bang out of order and irresponsible and that he was going to pay for the damage he'd caused. The guy and his friends couldn't apologize enough, and they pulled out a wad of notes and handed it straight to her. He told her that it was just a row that had got out of hand. Nicola threw a few swear words at him, and after apologizing again, they left.

It didn't take long to clear the bar, but the powder from the extinguisher had spread throughout the club and had settled on just about everything.

We had no choice but to shut the bar down. Luckily, there hadn't been any casualties apart from the girlfriend who was covered in powder.

I only found out about the conversation that Nicola had had with this guy after we'd cleared the bar, as I'd been busy clearing out the customers from the front entrance. Nicola had spoken to him with Peter standing just behind her by the rear doors, and once I'd locked the gates, I went back inside and joined Peter, Nicola, and a few of the others who had remained.

"Do you know who that was?" said Peter.

"I don't give a fuck who it was. This is our bar, and they had no right to do that. It was disrespectful," stated Nicola.

"Yeah, I agree with you, and they're going to pay for it too!" I said.

"That was the Scousers. They're all from Liverpool, and they're definitely not the type to mess with," said Peter.

"Like Nicola said, it was disrespectful, and I assure you they will pay for it."

"It's okay, Kurt. They've already paid and apologized over and over."

"I don't know how you got away with screaming and swearing at them like that. They tend to cause trouble wherever they go, and they don't normally have any qualms about hitting women either," said Peter.

"If they'd have touched her, I'd have killed them all" I replied.

"You don't understand. This group of individuals runs most of the drug scene out here, and they only really answer to a select few that also live out here. They always travel in groups, and if they get taken out, they'll come back in numbers for revenge. Like I said, Nicola was lucky to get away with that."

I asked Nicola how much they'd given her, and to our amazement we found there was over £800 in British currency. That should be more than enough to cover our losses. On reflection, it was probably best that I hadn't dealt with the Scousers instead of Nicola. They would have probably reacted differently if it had been a guy having a go at them.

The bar looked like it had been hit by a snow storm, and it was obvious that it was going to take some time to clear it all up. Luckily, if you can call it that, we had a few days to sort it out. Thank god for small mercies, as they say. You've got to stay positive in life or else you'll just sink in your own self-pity, and I wasn't about to do that.

We decided to leave the cleaning up for now, as Peter had invited us back to his place for breakfast. He wanted to take us on a tour of

Calahonda where he lived, so without delay the few of us who were left, which included Fallon and Kimberly, made our way down to his.

Peter lived in a rented time-share villa that Geordie Andy had sorted out for him. It was quite spacious with an outside terrace, and he also told us that he had the use of the residential swimming pool. It was very clean, apart from a few clothes that were scattered about the bedroom floor. Melanie told him off about this, much to his embarrassment.

While we were chatting, Fallon reminded me that I still hadn't taken her to see Danny yet, so I told her that we'd go and see him once we'd left Peter's.

We all ate the breakfast which Melanie cooked, and then as promised Peter took us on a grand tour of Calahonda. It was a small town—well, more like a village really—with row upon row of white villas leading down to a small purpose-built shopping precinct which was located at the edge of the main dual carriage way that led to Marbella. On the other side of the road was a large bar and, amongst other things, the beach.

"You see that bar over there. That was my bar, and it was very successful," said Peter.

"What happened to it?" I asked him.

"Well, it's a long story, but basically the owner went bankrupt and the banks foreclosed on the whole complex."

"I thought you said that you were the owner."

"I only held the lease on the bar, so when the bank took repossession of the freehold, they terminated my lease, and there was nothing that I could do about it. I lost everything."

"I'm sorry to hear that. It must have been awful."

"It was, but life goes go on, and I just had to pick up the pieces and get on with it. After all, there's no point in crying over spilt milk, is there?"

"No. My philosophy exactly."

"There's one other thing that you should know about me," he said.

"Oh, and what would that be?" I asked him.

"Well, last year I was up on a murder charge."

"I beg your pardon?" I said, feeling a little shocked at what he'd just said.

"Well, someone upset Melanie in the bar one night, and I ended up having a fight with him. I punched the guy a few times before he ran out of the bar. I then chased him down to the road, and he ran out in front of an oncoming vehicle and was killed instantly. The police tried to pin a murder charge on me, as they thought I'd pushed him in front of the car.

"Didn't the driver see what had happened?" I asked him.

"Unfortunately, he was also killed in the accident, so there were no witnesses, and as a result of that they eventually dropped the charges against me."

"So why are you telling me this?"

"Because many people have their own version of what happened that night, so I wanted to be open with you and let you hear it from the horse's mouth, so to speak."

"Okay, well, thanks for your honesty. I appreciate that. Just promise me that if we ever have an argument, you won't kill me, okay?" I said sarcastically.

"That's not funny," he said, and he started giggling to himself.

I was actually quite glad that he'd opened up to me about what had happened. It told me that he probably wanted to stay in his job for a while, and it also brought us closer together in a twisted sort of way.

We made our way back to the villa for one last drink before saying goodbye and then headed up to see Danny in hospital. When we got there, we found that they'd moved him to another room, and it took us a little time to find him because of the language barrier. He was very pleased to see us, and we sat down to fill him in on everything that had happened since the last time I'd been up there. I didn't tell him about the personal problems that we'd been going through, as Fallon and Kimberly were present at the time.

Danny's health had improved dramatically, and he told us that he would be able to leave the hospital in another couple of weeks but that he still wouldn't be able to work for some time. We stayed with Danny for another hour before heading back to Fuengirola, as we had now decided to have a go at the cleaning after all.

We were all now wide awake, and it was fast approaching midday. If we'd gone home now, we probably would have slept right through. Besides, you know what they say, many hands make light work. We stopped off on the way to pick up some cleaning products and some buckets and then went into the Stage Door to begin the big clean up. I was quite amazed to see how far the dust had spread. It had settled on practically everything. Kirby and Nicola took on the bar area, while I cleaned the seating, dance floor, and DJ booth. That left Fallon and Kimberly hovering and brushing down the walls and carpeted areas. Surprisingly enough, it only took about four hours to complete, and once we'd finished, it all looked as good as new.

The only damages that we could find were a few broken glasses and, of course, the empty fire extinguisher. I was pleased about this, as I'd spent quite a bit of money buying and setting up the bar, not to mention paying a year upfront on the villa in Mijas and the continuous rent on the bar. On top of that we had the cost of replacing the stock and wages, and we were down to our last ten grand in the bank, so the £800 that we'd received from the Scousers would help out quite a lot.

We left the bar and headed back to the villa to have a barbeque by way of thanks to the girls for helping out. I also told the girls that I was going to arrange a day out paint-balling for all of us. Peter had told me last night that he usually went once a month with some of the local staff from the London Bar and from Tramps bar next door. Apparently, Tony and Luciana also tagged along on occasion. Needless to say, the girls were very excited about going.

It was just coming up to five o'clock when we arrived at the villa, and there was still quite a bit of sunshine left to be had. Kirby sorted out the drinks while I lit the barbeque and stuck on some music. Nicola took Fallon and Kimberly into the bedroom and sorted out some costumes for them to borrow. I stuck some shorts on, and we messed about in the pool for an hour or so while we were waiting for the food to cook. I've got to say that all the girls looked pretty stunning lying out by the pool. Nicola's bikinis were a little tight on Fallon and Kimberly, as she had a slightly smaller bust size, but I wasn't about to complain, that's for sure!

I was just admiring the view and serving up the food. It turned out to be a really enjoyable evening, but eventually Fallon and Kimberly ordered a taxi, as they were now starting to get a little tired. After all, it had been a long couple of days. They thanked us for our hospitality, and there were kisses all around before they jumped into their cab and headed for home.

Time was getting on now. We'd been up for the best part of two days. I sat on the couch feeling a little tired myself now, so Nicola took my hand and said, "Why don't you let me take you to bed? You look exhausted."

"Mmm, that sounds like a great idea," I replied, getting to my feet.

"I think a massage might help you, and if you're not opposed to the idea, I could ask Kirby to join us. After all, you did say that you wouldn't be opposed to me exploring my sexuality, and now's as good a time as any. Well, what do you think?"

"Yeah, I suppose I did, didn't I? Okay, why not? Well give it a try and see how it goes, all right?"

Both Nicola and Kirby were delighted by my response, and the two of them led me into the bedroom for a couple of hours of sexual experimentation. It was obvious that Nicola and Kirby enjoyed themselves immensely, as did I. Nicola told me that it was the first time that she'd been with a girl and that she looked forward to it happening again. I wasn't sure how this would affect our relationship, as this was new to me as well, but for now at least there didn't seem to be any jealousy or animosity between us. In fact, quite the opposite—we seemed to grow stronger for it.

A lot had happened in the short space of time that we'd been out here. In general it had gone quite well, give or take a few glitches along the way, but I definitely hadn't seen this development between Nicola and Kirby coming. Still, as long as it didn't pose a threat to my relationship with Nicola, then of course I was more than happy to go along with it. Besides, the perks were wonderful, and it was obviously what Nicola wanted.

The next three weeks passed by without incident. We finished work on the Saturday morning at 6 a.m. as usual. Peter told us that he'd managed to book us all onto the next paint-balling event at the end of July, which was only a week or so away. Apparently, there'd be about twenty of us going in total, so it should be quite a good day out.

The time passed quickly, and before we knew it, we'd reached the last Saturday in July. The paint-balling event was nearing, and Danny was being let out of hospital today. This was great news, and I was more than happy to volunteer to pick him up. He'd been having quite a lot of physical therapy and was starting to get back on his feet, although he was still wheelchair-bound most of the time. I couldn't let him go back to his place on his own straight away, much as he wanted to, so I convinced him to stay with us for at least a few days.

I didn't take him straight back to the villa, as Nicola and Luciana had gone to the trouble of setting up a surprise party for him in the German restaurant close to Linekers. I drove Danny directly to the port and wheeled him around to the bar where a couple of dozen friends of his were waiting with the usual party poppers and silly hats. Danny was delighted to see them all turn out for him, and in between all the laughter and kisses he turned to me and just nodded as if to say thanks. In return, I tipped my baseball cap towards him in acknowledgement.

We had a great afternoon in the restaurant, and we finished off by making our way up to the London Bar, just taking in the warmth of the sun and the sound of the sea as the waves crashed onto the beach. If you closed your eyes for a second, it almost felt like a dream. As we walked along the promenade, we came across a group of musicians playing the tom-tom drums. They were actually very good, so we were more than happy to throw whatever change we had left into the hat that they had set out.

We carried on up to the London Bar and sat outside on the terrace. It was yet another beautiful day, and the streets were filled with tourists bustling around with their kids in tow.

Nicola and Kirby decided that they wanted to go shopping, and today was market day, or so we'd been told. Apparently there was a huge open-air market on the other side of the town. We finished our drinks and made our way up there. We had to park on the other side of the carriageway and then walk through the underpass. We emerged on the other side in front of what I could only describe as the biggest market that I'd ever seen! There were hundreds of stalls stretching back as far as the eye could see, and the place was absolutely heaving with people.

A lot of the stalls were like something you'd see at a boot sale, selling everything from new clothes to second-hand goods, and there were jewellery stalls all over the place. Most of them only sold women's jewellery, as they didn't really cater for men in Spain, apart from the odd wedding ring. The Spanish considered it gay for men to wear jewellery. Most of the clothing stalls were selling high-quality branded products, although I suspect that many of them were actually selling counterfeit goods.

We spent the best part of three hours at the market before finally making our way back to the villa to relax by the pool until it was time for us to get ready for the evening shift. No rest for the wicked, as they say!

Danny didn't want to stay in on his own, so we took him with us on the condition that he took it easy and didn't exert himself too much. This was the first time he'd been back in the club since the accident, and he was quite looking forward to it.

We met up with Peter and Simon at the London Bar for the usual drinks before going on to the Stage Door to prepare for another night of mayhem. Peter helped Danny down the stairs while I carried his wheelchair, and we all entered the bar together.

"I thought you said the place was covered in powder," said Danny.

"I can assure you that it was. It took five of us four hours to clean it up."

"Five of you!" replied Danny.

"Yes—me, Nicola, Kirby, and the two Swedes, Fallon and Kimberly."

"Oh, right, you managed to rope them all into it then?"

"Yeah, they're good girls, and as a reward for all their hard work, I've organized a day out paint-balling just outside Marbella."

"Oh, I'm so jealous," said Danny.

"Never mind. Maybe next time," I replied.

We finished preparing the bar, and once again we opened the doors to let the customers in. Danny wanted to sit outside on the door with me, as he didn't want to sit on his own inside while the bar was empty.

It wasn't long before we started filling up again. Danny, of course, lapped up the attention that he was getting on the door. I don't think I've ever seen one guy get kissed by so many girls at one time, and it wasn't long before Fallon and Kimberly came down the stairs to join us.

"Hey, Danny, it's great to see you up and about again," said Fallon, kissing him.

"Hiya, gorgeous! Thanks for visiting me in hospital. I really appreciated that."

"Anytime, sweetheart," she said.

Kimberly was next to give Danny a hug and a kiss. While she was talking to him, Fallon turned to me and said, "Hiya, sexy!"

"Hey, babe, you're looking very hot tonight," I replied.

"Thanks, I got dressed up just for you. What do you think?" she asked, giving me a twirl. She was wearing a small pair of denim shorts and a sleeveless black top that revealed her perfectly formed flat stomach and a pierced belly button. On her legs she we wearing knee-high black lace-up boots, and she'd platted her long blonde Swedish hair at the back just like Lara Croft from *Tomb Raider*.

"Well, between me and you, I think you look absolutely stunning—good enough to eat, you might say!"

"Well, if you feel hungry later we could always sneak off, and then you could help yourself as far as I'm concerned."

"You're a wicked girl, Fallon" I whispered to her.

"Yes, but very tempting all the same."

"You're not wrong there," I replied, smiling.

Fallon put her arms around me and slipped her fingers into the pockets of my jeans and gently kissed me on the lips. Then she backed off and asked me, "What's happening between you, Kirby, and Nicola then?"

"What do you mean?" I replied.

"I saw the way you looked at each other when we were all at the villa the other night. What's going on between the three of you?"

"I don't know what you mean."

"You know exactly what I mean, Kurt! Don't play innocent with me." she said.

"I am innocent, of whatever it is you're accusing me of," I said, laughing.

"I don't believe you. You're banging Kirby, aren't you? And Nicola's at it too, isn't she? I thought I was the only other girl in your life out here."

"Look, first of all, much as I think of you, Fallon, we were never an item. You took advantage of me whilst I was under the influence, and as much as enjoyed it, I did tell you at the time that I was happy in my relationship with Nicola. As far as me banging Kirby, as you put it, then the answer is yes, although it wasn't me that instigated it. I just went along with what Nicola wanted."

"I don't believe it!" said Fallon, looking a little upset at me for confirming her suspicions.

In the silent pause that followed, I turned my head to find Danny and Kimberly looking on, shocked at what they'd just overheard. Well, I guess that's let the cat out of the bag, I thought.

"Look, you mustn't say anything to anyone, okay?"

"Don't worry. My lips are sealed," said Danny.

"I knew it," said Kimberly, happy now that she'd finally found out about what had happened between me and Fallon. "Oh, and I promise not to say anything either. My lips are also sealed, although I'd be happy to part them for you, lover," she said, teasing me.

I gave Kimberly a hug and asked her to take Danny inside for me so that I could speak to Fallon in private.

"I'm really disappointed in you, Fallon. You gave me your word not to say anything about us."

"I really sorry, honey bunny, but I'm disappointed in you too! I thought that once Kirby had shown her true colours, it would show you that I was right about her and that would prove to you that she had an ulterior motive from the start. But now I find that's she's got both of you under her spell."

""You don't know the full story, Fallon, and I can assure you that I'm not under anyone's spell."

"If you wanted more fun, then I was always available to you. I thought I'd made that perfectly clear! In fact I'd have been happy to ask Kimberly to join in as well if it's threesomes you're into. I know she would have been delighted to participate. You wouldn't have been disappointed, I promise you."

"It wasn't like that. I didn't instigate anything. I just went along with something that Nicola wanted to try. That's all."

"Typical! First I lose a mate to Nicola, and now she's got you too!" she said, sounding very upset.

"Kirby hasn't 'got me' as you put it, all right? So don't get your knickers in a twist."

"So you admit that you did enjoy yourself when we were having sex then?"

"Of course, how could I not? You're a very beautiful and sexy girl."

"Well, if you're really not under Kirby's spell, then perhaps we could have a repeat performance again soon. That is unless you're too wrapped up in Kirby to want to mess around with me anymore."

"Look, don't get all jealous on me, okay? You mean a lot to me, so I'll think about it, all right?"

"You won't regret it, I promise you. Don't keep me waiting too long. I'm an impatient girl when I really want something, you know," she said, slowly kissing me again.

What else could I say? I didn't want Fallon going all vindictive on me. I've learnt from experience that women can be very destructive when they're emotionally unstable and suffering the pangs of jealousy. I couldn't really complain about it, as I'd dug my own grave, so to speak. For the moment at least, I'd just have to play her games for a while until I could figure a way out of this problem.

Most of the punters who were coming down to the bar tonight were already inside, and with Fallon cuddling up to me looking and smelling as good as she did, I thought that this would be a good time to go inside myself, so I left Peter on the door and walked Fallon inside.

As I approached the bar, I noticed that Nicola was chatting to a young couple. They turned out to be the Scouse couple that had been rowing in the bar the other night. Before I had the chance to say anything, the guy stepped forward to introduce himself.

"Hi, I'm Barry. I'm really sorry about the other night. I had a row with my girlfriend Katie, and she threw a drink over me, so I squirted her with the extinguisher and it wouldn't turn off. I know I was out of order, and I wanted to apologize in person."

"Look, Barry, you're right. You were in the wrong, but you've apologized and paid for the damage, so why don't we just put it behind us and start again, okay?" I said, holding out my hand to him.

Barry was pleased at my response and shook my hand. Then he introduced me to his girlfriend Katie. She was quite pretty, although maybe a little loud for my taste. Barry was very happy that I'd forgiven him, and he told me that by way of apology he'd arranged a treat for us on him. I was just about to ask him what he meant by that, when a group of lads entered the bar carrying a small set of drums. It was the group of musicians that we'd seen on the promenade earlier that day. Barry had taken it upon himself to pay them to perform in the bar with a couple of professional rappers that he knew.

It was too late to stop them. They were already here, and some of the customers had recognized one of the rappers as M.C. Mikey, who was very well known in the dance scene, so I thanked Barry and then went over to Simon to get him to announce their presence in the bar.

Simon put on a dance version of "Sweet Dreams" by Annie Lenox and handed a couple of mics to the rappers. The tom-tom players started playing along with the music, and M.C. Mikey and the other singer started rapping. I waked back to speak with Nicola, who still hadn't realized that they were playing live yet.

"What record is this then? I haven't heard this version before. Is it a remix?" she asked.

"No, sweetheart, they're playing it live," I replied, laughing.

"Wow! They're really good," she said. She was right. They were excellent. They played on for the last few hours, much to the delight of the customers.

I thanked Barry at the end of the night for bringing them down and invited him and Katie for the lock-in afterwards. I felt a little obliged to ask him. After all, he had contributed to everyone spending a lot more money than they otherwise would have.

Although Barry had his girlfriend with him, you could tell that he was quite a lonely guy. As I listened to him this evening, his constant attempts to crack jokes and grab the attention to the point of annoyance all seemed a little desperate to me. You could tell that his so-called girlfriend Katie didn't care too much for him either, as she would constantly try to undermine him at the drop of the hat. Underneath the confident character that he tried so hard to portray was a very lonely and insecure man. Unluckily for me, he seemed to latch on to me as if desperately trying to find a friend. I humoured him for a while, which was probably a mistake, as he now thought I was his mate! Don't get me wrong. He wasn't a horrible bloke, just a little over eager for me.

Once we'd cleared the bar and locked ourselves in, Barry stood up and pulled out a big bag of Charlie and poured it onto the bar. There must have been at least an ounce of powder sitting there. He proceeded to cut it into one long fat line and then gave me a wrapped up note.

"Help yourself and then pass it around," he said.

"You've got to be kidding," I replied.

"No, it's my way of making it up to you. You've got to let me do this. Please, I want to," he pleaded.

I couldn't be bothered to argue with him. I thought that if I agreed with him, he might just stop apologizing to me. I sniffed up a fair amount of the powder, which seemed very strong, and then one by one the dozen or so friends that were left followed my example. There was far too much for everyone to do in one line, so we all had another go and eventually polished it off.

After a while I started to feel a little queasy, so I unlocked the doors and went outside, where I immediately ran into Raymond the caretaker cleaning up.

"Morning, Raymond," I said reluctantly.

"Morning, Kurt. I have to talk to you about something very important!"

"Why? What's up now, Raymond?"

"Did you have live music last night?" he enquired.

"No, why do you ask?" I said, lying to him.

"Well, the people in the apartments above the shops have said that their cups and plates were jumping about with all the vibrations from the music last night. They are not very happy with you."

"Look, we didn't have any live music on, okay? And at the end of the day, this is a licensed music bar, so if they don't like it, then I'm afraid that's tough luck! Now if you don't mind, I'm busy."

Before he could say any more, I walked back inside and locked the doors behind me.

"That fucking bloke does my head in," I said out loud.

"What fucking bloke would that be?" asked Fallon. She'd walked into the corridor just as I'd locked the doors and overheard me talking to myself.

"Oh, no one you know. I was just sounding off about the caretaker. He winds me up."

"Ah, poor baby!" she said, cuddling up to me.

"What are you doing? Are you trying to get us caught?" I said, pushing her away.

"Hey! I thought you were going to make it up to me."

"I will, I promise! But not here. You'll get me killed."

"But I'm feeling really frisky right now."

"Fallon, I don't care if your hormones go into overdrive. You don't do that in here. And if you carry on, it won't happen at all. So be patient, all right?"

That seemed to do the trick, as she agreed to back off. Fallon blew me a kiss and headed back off towards the toilets. My head was still buzzing like fuck, and I felt overwhelmingly sick. I took several deep breaths to try and clear my head.

"You know the best thing to take the edge off the Charlie is to drink a glass of coke or fresh orange juice with lots of sugar in it," said Barry.

"Really? Are you sure? Because it sounds disgusting," I replied.

"Honestly, try it. I'm not joking. It sort of gives you a glucose rush and straightens out your head," he insisted.

As I felt so terrible, I had to take his word for it, although I must admit I did half-expect it to make me throw up. Still I followed his instructions and poured some sugar into a glass of orange juice and drank it very quickly. As I expected, it tasted awful. When you're on cocaine, your taste buds go a little haywire to the point where all you can taste is the sugar in everything you eat or drink. To my amazement though, within a few minutes of swallowing the drink, I stopped feeling sick, and although it didn't totally sort me out, it did take the edge off of the way I was feeling.

Soon after this, I decided to call it a night. We skipped breakfast, as we were all feeling a little wasted and caught a cab back to the villa.

We put Danny in Kirby's room and made up a bed for Kirby on the couch. Nicola then led me to the bedroom and made love to me with all the sexual sensations and passion that the Charlie brings.

Peter had arranged our paint-balling event for the next day, and the girls were eager to go shopping for something to wear, so after getting up on Monday morning, we drove up to Torremolinos, dropping Danny off at his apartment along the way. We spent quite a while traipsing around the shops until we came across an army surplus shop, where we kitted ourselves out with jumpsuits and American-style baseball caps. We looked like something from the A-Team. All we needed now was for B.A. Barakas to walk in, saying "I ain't getting on no plane, fool!" We had a lot of fun dressing up and took quite a few photos amidst all the laughter. We spent the next couple of hours on the beach and then left to pick Danny up. Then we headed back to the villa for a relaxing night in.

We got up at about 10 a.m. on Tuesday morning, and once we were ready, we made our way down to Linekers to meet up with the others, before driving down to the outskirts of Marbella to the paint-balling site.

When we arrived at the site, we were split into two groups, and we hired the guns and ammunition. We had to compete against each other to get a flag that was situated at the end of the course. I must admit that it was a lot harder than I'd expected, rolling about in the bushes and trying to avoid getting ambushed on the way. A few of us had got close to the end of the course, when Peter's team jumped out and finished us off. I'd never played before, but I can tell you this. When you get shot, especially up close, it hurts a hell of a lot!

After we took a refreshment break, the staff divided us into teams for a new game. They assigned each team its own area of the forest, gave us a flag each, and told us to defend it. The object of the game was to acquire the other flags whilst keeping you own, without getting shot. To make it fair, we all drew straws to decide the teams.

Nicola got teamed up with Peter and Luciana, while I got teamed up with a barman from Linekers called john and, of all people, Fallon. The remaining twelve were split into another four teams, and we were then led into the forest, where we were situated into our own areas. It was a bit like playing chess. You had to plan your moves very carefully. If you walked into another camp, you'd be shot to easily, and obviously if the three of you left your own flag, then you'd lose it and be out of the game anyway, so we decided that the best way forward would be for one person to stay and defend the flag while the other two went in search of the others.

As a team we decided that John would defend the flag while Fallon and I would go on the attack. We had been making our way through the forest for a while looking for the other camps, when we heard someone sneaking through the bushes. I grabbed Fallon, pulled her to the ground, and put my hand over her mouth so as not to alert the intruder. It wasn't long before Peter sneaked past us. He must have left Nicola and Luciana back at the camp so that he could attack on his own. He'd obviously played this game before! We were lying under some foliage in the wood, so it would have been far too risky to move and to try and shoot Peter, as he would have heard us, so we decided to let him pass.

Once I was sure that he was gone, I got back up and grabbed Fallon's hand to pull her up with me. Unfortunately her gun went off accidentally, shooting me in the stomach.

"Ow!" I yelled as the pellet hit me.

"Oh, I'm sorry. I didn't mean to do that. Did it hurt?" she asked, trying desperately not to laugh.

"Of course it fucking hurt!"

"Let me see," she said. I sat back down on the floor and opened my jumpsuit to find a big round bruise appearing on my stomach. "Well, you could say I owed you that."

"For what?" I asked her.

"For not giving me any more sugar since the last time we made love in my kitchen."

"Fallon, you know I'm with Nicola, and what happened before was definitely not something I'd planned!"

"Yes, and that was fine until I found out that you'd chosen to mess about with Kirby."

"Look, I said I'd make it up to you, didn't I?"

"I know, but I'm still waiting. I'm beginning to think you don't want to."

"I do, but it's finding the right moment when it's safe to do so."

"Well, I don't do safe, and you know what they say: there's no time like the present, is there?" she said, rubbing the bruise on my stomach.

"Fallon! We can't do this now. Someone might see us. It's too risky."

"Nicola's back guarding her camp with Luciana, and apart from Peter, who went past a while ago, I haven't heard anyone else, have you?" she said, sitting on top of me.

"Pack it in, Fallon. We'll get caught."

"Shh! Not if we're quiet, we won't," she whispered, putting a finger on my lips.

Fallon pulled open my jumpsuit and hitched her denim skirt up around her waist. She then slid her hand into my boxers, and it wasn't long before she was riding up and down on me again. She seemed to thrive on danger, which I've got to say was a terrific turn-on, and the need to keep our activities quiet made it all the more erotic and intense. After a few minutes or so, I rolled her over onto her back and then slowly made love to her, covering her mouth with my hand to try and keep the noise down. I must admit that although I'd been manoeuvred into this, I did find the danger of getting caught very exciting.

Once we'd got ourselves together, we made our way back to the camp, only to find that John had been shot and our flag was gone, effectively putting us out of the game. It came as no surprise that Peter's team had won, which made Nicola and Luciana very happy. They gloated about it all the way back to Fuengirola. It was obvious that everyone had enjoyed themselves—some more than others, I thought to myself. After a few drinks at Linekers to finish the day off, we left to pick up Danny, before heading back to the villa for a restful night at home.

The rest of the week passed fairly quickly. Before we knew it, Thursday night had come around again and we were getting ready to open up once more. We left the gates open for the queue to form while we prepared everything inside. Ten minutes later we heard someone banging on the doors. I opened up to find several police officers waiting outside with an official representative from the town hall.

"What's going on?" I asked them.

"Are you the owner of the bar?"

"Yes, how can I help you?"

"We've received some complaints about the noise, and as a result the town hall has decided to close you down until you can install a noise limiter to restrict the sound in the bar."

"You've got to be joking," I said to him.

"I assure you, this is no joke. You have been denounced by the tenants upstairs, and as a result of this we will be temporarily closing you down."

"Where would I get one of these noise limiters from?" I asked him.

"You will be inspected and tested for sound on Monday. After that we will inform you when and where to go and buy the necessary equipment. In the meantime you are being issued with a closure order, and your license will be temporarily suspended until the problem has been resolved."

"Look, mate, I've got a queue of people waiting outside. If I shut down now, it will cost me a fortune! Is there no way that you can postpone the closure? At least until Monday? Please!"

"I'm very sorry, but I have my orders, and we will post an officer in the nearby vicinity to make sure you abide by this order. Any attempt to open up to the public will result in the permanent closure of this bar."

There was absolutely nothing that I could do about it; the orders were signed by the mayor himself. In Spain mayors are not just figureheads; they have real power to meddle in the laws of their provinces. Basically, I was screwed! I had no choice but to send the customers away with an apology and to close the bar down.

I didn't see the point in sitting there feeling sorry for myself, so I locked up the Stage Door and walked down to the Underground to see how the competition was faring. Suffice to say, our closure had given them quite a boost. Still, there was nothing that we could do about it now, so we decided to chalk it up to experience and try to enjoy ourselves as much as we could, given the circumstances.

If I had a pound for every time someone asked me why we were closed, I'd be a rich man by now, I thought to myself. In the end we got fed up with explaining the closure to everyone and decided to call it a night.

Hopefully, we'd be able to sort out this mess on Monday.

Chapter Eight

The Reopening

Monday morning came around fast. I made my way down to the Stage Door to meet up with the sound engineer so that he could test the sound levels in the bar. I turned the music on as requested while one of his assistants went outside with some recording equipment and a walkie-talkie which he used to communicate with the engineer inside the bar. After a series of sound tests, we sat down at the captain's table to discuss the repercussions.

I pointed out that the noise loss would be drastically reduced when the bar was full of customers, as a certain amount of the sound would be absorbed by the people inside the bar, which they took on board. However, the final decision was that I would have to fit a noise limiter to restrict the sound to 105 decibels.

The sound engineer told me what shop to get the equipment from, and he also told me that as soon as I'd picked up the noise limiter, I would have to call him and he would arrange to come down and install it for me. The bar would have to stay closed until this was done.

I thanked him for his time, locked up, and went off to look for the shop they'd recommended. I wanted to get this sorted out as soon as possible! I was told that it was about half a mile down the main high street, so I headed off down towards it. Once I'd arrived at my destination, I found two audio shops next door to each other selling similar products.

I went into the one that had been recommended and approached a member of staff. He told me that the equipment that I needed would cost me £2,000, but unfortunately he didn't have one in stock. It would take at least three weeks to get it. If I had to close for that period of time, it would undoubtedly damage my business, so I asked him if there was any way that he could speed up the process. He told me that if I was prepared to pay him another £150, he could probably cut a week off that time. This was turning out to be a disaster. I walked out of the shop feeling quite annoyed at the situation I was in.

As I paced up and down trying to think, I noticed that the shop next door also sold noise limiters, so I went inside and spoke to a young Spanish girl. I asked her if she had the model I required in stock. It turned out that I was in luck, and even better, it was only going to cost me £1,200. Naturally, I was over the moon to hear this and handed her the piece of paper that the sound engineer had given me for the shop to sign.

"Oh, sorry, sir, but as much as I'd like to sell you this, I can't."

"Why? What are you talking about? You just said you had it in stock, didn't you?"

"Yes, sir, we do have it in stock, but the problem is that this form requires you to buy it from the shop next door. It is not a request, it is a command."

"What's the difference? It's the same machine isn't it?"

"I shouldn't tell you this, but the difference is that the shop next door is owned by the mayor's grandson."

"But that's outrageous! That's fraud!" I said, astonished at what she'd just told me.

"Yes, but I would be careful of who you accuse out here, especially if you have a business! I'm sorry, but that's just the way it is."

I left the shop absolutely fuming with anger at the blatant corruption that was happening to me. But she was right; I couldn't just accuse people in power if I wanted to survive out here. I had no choice but to accept it. I bit my lip and re-entered the thieving shop next door and ordered the noise limiter. I also begrudgingly paid the extra £150 to get it a week earlier.

In my bones I knew that this was going to be a major setback. Not only would I lose much-needed income, but it would also be difficult to build the trade back up again. People get fed up very quickly when they keep going to a place that's constantly closed down. On top of everything else, the lease payment was due this week. All in all, it would cost me around £3,000 for the equipment and rent, which would make a considerable dent in my bank balance!

So that was it. We were closed for at least two weeks and, as you could imagine, I was extremely upset about this development.

I rang Nicola to give her the bad news, and she suggested that we come up with something to explain the shutdown. This seemed like a good idea, so I arranged to meet her and Kirby in town to discuss it over a few drinks.

It didn't take long to come up with a plan. We decided to take the time to redecorate and update the look of the bar. Nicola suggested that we should put up a sign stating that we were reopening soon after refurbishment to try and generate some anticipation for the re-launch. We also decided that while it was closed, we'd re-tile the main floor and put in some ultraviolet lights over the bar. We estimated the cost to be around £800, which was exactly the amount of money that Nicola had received for the damage from the fire-extinguisher incident.

Consequently, we spent the next two weeks decorating and modernizing the bar. It wasn't difficult for me to achieve this, being a decorator by trade. When we'd finished the work the place looked fantastic, and on the following Monday I received a call from the corrupt shop telling me that my noise limiter had arrived. I was delighted with the news and immediately called the council rep to arrange for the engineer to come down and fit the equipment. I was told that the earliest they could do it would be on the Thursday afternoon, which would mean that because of the red tape at the town hall, I wouldn't be able to reopen until the Friday night, but at least I'd be open again!

We spent the next few days giving out promotional materials, and we ran an advert on the local English radio station to let people know about the reopening, and of course we restocked the bar and got everything ready.

When Thursday afternoon came around, we met the engineer as arranged to have the new equipment fitted. This took quite a while to complete, as they channelled pretty much every piece of media equipment through the limiter. The way the device worked was not just to restrict the sound in the bar but also to act as a data recorder for the town hall to give them information about the opening and closing times. I was also told that we could never turn it off; if we did so, then we would have to provide a written letter explaining the reason for doing so, or else we'd be subjected to a hefty fine. An engineer would come down once a month to take the readings from the limiter.

As far as the noise levels were concerned, each time the sound levels went past 105 decibels, you would get a warning noise for a few seconds. If you didn't reduce the sound, then it would cut the power to your system for ten seconds, which would be registered in the limiter for the council to see. It was obviously going to take some time to get used to it! Still, as long as we kept an eye on it, then I was sure we'd be okay.

Once they'd finished, the rep gave me the paperwork to enable us to reopen the bar for tomorrow night. My personal impression was that I felt that it was actually louder now than it was before we'd fitted the limiter. Still, at least we were now all-systems-go again, which I for one felt very happy about. We locked up the Stage Door and made our way down to the London Bar to celebrate! Although I had been pretty sure that I'd get the nod from the council to reopen, it was still quite a relief to get it out of the way.

It was still only 8.30 p.m., but the bar was packed full of people. There seemed to be some sort of party going on inside, and as a result we weren't able to get a table inside the bar, so Nicola and Kirby went back outside and grabbed a table on the terrace. Meanwhile I made my way up to the bar and asked the barman what was going on. He told me that their ex-barmaid Keeley had returned from the UK and was celebrating the fact that she just been offered some work as a result of the *Sun* newspapers page-three girl interviews.

Looking down the length of the bar, I spotted Keeley joking around with a group of girls. I caught her eye, gave her a wave, and then ordered some drinks. It wasn't long before I got the tap on the shoulder from Keeley. I turned around to greet her, and she predictably threw her arms around me and planted a big kiss on my lips.

"Hiya, gorgeous! I see you're back then. I take it the photo shoot went well then?"

"Oh god, I've got so much to tell you. I had the best time in England. Everything went better than expected."

"Yeah, that sounds great. Tell me more."

"Well, for starters the *Sun* newspaper is considering me for the new page-three girl of the year competition which there going to play out in their newspaper with a public vote to decide the winner, and they have also put me forward to a top modelling agency."

"That's terrific news. It sounds very exciting. So what are you doing back here then? Surely you've not come back to work as a barmaid?"

"No, silly, I've come back to pick up the rest of my stuff."

"So is that the only reason you came back?"

"No, definitely not! I also came back to see my friends and, of course, to see you. What happened with you and Nicola in the end?"

"Well, after a long heart-to-heart, we managed to patch up our differences. And talking of Nicola, I'd better take these drinks out to her before I get into trouble. I'll try and catch up with you later, okay, sweetheart?"

"Great! I'll hold you to that. Make sure you don't forget," she said, kissing me on the lips once again.

Unfortunately, as she did this, Nicola walked in the bar and, suffice to say, she wasn't too impressed by what she saw. Nicola pounced on Keeley, pulling her hair in an attempt to get her off me.

"What the fuck's going on? We're sitting outside waiting for you while you're in here cavorting with this little whore!"

"Whoa! Ease up, Nicola. It's not what you think, okay?"

"It looks pretty obvious to me what's going on. Every time you're near this slag, you get all flirty with her. What's that all about?"

"Hey, now wait just a minute. Who the hell do you think you are, calling me a slag and a whore?" said Keeley aggressively.

"I'll call you whatever the hell I like, you bitch, and in future keep your dirty little hands off my fella. He's far too good for the likes of you!"

"Is that right? Because it didn't bother him when he was banging me the last time I was here."

"You're a fucking liar!" shouted Nicola.

The pair of them pounced on each other, pulling hair, scratching, and screeching like a couple of wild animals. I jumped in between them in an attempt to separate them, and after a couple of minutes with the help of some of the punters in the bar, I succeeded in pulling them apart. I dragged Nicola out of the bar, kicking and screaming all the way. Once we were outside, I grabbed hold of Nicola to try and reason with her.

"Nicola! Nicola, what the fuck's got into you? Calm down!"

"You had your tongue down her throat. How could you do that to me? I thought you loved me!"

"I do love you, and I didn't have my tongue down her throat. The kiss didn't mean anything. She was just greeting me. That's all."

"If it was so innocent, then why did she say that you were banging her? I suppose that she just fell on to your dick as well!"

"She just said that to wind you up, probably because you called her a whore."

"I'll do more than just insult her."

"Nicola! This isn't helping anything. Now calm down and we'll sort it out, okay?" I said angrily.

"No, I won't calm down! You were cheating on me. Admit it!" she demanded.

There was no way that I was going to admit anything, especially when she was in this state.

"I'm telling you the truth. Nothing's happened between me and Keeley. Look, Nicola, relationships are based on trust, so believe or don't believe. It's your decision, but if you don't believe me, then I guess we don't have much of a relationship any more. It's up to you, Nicola. Make your choice."

"Don't try and blackmail me. I caught you red-handed. It was obvious what was happening. I'm going back inside to have it out with that little slag in there."

"Okay, fine, do what you fucking like. I've had enough of this shit!"

I turned my back on Nicola and walked away while she screamed obscenities at me. I headed up towards the taxi rank and got the cabbie to drive me to Torremolinos, as I wasn't in the mood to bump into anyone I knew. I wasn't sure whether Nicola and I would recover from this setback, and quite frankly, at this moment in time I didn't really give a fuck either way. I couldn't believe that this had just happened. Just when we seemed to be sorting things out, something always comes along and kicks us back down again!

I spent the next few hours getting slowly plastered, and then I got a phone call from Keeley of all people.

"Hey, Kurt, how are you doing?"

"Oh, I'm okay, I guess. The question is, how are you? I suppose Nicola came back in the bar and caused a scene."

"No, actually she disappeared with Kirby not long after you. So where are you?"

"To be honest, I couldn't be bothered to hang around getting insulted in the street by Nicola, so I caught a cab to Torremolinos."

"I could meet you there if you want."

"I don't know, Keeley. I'm in enough trouble as it is."

"Well, I can't let you sit there all alone. After all it was sort of my fault that Nicola got angry in the first place."

"Well, I must admit, telling her that I was banging you didn't really help the situation," I said sarcastically.

"Don't! I can't believe I said that. I'm really sorry. So can I come down and join you?" she asked again.

"It's up to you, Keeley. If you really want to, then I guess that's okay with me."

"Great. I'll meet you at the Palladium nightclub. It's on the main road in Torremolinos that leads to Malaga. I'll see you there in about twenty minutes, okay?"

I was probably doing the wrong thing, but drinking alone was never much fun, so I finished up my brandy and then slowly made my way up the hill past all the shops and bars and eventually arrived at the entrance to the Palladium, where Keeley was now waiting for me. She was with a couple of girlfriends who had tagged along with her. Once we'd got all the hugs and kisses out of the way, we all went inside.

It was nothing like I'd expected. The large floor area was divided into two halves. On one side there was the usual dance floor, and on the other side was a swimming pool, separated by a thick glass panel. Effectively, you were dancing next to the swimmers in the pool. It was incredible. We made our way up to the bar area, which was situated at the back of the club facing the pool. We were told by the barmaid that if we wanted to go for a swim later, then we could hire some costumes and a towel for a small fee. Quite a novel idea, I thought to myself.

I grabbed some drinks, and we found a table close to the dance floor. As soon as I'd put the drinks down, Keeley and her friends grabbed hold of me and pulled me onto the dance floor. The DJ was playing a mixture of dance music and classic chart tunes. He was very good; there seemed to be a very relaxed atmosphere in here.

Keeley told me that this place was very popular with the dance crowd and as a result of that, many of them were on some sort of social drug. In fact, while we were up dancing, a girl approached us and offered us some ecstasy. I've got to say that I've never been a big fan of taking pills, so I declined the offer, as did Keeley, although the girls that had come with her were only too happy to participate.

After an hour or so we were starting to feel the heat in there, so we decided to take the barmaid up on her earlier offer and hired some costumes for a swim. I've got to say the coolness of the water was extremely refreshing and definitely had a sobering effect on me.

We messed about in the pool for a bit before Keeley swam up to me and said, "I'm really sorry about saying that to Nicola. It was unforgivable of me."

"Yes, it was, but what's done is done."

"Do you think you can salvage the situation? I'm happy to tell her that I said it out of spite because of what she called me."

"To be honest with you, Keeley, I don't think it would make a lot of difference. Nicola can be a very stubborn girl. It would probably be best if you kept your distance right now. She'd only think that you were conspiring with me to cover something up, but thanks for offering anyway."

"So what are you going to do now? Are you going back to sort it out or not."

"I hadn't really thought that far ahead. One thing I do know is that I don't want to go back and listen to that crap tonight."

"Well, I can't let you sleep in the street, so I think the best thing you can do is to come back to mine. I'll make it worth your while."

"It's a tempting offer, but I wouldn't want to be a burden to you, Keeley."

"You could never be a burden to me, Kurt. I want you to come back with me. Besides, I've got something I want to ask you."

"Oh, and what would that be?"

"Well, come back and you'll find out," she said, giggling.

I agreed to return with her, which obviously pleased her quite a lot. I pulled the hair away from her face, thanked her for being here for me, and kissed her gently on the lips.

"Come on then, let's get out of here," I said to her.

Keeley said goodbye to her mates, as they weren't quite ready to leave yet. We then jumped in a cab and made our way back to her apartment in Fuengirola.

Keeley fixed us some drinks, and we sat down on the couch together. Looking around at all the boxes and cases everywhere, it was obvious to me that she was in the process of packing up her stuff.

"So what's happening with your apartment then?"

"Well, because of the developments in my modelling career, it seemed an unnecessary expense."

"I take it that means you're returning permanently to the UK."

"I'm sorry, babe, but I have the opportunity to do something that I've worked towards all my life. Surely you of all people can understand that. The thing is, the main reason I came back was to see you."

"I don't understand. You're talking in riddles."

"Look, the truth is that until I bumped into you I had tunnel vision. I only ever had one thing on my mind, and that was my career. But then I met you and it gave me something else to think about. I couldn't get you out of my head, and as a result I've been confused ever since about what I want to do with my life."

"I don't understand. We've only met a few times and only slept together once, albeit a very sexual experience. Why would that make you second-guess your future, bearing in mind that I'm already in a relationship? Don't get me wrong. I'm extremely flattered. You're a very beautiful girl. Any man would be pleased to have you as their partner, but you have your whole career ahead of you. That's not something you give up lightly, Keeley!"

"You see, that's what I love about you. You're not selfish. I can talk to you openly and know you'll respond with honesty, I love that. I don't know what it is, but when I'm with you I feel like I've found a soul-mate, and in my book that's also not something you give up lightly."

"Look, Keeley, I won't deny that there's chemistry between us. I think that's plain to see. But you can't just abandon your dreams. If we were to become a couple, given time you would have regrets in your heart, always wondering what might have been. Eventually you would begin to resent me, and to be honest with you, I'd never forgive myself for taking away your opportunity to shine as a top model, which is something that I think you can achieve. It would be wrong of me to deprive you of that."

Keeley just sat there for a few moments thinking about what I'd just said.

"Are you sure? If things don't work out with you and Nicola, then you could come back to England with me, and then I could have my cake and eat it too," she replied with a laugh.

"Hmm, sounds tempting, but I've got unfinished business here, whether or not it works out between me and Nicola. I'm chasing my own dreams with the club, just as you're chasing yours. So why don't we play out our futures for a while and see what happens? If it's meant to be between us, then it will still happen. I'm not going anywhere soon, so go and follow your career. I'll still be here in a few months' time, and by then you'll have a better idea of whether you still feel the same way or not."

"I'm so jealous of Nicola. She doesn't know what she's throwing away. I'm going to catch a flight back home tomorrow, but I will stay in touch, and who knows what the future might hold for us both? In the meantime, as this will be the last time I see you for a while, I'd like to leave you with a memory of me that you'll find hard to forget."

"Hmm, and what do you have in mind?" I asked her.

"Just sit back and enjoy," she said, getting up.

Keeley walked across the room and put on some music. Then she turned towards me and proceeded to do a striptease, caressing herself as she slowly removed each piece of clothing until she was totally naked, revealing that stunning body of hers. She then stripped me down to my boxers and performed a very erotic lap dance, which had me so turned on that I could no longer control myself. I stood up, took her in my arms, and carried her into the bedroom. We fell onto the bed, passionately kissing, caressing, and touching every inch of each other. It wasn't long before we were making love to one another, eventually ending up on the floor, both sweating and exhausted from the sexual activity that had just taken place.

"Wow! That was incredible. You truly are the sexiest girl I've ever had the pleasure of making love to."

Keeley just smiled at me and then got up and slipped under the duvet.

"Come to bed. I want to feel you against me while I sleep," she said.

"Okay, but I'm not sure I'll be able to sleep feeling your body pressed up against me all night. I might have to take advantage of you again," I said, giggling.

"Hmm, well, if you feel the urge in the night, then don't let me stop you. Take all the advantage you want," she said in that sexy voice of hers.

The morning came around before we knew it. After one more round of sexual passion, we got up, showered, and got dressed. We had breakfast, and then I accompanied her to the airport in a cab.

"Well, good luck, Keeley. I know you'll do well. Just promise me that you won't forget me, okay?"

"I could never forget you, Kurt, and this isn't goodbye, it's more like I'll see you later. Look out for me in the *Sun*. I'll call you if that's okay."

"Hey, I'd be upset if you didn't."

"Bye, babes, take care," she said, hugging me tightly.

I held her in my arms for a few minutes before kissing her goodbye and then saw her through the departure gates, leaving me wondering whether or not I'd made the right decision to let her go.

I left the airport in a bit of a confused state. I hadn't known Keeley that long, but she had had a profound effect on me. I felt the connection between us as strongly as she did, but although I know it sounds hypocritical of me, I still owed it to Nicola to try and sort things out.

I wasn't sure what would happen next, but there was only one way to find that out. So I jumped in a cab and headed back to Mijas. I entered the villa to find Nicola and Kirby in the kitchen.

"Hey, Nicola, have you calmed down enough to talk yet?"

"I'm sorry, Kurt, but I don't think there's anything left to talk about. In fact I've decided that I don't want this anymore. You can keep the club, it's all yours. I don't want anything else to do with it!"

"What do you mean? Do you realize what you are saying! Surely we can sort this out?"

"I'm sorry, Kurt, but my mind's made up. In fact Kirby has spoken to her previous landlord and he's agreed to give her the apartment back. I'm going to move in with her."

"What! I don't believe I'm hearing this. What are you going to do for money?"

"Kirby has some money put by, and . . . I wasn't totally honest with you about the amount of money I'd raised against my flat in England."

"What are you talking about? Why would you lie to me about that?"

"I didn't see it as a lie. I was just being cautious, planning ahead, so to speak, just in case something went wrong. You know what I'm like."

"I used to think so, but it seems I was wrong about that too."

"Between us we're going to try and set up an English hairdresser's out here."

"So I was sitting here worrying about where our next penny was coming from, while all the time you've been sitting on your own little nest egg. And you think I'm deceitful!"

"Look, Kurt, it was there for the both of us, but circumstances have changed."

"And when were you going to tell me about the money?"

"Look, I'm sorry, but it's over between us. There's nothing more to say! Goodbye, Kurt."

Nicola left the villa in tears, closely followed by Kirby.

This was a very low period in my life, and I won't deny that I shed a few tears myself over the loss of Nicola, but the truth was that at the end of the day I'd brought this on myself. Even so, the fact that I was so upset showed how close I'd actually been to Nicola. It was a shame that it had to come to this, but as terrible as I felt, I still had a business to run, and moping around here wasn't going to help me.

I pulled myself together and made a call to Tony at Linekers. I asked him to help me find temporary cover for the next couple of nights behind the bar. Naturally, he fired thirty questions at me, which I deflected. I just told him that I'd explain later. I'd arranged to meet up with the remaining staff in the usual place, and after I'd hung up the phone, I made my way down to Fuengirola town.

There had been quite a lot of promotional material given out already, and of course I'd arranged for several flier girls to work on the streets tonight, so I was hoping for a big turnout. I didn't know whether Nicola and Kirby would show up tonight, which is why I'd asked Tony to help me arrange for cover.

After meeting everyone in the London Bar, we all made our way up to the Stage Door to prepare for the reopening. Tony had persuaded Luciana and one of the other Linekers staff to work behind the bar for me this weekend, which I was very grateful for. I told Tony and Luciana that Nicola and I had split up following an argument. They both seemed quite sad about it and also very surprised, but they were very supportive about my situation.

There was no sign of Nicola before or after we opened. She was obviously serious about the break up.

It turned out to be a very busy night. In fact, we were packed to the rafters. The noise limiter wasn't too much of a problem, and the music was still loud enough to keep the punters happy. Everyone seemed to be enjoying themselves, and Danny was back on the decks, which was great news. We'd had a really good night, but I didn't feel elated like I should have. I guess I was expecting Nicola to come through the door with that big smile on her face, but she never came!

I didn't hang around for too long after we closed up, as I really wasn't in the mood, so I made my way home to wallow in my own self-pity. I sat up for a while talking to myself. I found myself doing this more and more, especially when I had a lot on my mind. I suppose you could say that I draw my strength from myself.

The long and the short of it was that what had happened between Nicola and me was now in the past. For me to succeed out here, I had to put it behind me and drive on regardless. Like I've said before, positivity promotes positivity, just as negativity is a cancer that spreads, so from now on I was going to enjoy myself and work hard to succeed. I eventually fell asleep on the couch, drink still in hand, and didn't wake up until the early evening.

I jumped into the shower, and after a strong cup of coffee, I made my way into Fuengirola to see if I could sort out some transport. Nicola had taken her car when she left, which left me on foot or in cabs. There were a few garages in town, so I went around them to see what I could find. In the end I brought a second-hand Suzuki jeep for £1,500. I made a phone call to Rosa to sort out some insurance, and after that I was ready to go.

I drove down to the Stage Door, parked up, and went inside, locking the gates behind me. I still hadn't cleaned up from last night's reopening, and as I was now on my own, I was eager to get started. It didn't take too long to get everything done, although the girls' toilets were in a disgraceful state. They say that lads are messy, but believe me when I say that the girls were far worse than the boys, throwing toilet paper and tampons everywhere, not to mention bits of hair and makeup, amongst other things.

I didn't finish cleaning up and restocking the bar until about 9 p.m. I was now starting to feel pretty hungry. I locked up the bar and walked down to the port to Jimmy's bar and sat down on the terrace for something to eat. I was halfway through my dinner when I was joined by Geordie Andy who had spotted me as he was walking by.

"Hey, Kurt, how are you doing? Sorry to hear about you and Nicola splitting up."

"I'm good, thanks. But who told you about the break-up?"

"Actually, I saw her this morning in town with Kirby. She told me herself."

"How did she look? Was she okay?"

"Yes, she seemed quite happy with Kirby, considering what had happened between you. She was visiting estate agents," he replied.

Time was getting on now, so I finished eating and made my way up to the London Bar with Geordie to meet up with the others before walking over to the Stage Door. It wasn't long before we were opening the doors again, and the club started filling up. I stood at the door meeting and greeting the customers for the first couple of hours, while Danny and Simon took care of the decks. I felt it was important for me to be on the door, as I was trying to rebuild my trade after the shutdown. I'd probably only have about another six weeks or so left of the season, so it was important that I drew in as much custom as possible to get through the winter months.

Geordie Andy hadn't walked up with us to the Stage Door earlier, as he had a few things to do. At about 2.30 he made his appearance with a couple of guys that he said worked with him. I shook their hands and let them into the club without charge. Shortly after that, Kimberly and Fallon came down the steps. I didn't think it would be long before I saw the pair of them; in fact, I was surprise that I hadn't seen them last night.

"Hey, honey bunny," said Fallon, giving me a hug.

"Hiya, gorgeous. What have you two been up to then?"

"Well, we've been too Gibraltar for the last couple of days with Kimberly's parents. They came to stay with us for a few days."

"Oh right, so you haven't heard yet then?"

"Heard what?" they both asked.

"Well, it seems that me and Nicola have now split up and she's moved in with Kirby."

"No! I don't believe it. I knew Kirby could be manipulative, but I never thought she'd go that far!"

"Well, there's a little more to it than that. It wasn't Kirby's fault."

"What do you mean?"

"Nicola caught me kissing Keeley in the London Bar, and she went nuts."

"Kurt! So you brought this on yourself then? No sympathy from me then, I'm afraid."

"Yes, I guess you could say that I got what I deserved."

"Well, look on the bright side. At least you're a free agent now," said Kimberly as she kissed me on the cheek.

"Hey, hands off! He's mine," said Fallon.

"Take it easy, girls. There's plenty of me to go around," I joked.

I led the girls inside and walked them up to the bar to get them a drink. I stayed there chatting with them for a while before relieving Danny on the decks where I stayed for just over an hour before Simon took over to play the evening out.

All in all it had been a successful reopening. The tills were full and everyone seemed to go home happy, but I still felt a little empty without Nicola and Kirby's presence in the bar.

Once all the punters had cleared the bar, I locked up, leaving only a select few for the usual lock-in. I decided at that point that I wasn't going to dwell on the past and be miserable, so I joined Fallon and Kimberly at the bar to take my mind off Nicola. The pair of them were a little worse for wear after consuming a considerable amount of alcohol.

"Hiya, girls! You both look like you've been enjoying yourselves a little too much."

"Maybe just a little," said Kimberly.

"So is it really over between you and Nicola then?" asked Fallon.

"Yes, but I'd rather not talk about it if you don't mind."

"Oh, poor baby, you're still suffering, aren't you? Well, there's no way I'm letting you go home alone tonight feeling like that."

"It's alright, Fallon. I'll be okay, really!"

"No, Fallon's right. We can't have you sitting at home alone all depressed."

"So what do you suggest then?" I asked.

"Well, I think you should come back and stay with us," said Fallon.

""Hmm, that sounds like fun. Okay, but as long as you promise not to wear me out too much," I said, laughing.

"From what Fallon tells me, it's more likely that you'll wear us out first," replied Kimberly, giggling.

After the usual Charlie session, I locked up the bar and made my way back with the girls for what was to be my first sexual encounter as a single guy since meeting Nicola. I was determined to enjoy myself. I was feeling extremely horny by the time I entered Fallon's apartment, as were the girls, especially Kimberly, who'd been trying her hardest to get into my pants since the moment I'd first met her.

As soon as we'd closed the door, Kimberly and Fallon led me into the bedroom. Before long we were all messing about on the bed practically naked. The sexual excitement in the room, combined with the effects of the cocaine that we'd taken earlier, was intense and intoxicating in the extreme. Before I knew it, Kimberly was sitting on top of me. She had a similar body to Fallon's, with firm upturned breasts that were sensitive to the touch (which I took full advantage of), and her skin was smooth and silky. I could see why Fallon took so much pleasure in her—a pleasure that I fully intended to enjoy as much as I could. It seemed that Kimberly felt the same way. It wasn't long before she was riding me like a rodeo horse, with Fallon's hands caressing the pair of us. Fallon was taking great pleasure in watching me having sex with Kimberly, and after we climaxed, she didn't give me too much time to recover before having her way with me too. By this time Fallon was extremely turned on, and nothing was going to stop her. The sex between us last time had been intense, but this was something else. She was practically feral in her eagerness to shag me. Having two beautiful girls fuck the shit out of me was . . . well . . . all I can say was that it felt incredibly sexy!

We slept for several hours after that marathon of sex, each one of us totally exhausted.

I woke up at about 6 p.m. that evening in Fallon's bed with Kimberly's soft warm body cuddled up behind me and her arm trailing over my chest. Fallon was already up. I could hear the shower running, so I decided to join her. I stepped into the shower behind Fallon and slipped my arms around her soap-soaked body, kissed her neck, and whispered, "Morning, gorgeous. I really enjoyed last night."

"I should think you did, with two Swedes shagging the crap out of you," she said, turning around to face me.

"Well you two had your way with me last night, so I guess it's up to me to return the favour."

"Anything you say, Kurt" she said smiling.

It was my turn to take advantage of her, and I didn't disappoint!

We eventually made our way back into the bedroom to wake up Kimberly. Then Fallon knocked up some breakfast, which we ate on the patio whilst going over last night's events. I could see that I was going to have a lot of fun with these two!

We finished getting ready and then made our way into town and then onto the Stage Door to clean up and restock after last night's session.

I spent quite a lot of time in Fallon and Kimberly's company over the next four weeks, and they were only too happy to help in the bar. Things had seemed to settle down again. The only problem was that the trade was now starting to drop off as the season was coming to an end. Many of the local English workers were going home for the winter, and it was obvious that it wouldn't be too long before I lost most of my custom and consequently my income.

The last time I'd checked, I had about five grand in the bank. I should have had more, but my habitual use of cocaine had made a considerable dent in my finances. I was still renting the villa, although most of the time I was at Fallon's.

Kimberly was getting ready to return to Sweden, as she had only intended to stay for the summer. Although she loved it out here, she was looking forward to going home to see her family and friends.

Danny was also flying back to the UK to see his family for a few weeks. This wouldn't be a problem because, as I said, the trade was now slowly ebbing away, which was something I'd have to address.

Keeley had entered the *Sun*'s page-three competition and won. I rang her up to congratulate her, and she was very pleased to hear my voice. She told me that she'd been very busy doing various photo shoots and was having a great time. She also said that she'd pay me a visit as soon as she could but that she was extremely busy at the moment. It was good to hear her voice again.

Many of my rivals were now closing down for the winter, but unfortunately I didn't have that luxury, as I'd soon run out of money with my doors closed. If I couldn't generate more trade soon, then I'd have to consider reducing the staff. The next two weeks passed by, and, as predicted, the customers disappeared. I called a meeting at the London Bar with all the staff to talk about the problems at hand.

Kimberly had now returned to Sweden, and I was still seeing Fallon, although I stopped short of moving in with her. I suppose you could say that we'd formed a strong bond together. It wasn't the same as what I'd had with Nicola—more on the physical side, I suppose. I still missed Nicola a lot, although I never let on to Fallon how I felt.

I arrived with Fallon at the London Bar at 8 p.m. on the Monday evening to find all the staff waiting for me.

"So the reason we're here is because there isn't enough trade to carry on employing all of you. The truth is, our trade is gone, so unless anyone has any suggestions, then I'm going to have to terminate most of your jobs."

Confirming their suspicions wasn't much fun, but they had to know the truth. We chatted for some time, and several suggestions came up, ranging from theme nights to live music. Even pole-dancing was suggested, which brought fits of laughter from everyone.

But the best suggestion came from Geordie Andy, who come along to the meeting with Peter, my doorman. He said that he knew a Spanish DJ called Minola who had a big following in the Spanish trance scene. He had his own bar but was looking for new places to perform in. Geordie offered to introduce me to him, which I agreed to. If I could get him to play in my bar, then it was possible that I could generate a new customer base with the Spanish youngsters. I thought that if I could secure that trade, then it should be enough to see me through the winter months. Geordie rang Minola and set up a meeting for tomorrow night at his bar which was situated just outside Malaga. I was told that he spoke fairly good English, which would obviously be very helpful to me.

Most of the staff went their separate ways except for Fallon and Geordie, so I left them at the table chatting while I went to get another round of drinks in. As I turned around to return to the table, I was surprised to see Nicola and Kirby enter the bar with Luciana. This was the first time I'd seen her in here for a while, and after I'd placed the drinks on the table, I went over to greet them with the usual hugs and kisses. I invited them to join us at the table and ordered some extra drinks.

We stayed in the bar for a few hours just chatting and reminiscing. It was quite a good atmosphere. I managed to get a few minutes alone with Nicola while the others were in the loo sniffing power.

There was an awkward silence for a moment, and then Nicola said, "It's okay, you know."

"What do you mean?" I asked her.

"I mean, I know you're seeing Fallon, and I've accepted that now. Rather her than Keeley any day."

"You still haven't got over the Keeley thing, have you?"

"Kurt, I need you to tell me the truth about what happened between you. I want to know. You owe me that much."

"I owe you! If I recall, you're the one who betrayed me and lied to me."

"So, did you make love to Keeley or not?"

"Look, if you want the truth, then here it is. I caught you cavorting with Kirby behind my back. I trusted you, and you let me down."

"But we never had sex together until after you returned from our argument."

"The level of contact was irrelevant. Whether you dipped your toe in the water or dived right in makes no difference. In my mind, you deceived me and I felt let down. When I left the villa, I bumped into Keeley and ended up pouring my troubles out on her. Before I knew it, I was back at her place making love to her in the heat of the moment. I accept I was wrong to do that, but you weren't innocent in all this."

"No, I guess I wasn't, but you went too far. I couldn't forgive you for that because my last boyfriend also betrayed me. I'm sorry it came to this. I thought we had a long future together. Thanks for at least being honest with me now. I hope we can at least salvage a friendship out of all this mess. A piece of my heart will always be with you, Kurt," she said with a tear in her eye.

"Hey, I'll always be there for you as a friend if that's what you want, so cheer up, princess. You know I don't like seeing you sad. Now let me get some more drinks in, okay?"

"Okay, thanks, Kurt," she said as I walked towards the bar.

By the time I'd returned with the drinks everyone was back at the table. It was good to have all the gang back together again, even if it was for just one night. We stayed in there until they closed up and then said our goodnights and went our separate ways.

It was now late afternoon, and Geordie had arranged a meeting with Minola at his house, which was situated on the outskirts of Malaga. I picked Geordie up at the port in Fuengirola, and we made the drive up to Minola's. Eventually we pulled into a long high street and then turned left down what seemed to be an old dirt track. At the end of the road there were a few small shops and a row of old houses that adjoined a small rundown bar with a large fenced-in terrace. We got out of the car, and I followed Geordie up to the front door of the house nearest to the bar and rang the bell. The door opened and we were greeted by Minola who welcomed us inside.

He was Spanish in complexion, about five foot ten, with cropped hair. He seemed very laid back and had a permanent smile on his face. He made me feel very welcome and came across as very sincere. Minola told me that his father had died a couple of years ago and left him the house and the lease on the bar next door.

I sounded him out on our idea of him bringing the Spanish crowd to the Stage Door, and I let him know that I was prepared to give him a share of the door money for his troubles. I also told him that he could drink as much as he wanted for free while he was working in there. I thought that that might push his buttons, as Geordie had told me earlier that he had a passion for whisky, which was a very popular drink with most of the Spanish guys.

Minola seemed very interested in my proposal and invited us to stay for dinner, which we duly accepted. He took me on a tour of his house while his girlfriend Danni, a young English girl, prepared the meal. There was lots of music memorabilia lying around his house, from photos and posters to equipment, records, and event fliers. He had been a DJ in the Spanish dance scene for many years now, and judging by the photos and posters where he was generally top billing, a very popular one at that.

We eventually sat down to a delicious dinner and then relaxed in his garden with a couple of bottles of wine. Before we knew it, it was 10.30 p.m. Minola asked us to join him as he had to open up the bar. He locked up the house, and we walked the short distance to his bar and went inside.

It was very sparingly decorated in black and luminous colours that lit up when the fluorescent lights went on. There was very little bar equipment, and it had no tills or lager pumps, just crates and fridges. Minola assured me that it would be busy within the hour and asked us to help him get it ready. Sure enough, the punters started to arrive. Before long it was so busy inside that most of the people had to stand outside on the terraces. I must admit I was very surprised that he could fill up such a rickety old shack of a bar so easily. Even more surprising was that one of his best DJs was a beautiful young seventeen-year-old Spanish girl with long dark ringlet hair. She really rocked the place! Minola told me that her name was Mellissa. She was quite small, only about five foot two, but very well proportioned, with piercingly beautiful brown eyes.

Minola introduced me to her, telling me that she would be an asset to my business if I was happy to let her come along and play in the Stage Door with him. Mellissa's English was generally quite good, and anything I didn't understand Minola was happy to translate for me. It was becoming apparent to me that if I was going to survive out here, it would probably be wise to learn the language.

I complimented Mellissa on her DJ skills and, of course, on her looks and especially her eyes. Mellissa smiled and glanced down, blushing from the compliment I'd just paid her. I've got to say that she looked extremely cute when she was embarrassed. Minola asked her if she'd be interested in playing at the Stage Door with him, and she seemed very excited at the prospect.

We were getting on quite well together, and there seemed to be quite a lot of flirting between the two of us, but then our conversation was cut short by the arrival of the boyfriend, a young Spanish lad of about the same age. It was obvious that he wasn't too keen on her talking to me, so I made my excuses, kissed her on the cheek, and left her to argue with her over-possessive partner.

"She likes you. I can tell," said Minola, smiling.

"What makes you think that?

"Kurt, she couldn't take her eyes off you."

"Really? Well, she was very pretty, so I guess I'm quite flattered."

"So, Kurt, I've decided. I play for you. We be good friends, yes?"

"Yeah, I'd like that very much."

"I think this will be very lucrative for both of us."

"I hope so, Minola. I hope so."

We stayed on for the lock-in. Like the English, Minola and his friends were very much into cocaine. It seemed to be widely used out here by all nationalities. We stayed up drinking and chatting until the early hours, when Minola invited us to stay at his for the night, which we were very pleased to accept.

We woke up the next day at about midday and Minola insisted that we eat breakfast before making the drive back to Fuengirola. Afterwards I thanked him for his hospitality and we bid him goodbye.

Last night couldn't have gone any better. I had a great feeling about my new-found friendship. Things looked extremely promising.

Minola had a gig to do on Thursday night, so we agreed that his first night would be on the Friday. Over the next few days with Fallon's and Danny's help, we distributed loads of Spanish fliers all over town and put up posters in the local record shops and bars. Thursday night went off very quietly with only about thirty people in the bar. It cost me more in stock and wages to open up than I made over the bar, so as you can imagine I was quite pleased to see Friday night come around.

Minola said that he would meet us at the Stage Door at about midnight. I'd told Simon the previous night that I wouldn't need him this weekend. He wasn't too happy about it, but that's life, I guess. We prepared the Stage Door as usual. Fallon and Luciana manned the bar, while Danny started on the decks. I'd advertised that we'd be open from 12.30 a.m. with Minola being on top of the billing, as well as Mellissa and, of course, my own DJ Danny.

It was approaching one o'clock before Minola arrived. He apologized for being late. Apparently, he'd had a very busy night in his own bar. Up until the time Minola arrived, we'd only managed to attract about forty customers, so I was quite pleased to see him. He'd brought about twenty people with him, which helped the bar look a little busier. I poured Minola a large whisky and led him behind the bar and up to the DJ booth and left him in Danny's capable hands. Once acquainted with the equipment, he took over from Danny and started playing his trance music.

Over the next hour the Spanish crowd slowly arrived in groups of ten or twelve, but sure enough they came and filled the bar. The Spanish kids were different to the English. They didn't spend their money anywhere near as freely, and they rarely brought a round of drinks for each other. They much preferred to adopt a buy-your-own type of policy. Their dress sense was smart but casual. Most of the girls tended to wear those sexy hipster trousers and shorts. It was also fairly obvious that most of them were pretty wasted on one sort of drug or another. But all in all we had a great night. In fact, It was the first night in a while that I'd turned a decent profit, which I was extremely relieved about.

At the end of the night I thanked Minola and settled up with him. Then I locked up and made my way down to Jimmy's with Tony and the staff for breakfast.

"Well, I've got to hand it to you Kurt. That was a great night!" said Tony.

"Yeah, I agree. The music was brilliant," said Luciana and Fallon.

"Do you think so?"

"Yes we do. You must be getting old," said Fallon, laughing.

"Hey, don't be so cheeky or I'll put you over my knee!"

"Ooh, is that a promise? You'll have to smack me hard, as I'm a very naughty girl," said Fallon, laughing.

"Behave yourself," I said to her.

"You know that's something that she finds very hard to do, don't you, Kurt?" said Luciana, giggling out loud.

I finished my breakfast and said goodnight to the others. Then Fallon and I made our way up towards her place in Los Boliches.

"I really enjoyed tonight, Kurt," said Fallon, hanging on to my arm.

"Yeah, it was quite successful, wasn't it?"

"It was, so I think we should celebrate. I've got some jelly and ice cream in the fridge if you fancy it."

"Thanks, babe, but I don't think I could eat another thing. I'm stuffed!"

"Who said anything about eating it?" said Fallon with a big smile on her face.

"You know, you never fail to surprise me—in a great way, of course."

"You know you can't resist this sexy body of mine!"

"You're not wrong there," I said, putting my arm around her.

Fallon always kept me on my toes sexually. In fact, I'd go as far as to say that she was a bit of a nymphomaniac. Not that I was complaining—far from it! As I've said before, she was a very sexy girl. A little wild sometimes, but I wouldn't change a thing about her.

I'd arranged the same set up for Saturday night, with Minola and his crew coming down again, so I hoped we'd be just as busy. It looked as though I'd found a solution to the money problems for now, which would allow me to sleep a little easier tonight. For that at least I was grateful.

Saturday afternoon came around quickly. As usual the sun was out in force. Fallon had decided to spend the rest of the day on the beach. We were now at the end of the season, so the beaches were relatively empty. Most of the big bars and clubs were closing up for the winter months, as the tourist boom was now well and truly over. The town's businesses were practically working with a skeleton staff, and I'd heard it said that unemployment in the town was over twenty per cent! The jet skis and water sports had packed up for the winter too, but the two things that still hadn't deserted us were the sunshine and the way of life out here. I'm pretty sure that, given the choice, if you'd experienced living out here, most people would never want to leave. Why would you? I'd have to say it's definitely worth the struggle.

The good thing about less people being around is that everything gets a lot cheaper and you don't have to queue to get a sun lounger. I laid down under the shade of the parasol next to Fallon, who was basking in the full glory of the sun. I'm so jealous of people who can do that. Unfortunately, as I've said before, I can't do it through fear of pain and resembling a lobster. I've been badly burnt by the sun in the past, and it's not something that I'd like to repeat! Don't get me wrong. I love the heat of the sun, but I know my limits and I try hard to stick to them.

We fooled around in and out of the water for a couple of hours before packing up and heading into town for refreshments. Soon after that, we headed back to the villa to relax by the pool for the rest of the evening.

When we were ready, we left and headed back down the Mijas hill towards Fuengirola to meet up with the rest of the staff and then on to the Stage Door. It was just coming up to midnight as we rounded the corner. To our surprise, there must have been a queue of about 100 people already waiting outside the gates. At the front of the queue stood Minola and a group of his entourage, including the beautiful Spanish DJ Mellissa.

"Minola, What are you doing here? You're half an hour early. We haven't even set up yet."

"Hello, Kurt. We finish early tonight. So I think I come sooner. More time that way, yes?"

"Yes, but you should have called. At least given me some sort of warning."

"Okay, next time I warn you, yes?"

"Yes, please do. Anyway you're here now, so let's go inside and quickly get set up. After all, we don't want to keep your audience waiting, do we?"

"I agree," said Minola.

"*Hola*, Mellissa. How are you?" I asked, kissing the back of her hand.

"Very good gracious," she replied in broken English. Minola told me that he'd been helping her improve her English, but as she lived in a small village, she didn't often get a chance to use it.

We entered the bar, and after a mad rush to get things ready, we opened the doors to let the influx of people inside. Minola had done us proud tonight; it was obvious that the word was spreading about this new venue that they could use.

Minola started the music off to warm up the crowd, while I worked the door with Peter. It didn't take long before we were turning people away at the door, so I left Peter to it and went inside. Mellissa and Danny were now working the decks together, and Minola was drinking whisky at the bar with a couple of Spanish lads. He beckoned me over and then introduced them to me.

The first one was called Julio, pronounced with the letter H. He was of average height and build, with the usual short dark Spanish hair. He didn't speak too much English but stuck out his hand to greet me anyway. Next he introduced me to a guy called Socar. He was slightly overweight, spoke good English, and came across as a very confident character.

Minola pulled me to one side to tell me that the two of them were gypsies, better known locally as *Gitana*. The gypsies were feared and respected amongst the young Spanish but generally unknown to the English. It turned out that these two lads were quite high up in the chain of command, so I guess I was sort of privileged to meet them. I made them both feel welcome, saying that a friend of Minola's was a friend of mine, and I asked Fallon to give them a drink on the house.

Minola nodded his head in appreciation, and then I left him to it, as I fancied a spin on the decks myself now. I relieved Danny, but Mellissa wanted to stay on to help me with the selection of the music, as Euro trance was not really my bag. Mellissa was like a live wire. She had so much passion for music and never stopped smiling, and although there was a minor language barrier, we were both strongly drawn to each other. She had a youthful energy and naivety about her that was a breath of fresh air. I played on for about an hour before reluctantly leaving her in the capable hands of Minola.

Besides, I was starting to get a few strange looks from Fallon now, so I thought it best to leave them to it and pay a little attention to her. I didn't want another scene in here!

"Hey, Fallon, how are you holding up, sweetheart?"

"I'm good, thanks. I see you're getting quite friendly with Mellissa. I can see why you fancy her. She's very attractive."

"Hey, don't be like that. You don't have to worry. I'm not about to run off with her, so don't get so jealous, okay?"

"Kurt, you know that as a Swede I'm very open-minded, but I really enjoy our relationship, and I don't want to lose what we have."

"You've got nothing to worry about, sweetheart, although you're right—she is very pretty."

"Kurt! Don't tease me."

"I thought you liked me to tease you," I said, kissing her. Fallon just smiled and kissed me back, before serving the next customer. She looked a lot happier, much to my relief.

It was a very profitable night once again, and after seeing the customers out, we had the usual lock-in to celebrate. Minola and his crew were the first to leave, and I walked him to his car outside to see him off. I shook his hand and thanked him again. Then I gave Mellissa a hug and a kiss to thank her too and went back inside to re-join the others.

The weekend had been a complete success—much better than I could have hoped for. Hopefully, Minola's introduction to the Stage Door would continue to help me get through the winter months.

CHAPTER NINE

The Winter Months

It was now Tuesday afternoon. The bar had been cleaned and restocked, and Fallon and I had decided to go water skiing in Marbella. I'd never tried it before, but I was quite looking forward to it. We'd brought a couple of wetsuits in town earlier, as we didn't want to use the hired ones. I've tried them before, and I can tell you, they're not too flattering. We made a private booking to water ski, as most of the water sports businesses were now closed down.

Fallon was first in the water, and I've got to say she skied like a professional. She'd obviously done it before! I should have guessed really, after all she was a very sporty girl, regularly going down the gym and attending various fitness classes. She loved doing risky things, and a lot of the time she seemed to have more energy than I knew how to cope with!

Fallon was out on the water for around thirty minutes before handing over the reins to me. I hit the water running and firing on all cylinders, gliding along like a swan. Unfortunately, it wasn't long before I plunged into the water head first in a tangled mess. From that moment on, as much as I tried, I just couldn't get back on my feet. I must have swallowed a gallon of sea water by the time we pulled back up on the beach. I staggered back towards Fallon, who was hysterically laughing her tits off.

"Hey, what's so funny?"

"You look like a drowned rat."

"Well, thanks for your concern. I'm okay, thanks, or at least I will be after I've finished being sick!" I said sarcastically.

"I'm so sorry," she said, roaring with laughter.

"Actually, besides the fact that I nearly drowned, I quite enjoyed myself, but I definitely won't be doing it again in a hurry!"

"Ah, poor baby, come here," she said, stretching out her arms out to cuddle me.

We stayed on the beach for another hour before changing and wandering up onto the promenade. We then crossed the road to stop at one of the sea front bars. I was going to suggest food, but my stomach was still a little upset from all the salt water that I'd swallowed earlier. As we sat on the terrace, Fallon spotted some familiar faces walking past.

"Hey! Don't say hello then," she shouted out. It was Peter and Melanie walking along with Simon.

"Hiya! What are you three doing here?" I asked them.

"We could ask the same about you."

We both stood up to greet them and asked them to join us. Simon told us that, thanks to Peter, he had been given a trial night at one of the top clubs in town.

"Hey, that's great. I'm sure you'll do well. You're a good DJ, Simon. It's a shame I had to let you go. I'm sorry about that."

"That's okay, Kurt. Don't worry about it. No hard feelings, okay?"

"Look, I know the manager at the club he's playing in tonight. It's a ticket-only event, as are most of the top clubs in Marbella. Why don't you hang around, and I'll get you both in tonight. It would also be away of supporting Simon," said Peter.

We stayed in the bar until 10 p.m. before making our way into town. Peter led us up to a large building with a long entrance that had a lighted canopy leading up to the front doors. As we approached, the bouncers asked us for our tickets. Peter stepped forward and had a word with them, and before you could say jack flash, we were ushered inside.

It was far more upmarket than the Stage Door. Everything inside was like new, and it was very spacious and classy throughout. Apart from the rich seating material and well lit dance floor, there was also several podiums scattered around with scantily clad girls dancing on them.

Peter introduced me to the owner, whose name was Kieran, while Simon made his way up to the DJ booth. Kieran showed us to a table and gave us a complimentary bottle of champagne to start the night off with, and then left us to it. We'd had quite a bit to drink by now, so Peter offered us a line of coke to sober us up a little, which we gratefully accepted.

Simon played a great set on the decks, which got most of the people up dancing, including us. It turned out to be a great night, and between the coke sniffing, dancing, and free bottles of bubbly, both Fallon and I really enjoyed ourselves.

On top of everything else, at the end of the evening Simon was offered a full-time resident DJ position, so it had turned out to be quite a successful night all around. As we left the club, Peter told us that they were going on to a friend's house and were going to drop Simon off on the way. I thanked him for the night out, and we jumped into a cab and headed back to the villa for some rest and play, although not necessarily in that order!

Thursday night came around, and we opened up at 1 a.m. We only had about a dozen customers for the first hour or so, but then Barry the Scouser and a few of his friends arrived. They propped up the bar for a couple of hours, buying a round of drinks every ten minutes like it was a competition or something, slowly getting louder and louder.

At about 4.30 a.m., I went up to Danny to see how he was. I'd only been chatting to him for a few minutes when an argument broke out at the bar, so I quickly made my way back there to find out what was going on. One of the Scousers called Ian was arguing with Fallon, who was now close to tears, and Peter was right in between them, trying desperately to calm the situation.

"Whoa! Calm down! What's the problem?" I asked Ian.

"I gave her a ten mil note, and she gave me change for a five. I want my money now," he demanded.

I felt like telling him to piss off, as I'm pretty sure Fallon wouldn't have done that deliberately, but I humoured him and checked the tills for the ten mil note, which was worth about £50. Most people never used bigger than a five mil note, so if she had made a mistake, it would have been in the till, but it wasn't.

"You must have been mistaken, as we don't have a ten mil note in the till," I told him.

"I gave that bitch a ten mil note, and I want the right change now," he snapped at me.

"Hey, you're not listening to me, mate. I don't have a ten mil note, so you're not getting any more change, okay?"

Ian grabbed a bottle off of the bar and raised it up in an attempt to strike me with it, but before he could, Peter grabbed his arm and twisted it behind his back, forcing him to drop the bottle, and then he pinned him against the bar. Two of the Scousers who were with him immediately turned towards Peter, grabbing whatever they could off of the bar to use as weapons. Seeing this, Peter pulled out a knife and brandished it towards them, saying, "Put the fucking bottles and glasses down or I swear I'll kill the lot of you!"

They could tell that he was serious, and after a heated exchange, they reluctantly lowered their weapons.

"Now take this piece of shit and get the fuck out of here and don't come back!" he shouted at them, still brandishing the knife.

"Okay, we're going. Calm down. We don't want any more trouble, okay?"

Barry and his other couple of mates grabbed hold of Ian and made a sharp exit.

"Whoa! Thanks, Peter. That was touch and go for a moment there," I said.

"You're not kidding. I wasn't sure they'd back off, but one thing's for sure though, they'll be back. This won't be the end of it!" he replied.

"Well, I hope you're wrong, but thanks anyway."

The few customers who were in here when the Scousers kicked off had already left, so we didn't see the point in staying open any longer. Besides, there was a good chance that the Scousers might return in force, so we decided to lock up and have an early night instead. Hopefully, in the cold light of day they would forget about it, and it would all blow over.

As we walked away from the Stage Door and headed down towards the taxi rank, we bumped into Simon who had his face all bandaged up.

"Where is he? Has he gone yet?" he asked me.

"Simon, what the hell are you going on about? And what happened to your face?"

"Him! That bastard, your doorman Peter! He cut my face!" he blurted out.

"What the fuck are you talking about? Why the hell would Peter do that? It was only last night that he got you a job!"

"Yeah, and when he dropped me off last night, he ran up behind me as I approached my front door and slashed me across the face with that knife of his."

"I don't believe you. Why would he do that? What did you do to provoke him?"

"I didn't do anything. He just went crazy. He's a mad man, and he's going to pay for what he did." Simon unwrapped his bandages to reveal a long gash down the right side of his face. It looked pretty gruesome. "I want you to sack him. It's the least you can do for me," he demanded.

"Hey, I don't know the full story yet. At the moment I've only got your word on what happened. I'll look into it, okay? Now do yourself a favour and go home, all right?"

"He's gonna pay," he said angrily, walking away from us.

"I can't believe what I've just heard, can you?" said Fallon.

"No, I can't, so I think we should find out what really happened."

I knew Peter wouldn't have gone far, so I called him on the mobile to see where he was. Unfortunately, he'd already got into a cab and was heading back towards his home. I told him that I needed to speak to him face to face urgently, so he invited us to meet him at his place in Calahonda. I hung up the phone and we jumped into a taxi and drove down there.

I knocked on Peter's front door about twenty minutes later. He invited us in, and we went into the front room.

"So, what's wrong? What's all this about?" he asked.

"I've just had Simon mouthing off to me in Fuengirola, accusing you of cutting his face. What's going on, Peter?"

"He had it coming to him."

"What? So you did cut him then? I can't believe it! You were in such good spirits when we left you in Marbella. What happened?"

"It's a private matter, okay?" he snapped.

"Well, actually it's not. I'm sorry, Peter, but I'm not sure that I feel comfortable employing someone who just ups and stabs people for little or no apparent reason."

"No reason! Is that what he told you? Well it's a lie. On the way back from Marbella, I stopped to get some petrol. When I got back in the car, Melanie was really quiet. I asked her what was the matter, but she wouldn't tell me. So I carried on and dropped Simon off. Once he stepped out of the car, I asked her again, demanding that she tell me what was wrong."

"And what did she say?" I asked him.

"She broke down in tears, telling me that while I was in the garage, Simon tried it on with her. When she refused his advances, he grabbed her by the throat and forced a kiss on her whilst fondling her breast. She tried to push him off, but he squeezed her throat a little tighter and warned her not to say anything to me or otherwise he'd cut her throat. She was terrified and sobbing uncontrollably by now. I jumped out of the car and ran up to him, and as he turned around, I slashed him across his face and then kicked him to the floor. I told him that he was lucky I hadn't killed him for what he'd done. I got back in the car and drove Melanie home to console her."

Melanie showed us the bruises around her neck and started crying. Fallon sat down and put her arms around Melanie to comfort her.

"Well in that case, I think he got what he deserved. I hope you're okay, Melanie."

"If he got what he deserved, he'd be dead right now," said Peter angrily.

"Well, I'm glad he's not dead, otherwise you'd be in jail right now, but I can assure you that he won't be welcome around me any more. That's for sure!"

We didn't stay much longer, as we didn't want to impose on them. It had obviously been a shocking experience to Melanie. I had no sympathy for Simon whatsoever and if he had any sense, he'd stay as far away from Peter as possible. I don't think he'll get away so lightly the next time they meet!

Friday night came around. I was glad of this, as it was going to be Minola's second weekend. Hopefully, it would be as lucrative as the last. At 8 p.m., I made my way down to the Stage Door to sort out the stock, while Fallon headed up to the London Bar, as she had a few people to see. For a change, Pablo turned up on time with the stock, and I set about restocking the shelves and fridges.

At about 9 p.m., I received a surprise phone call from Keeley of all people. I hadn't spoken to her in a couple of weeks, so I was quite pleased to hear her voice.

"Hey, baby, long time, no hear."

"Yeah, sorry, Kurt, I've been really busy. So how have you been?"

"I'm okay, although it has to be said that business has been a little slow, but I've managed to find a temporary solution with a Spanish DJ called Minola, and it's showing promise. So what about you? Tell me what you've been up to."

"Oh, you know, lots of photo shoots and different locations. I've got a surprise for you."

"Oh, what's that then? Something good, I hope."

"You could say that. I'm scheduled to do a photo shoot in Malaga for a magazine in a months' time. I'll be in town for a couple of days, and I was hoping we could spend that time together. What do you think?"

"I think that sounds terrific. I look forward to seeing you again."

It always gave me a lift to hear Keeley's voice, although I don't suppose that Fallon would be too happy to know that she was going to be returning, even if it was for only a couple of days. I'd have to think of something when the time came to keep Fallon out of the way.

I finished my conversation with Keeley and then locked up the Stage Door and walked down towards the port. As I passed the bowling alley, I saw a familiar face walking towards me. It was Simon, and the minute I saw him my hackles went up!

"Kurt, have you sacked him yet?" he asked me.

"You'd better get the fuck away from me. I've spoken to Peter and Melanie. What you did was disgraceful, and you got what you deserved," I said, pointing a finger at his face.

"But she came on to me!" he insisted.

"You're a fucking liar. You're not welcome in my bar any more, and I'd be happy if I never saw you again. You disgust me. Now fuck off before I kick the shit out of you."

Simon quickly had it away on his toes, which was a wise move, as I was about to thump him. I carried on walking towards the London Bar, where I met up with Fallon and the others for a couple of drinks before making our way back to the Stage Door. We opened the doors at about 12.30 a.m. and let in the thirty or forty people waiting outside. As usual, Danny started the night off. Minola wasn't due until after 1 a.m., and over the next half an hour we started to fill up with mostly Spanish customers.

Everything seemed to be going well until an argument broke out on the dance floor between a Spanish lad and, of all people, a young Scouse lad. These Scousers just don't seem to be able to behave themselves! I walked over and grabbed hold of the pair of them, telling them both to calm down. I fully intended to throw the Scouser out, but to my surprise the other Spanish customers sided against their own. It turned out on this occasion at least that it wasn't the Scouser's fault. The Spanish lad turned out to be one of the local gypsies and seemed bent on causing trouble, so I frog-marched him out of the bar and barred him from coming back, much to his annoyance.

Soon after that Minola arrived, followed by a queue of people that filled up the bar. I was disappointed to see that Mellissa wasn't with him tonight, but he had brought along a young DJ called Paul. Minola told me that he was very up and coming in the Spanish dance scene.

Paul took over from Danny. He had an immediate impact on the punters, and he had them all up dancing in no time. The atmosphere in here now was very good, and as I stood at the bar looking on, the Scouse lad from earlier approached me with one of his friends.

"Hey, thanks for earlier. Can I buy you a drink?" he asked me.

"I'm okay at the moment, thanks."

"I'm Steve by the way, and this is my mate Wilf."

"Pleased to meet you, lads. You can call me Kurt as long as you behave yourselves."

"Sure, okay, and don't worry. We're not looking for any trouble."

"Glad to hear it," I said.

I turned around to see Minola chatting to Peter by the door, so I got Fallon to pour out a whisky and took it over to him. The customers were now backed up past the door. We were now full to the brim. Danny and Luciana were working behind the bar to help Fallon out as the punters were now queuing up to get served. Luciana had come down with us on her own, earlier as Tony had to work late tonight at a private gig in Torremolinos.

Everything went smoothly until about 4 a.m., when there was a commotion at the door. I went over to see what was occurring, and I found Minola arguing with some thirty-year-old Spanish guy.

"Hey, what the fuck's going on?" I asked them.

"I don't want this guy in here. He's nothing but trouble, and I won't stay here if you let him in," said Minola angrily.

"If I want to come in here, I will. It's not up to you," said the Spanish guy, pointing aggressively at Minola.

"Look, mate, I'm the owner, and I'm telling you that you're not welcome here, so do yourself a favour and go somewhere else, okay?"

"If I want to come in, I will, okay? You're not going to be able to stop me."

"We'll fucking see about that," I said.

Peter stepped in, grabbed hold of him, and physically threw him out.

"What the hell was all that about" I asked Minola.

"He is a gypsy, and he has caused my family trouble in the past."

"Ok, fair enough. Now go and play some music and calm down."

"You are a good friend to me," he said, giving me a hug.

Everything calmed down for about half an hour, but then another argument erupted in the entrance corridor. I rushed through the office and out into the corridor to find that the Spanish guy we'd thrown out earlier had returned with a couple of mates who were obviously intent on causing trouble. Peter wrestled with the biggest guy, who was trying his hardest to get through into the main bar, while I came up against one of the other two guys. He was wielding a knife and spouting off in Spanish. I approached him cautiously with my hands raised and asked him to calm down and to lower the knife in Spanish.

"*Tranquilo! Tranquilo. No cutas,*" I said.

In the split second when he lowered the knife, a couple of punters grabbed hold of him, and I immediately punched him several times in the face, dropping him to his knees. This was all the customers needed to finish him off, before dragging him out of the bar. Seeing this, the third guy obviously didn't fancy his chances and ran off in a hurry, leaving the big guy, who now had Peter in a head lock. He was about to smash a glass in his face. I rushed over to help Peter, and landed a couple of good punches on his attacker. Apart from making him drop the glass, this didn't seem to wobble him at all.

Fallon grabbed a tin of CS gas that Peter liked to keep behind the bar for emergencies and squirted it at the big guy. It had little effect, so I took it off of her, grabbed him by the hair, and unloaded most of the can into his face. This practically felled the guy. Up to now most of the punters had given this huge bloke a wide berth for obvious reasons, but as he collapsed from the stinging effects of the gas, they just pounced on him, raining down punches and kicks until he eventually crawled out of the bar, leaving a trail of blood behind him.

Once he was outside the gate, I locked it behind him to stop any repeat performances and went back inside to see how Peter was. I found him sitting at the captain's table with his face in his hands. Unfortunately, Peter had been a little too close to the big guy and had also been hit by the spread of the gas, which had burnt his eyes and face.

Apart from this casualty, the feeling in the bar was one of elation and excitement at winning this victory. One of the customers who had been in the corridor earlier had also suffered a cut across the palm of his hand

and was bleeding quite heavily, so his friend decided to take him to the hospital just as a precaution.

I walked outside with them and opened the gate to let them out. The two trouble makers were still waiting outside. They were a little worse for the wear now and absolutely caked in blood. I couldn't really understand why they would hang around. After all, they'd just got a right pasting inside. I told the big guy who was nearest to the gate to go home, and he immediately threw a punch at me that landed on the side of my left eye, slightly cutting me. I still had what was left of the CS gas canister in my hand, so I squirted it towards him, which had the effect of backing him up long enough to lock the gates back up again.

Two minutes later the police arrived, and after speaking to the trouble makers, they demanded that I open the gates. One of the officers spoke to me in broken English, and I told him that these guys had come into the bar with knifes and started fighting, cutting one of my customers who was now on his way to the hospital. I told him that someone had let off a CS gas canister and that after a long scuffle we'd managed to drag them out of the bar and lock the gates behind us. I also told him that my bouncer had been gassed in the face and showed him the injury that I'd sustained in the fight whilst trying to protect my bar and customers. The police officer promptly arrested me and Peter, and I threw the keys to Fallon, who'd now joined us outside.

"Lock the gates behind me, and whatever you do, don't close the bar!"

"But we don't have a bouncer now," said Fallon, looking very worried.

"It's okay. Minola will look after you, and Tony will be down soon. Don't worry. I'll be okay."

"Okay," said Fallon, kissing me on the cheek.

Fallon and the others went back inside. The police took both us and the gypsies to the station, where they separated us and stuck me and Peter in a large room that was completely empty except for a table and some chairs, where they questioned us for some time. It took quite a while to get our statements, as the station officers didn't speak very good English, and Peter constantly complained about his eyes throughout the interview. In the end, they let me go at about 8 a.m., and they took Peter to the hospital in Marbella, telling us both that they would be in touch in the future.

The first place I headed for was the Stage Door to try and find Fallon. I approached the gates, only to find them locked up. I couldn't hear any sounds coming from inside the bar, so I rang the bell on the off chance that they were having a lock-in. I didn't have to wait too long before the doors burst open and Minola of all people stuck his head out, quickly followed by Fallon.

"Kurt, Kurt, I'm very pleased to see you," said Minola.

"How come you're still here?" I asked him.

"Kurt, I go nowhere till you return. You are my friend."

"You don't know the half of it," said Fallon, wrapping herself around me.

"Hey, baby, I'm pleased to see you too. So what's going on in here then?" I asked her.

"Come inside and I'll tell you all about it," said Fallon.

Minola locked the gates and we went inside. As I entered the main bar, a cheer went out from the fifty or so people still inside.

"What's going on?" I asked, looking very surprised.

"None of them wanted to go. In fact, Tony and Luciana had to help me talk them out of rescuing you from the cop shop," said Fallon.

"What do you mean?"

"I mean this lot was going to go down and physically break you out," she said, giggling.

"That's insane, but very touching. Thanks, I appreciate the sentiment, but I'm glad you didn't," I said, hugging Minola.

"Hey, Kurt, I hear you gassed Peter. I can't believe you got away with that!" said Tony, laughing.

"Yeah, I know. Can you believe that he didn't stop whining all the time we were in the police station?"

We both started laughing out loud. I turned to everyone who had stayed, thanked them, and gave them a free drink on the house. I must have heard the story about what had happened twenty times over the next half hour from different people. Tony had arrived about ten minutes after we were carted away, and between him and Minola's crowd they kept everything running smoothly. Tony couldn't stop talking about all the blood on the steps outside that he'd mopped up, and he just couldn't get over the fact that I'd gassed Peter and got away with it. It had turned out to be quite an eventful night, and in a strange sort of way I really enjoyed myself.

We kicked out at about 9.30 a.m., and a few of us went down to Scottie's for the ritual breakfast. Minola joined us for a while, and we spent the next hour just chatting and joking about the night's events. While we were sitting there, I got a call from Peter to say that he'd been released from hospital with a clean bill of health apart from the sore eyes. He told me that he'd see me tonight and then hung up the phone. Eventually, Minola said goodbye, followed by Tony and Luciana. Danny left next, leaving just me and Fallon to finish up before heading back to the villa to unwind. We slept for about eight hours and then got up to lie by the pool for a while.

We still had a few hours to kill before starting again, so Fallon suggested that we get some food inside us. Since I'd been out here, I'd seen many Spanish restaurants advertising the paella dishes. As I've said before, I'm not one for eating foreign dishes, especially fish—except for the obvious cod and chips. I like prawns as long as they're served up as scampi, but I do have a problem eating things that stare back at me, which is why I hadn't tried it before. But Fallon knew of a place that made the paella up for you with chicken and no prawns if that's what you wanted, so I agreed to try some.

We ordered the paella dishes with some drinks. It took about forty-five minutes to cook. When it finally arrived, it was served up in a couple of extremely hot black porcelain bowls, and I've got to say it was absolutely delicious!

I was glad to get a good hot meal inside me before that Saturday night shift began. I was regularly taking a small amount of cocaine now socially with the others, but on the Saturday night, because it was the last night in the working week, we usually went a little over the top, and as a result of this we tended not to eat to anything for a while.

We stayed in the restaurant a little longer before meeting up with the others and moving on to get the Stage Door ready. Just as we were about to open the doors, my mobile rang. It was Minola.

"Hello, Kurt. I'm going to be a little late tonight, as I'm with my friend at his sister's wedding reception."

"What do you mean by late?" I asked him.

"Probably about 3 a.m. Unless you want me to bring them all down to yours," he joked.

"Well, if it gets you here sooner, then, yeah, bring them down."

"But Kurt, I cannot let them pay at the door. It is family and friends, you see."

"Okay, I'll let them in free this time as long as you think I'll make enough money behind the bar tonight."

"Kurt, they have many relatives down from all over Spain with lots of cash in their pockets."

"Well, that's good enough for me then. How many of them should I expect?"

"Well, I think maybe 200 will come. Is that okay?"

"Sure, why not? I'll restrict the door to only sixty customers so that we can fit them all in."

"Okay, I see you soon," said Minola.

I hung up the phone and gave Peter a sign to put up on the gate to let the customers know about the restricted access. We opened at about 12.30 a.m., and the first twenty people trickled inside. Luciana jumped behind the bar with Fallon again, and it wasn't long before the wedding party arrived. I'd reserved the captain's table for the bride and groom, and once they were all inside, Fallon brought over a complimentary bottle of champagne for the newlyweds.

By now we were already turning people away at the door, so we decided the best thing we could do would be to close the gates. I gave Peter the keys so that he could let anyone out that wanted to leave and turned to go back inside, when a group of three lads approached the gates only to find them locked.

"Kurt, Kurt, you can let us in, yes?" one of them said to me in a Spanish accent. I turned around to see Socar the gypsy and a couple of his friends standing there.

"Well, actually we are over full already, mate, and if I let you in, then everyone else will want to come in, and I really don't have the room. Sorry."

"Please, Kurt I have to meet someone inside, and we have come a long way to get here. You would be doing me a big favour."

"Okay, I'll let you in this time, but you owe me one, all right?"

"*Gracias*, Kurt. I won't forget it."

I got Peter to open the gates for them amidst a bevy of dirty looks from the punters who were hanging around outside waiting for people to leave so that they too could gain entry.

There was a real friendly atmosphere in the bar tonight. I guess that had something to do with the majority of the customers being related as opposed to having lots of individuals in the bar. Minola seemed to know just about everyone in the bar, and after a couple of hours of mingling and playing on the decks, he joined the bride and groom for a drink at the captain's table.

"Kurt, Kurt! The bride and groom would like you to join them so that they can raise a toast to you to say thank you for this evening," said Minola.

I walked over to the table to accept the toast and raised a toast of my own to the newlyweds and wished them all the best for the future, which they seemed to appreciate. I then sat down between Minola and several women who were chatting away in Spanish and giggling amongst themselves.

"What are they saying?" I asked Minola.

"This is the bride's sister Adriana, and her two friends are called Isabel and Leticia. Isabel was telling her friends that she thinks you are very handsome."

"Tell her that I'm flattered and that I think that she is very beautiful."

Minola repeated what I'd said, which made Isabel blush, much to the amusement of her friends who were quick to tease her about it. Isabel was a very pretty girl with long dark hair and beautiful green eyes. She was in her twenties, and I'd estimate that she was about five foot five tall. She didn't speak a word of English, but with the use of Minola as the translator and Leticia who spoke a little English, I seemed to get on quite well with her.

While we were sitting there chatting, Adriana asked Minola if he could put on a CD that she'd brought along and supply Isabel with a mic so that she could sing along to it, which he happily agreed to. Minola told me that Isabel was a professional cabaret singer, so I was quite looking forward to seeing how good she really was.

Minola gave me the CD, which I passed to Danny to play, and I collected a microphone and passed it to Isabel who was now standing by the bar with Leticia. The song came on, and with the help of her friend she began to sing a beautiful Spanish ballad, and I've got to say she had a phenomenal voice! Obviously she sung the whole song in Spanish, and although I couldn't understand a word of the song, the emotion in her voice completely sold it to me. She finished off to the sound of rapturous applause from just about everybody in the bar.

While I was congratulating Isabel, Minola took the opportunity to say something to Leticia, and she immediately passed me the mic and asked me in broken English to sing for them.

"What did you say to her?" I asked Minola.

"I just told her that I'd heard you are also a good singer."

"Well, I've sung in a few bands, but . . ."

"No buts, Kurt. I have promised now. You will sing for us, yes?"

By now Isobel and Leticia had announced to everyone that I was going to sing, so I didn't seem to have much choice!

"Okay, if it keeps you all happy, then I'll sing," I said.

Before I'd met Nicola I used to sing in several bands, as well as taking part in the odd talent contest, and I also used to write or work with writers to produce my own tracks. As a result of this, I had several CDs of my own songs that I'd recorded in studios in England which were kept behind the DJ booth.

I asked Danny to put one of them on, and I sang along to a track called "Heartache", which ironically was about a failing relationship. That was something that I knew a lot about given my recent breakup with Nicola. It was a sort of light rock sound with a guitar and a saxophone backing track. It was quite an emotionally driven song, and it was also arguably the best track I'd ever done, so I knew that I'd perform it well, which I did, much to the delight of the crowd.

Isabel told Minola that she was very impressed and that she thought I should sing professionally. By the attention that she was now paying me, it was obvious that she was about to make a move on me, but before she could do so, Fallon stepped in.

"Wow, you were great babe. You should sing more often," she said, and she kissed me passionately on the lips. This definitely had the effect of backing Isabel off. It was probably done deliberately by Fallon as a way of marking her territory. I introduced Fallon to Isabel and Leticia, and we both joined the bride and groom at the captain's table to celebrate with them, leaving Kirby and Luciana behind the bar for the last couple of hours.

At the end of the evening I joined Peter on the door to thank everyone for coming as they left, and finally the taxis arrived for the newlyweds and the bride's close friends and family, and they left, thanking me as they went.

Isabel was last out of the door. I gave her a hug and a kiss on the cheek and then bid her goodbye. I guess you could say that that was the one that got away. Still, I can't really blame Fallon for doing what she did; after all, she was only protecting what she had. We had a short lock-in afterwards, during which time Minola told me that he had a proposition for me.

"So, Minola, tell me about this idea of yours."

Minola went on to tell me that the Spanish youths aged between twelve and sixteen had recently lost their youth centre in Fuengirola due to lack of funding and were looking for somewhere to go in the evenings. He suggested that we held a disco night for them on one of our closed nights to run from about 8 p.m. until midnight. We would only sell soft drinks, and we could charge them on the door. He also told me that he would take care of the advertising, and as we'd only need minimal staff to run it that way, it was reasonable to assume that there could be reasonable profits to be made from it.

"It sounds like a great idea, and I take it you'll be working the decks?"

"Well, actually I will help you with the door, and if you don't object, I would like Mellissa to play the music. It will be good practice for her," said Minola.

"Okay, that sounds great, and, no, I don't have any objection to Mellissa playing. When do you want to start?"

"We could start this Tuesday night if it is okay with you."

"That's a little short notice, but I'm sure we'll manage."

"Great! I will get right on it, and Mellissa will be very pleased."

"That's settled then. Can I get you one more whisky before I lock up?"

Minola was never one to turn down a free whisky, and he gratefully accepted my offer. Soon after that we called it a night and locked up the bar. I saw Minola into a cab and then drove back to the villa with Fallon and went inside.

"So what was that kiss in the bar for earlier?" I asked Fallon, knowing full well what it was about.

"That kiss, honey bunny, was to make sure you slept with me tonight and not her."

"I don't know what you mean," I said innocently.

"Don't tease me, Kurt. You know I'm talking about Isabel. She was practically undressing you with her eyes!"

"Fallon, you were jealous, weren't you?"

"No! Well, maybe, but you were flirting with her."

"Flirting is part of being a good host. It doesn't mean that I'm going to jump into bed with them."

"Okay, I'm sorry. I'm not usually like this. I guess I really like being with you. Is that so bad?"

"No, sweetheart, that's good, because I enjoy your company too. Why wouldn't I? You're a very beautiful girl, and you definitely know how to push my buttons," I said, hugging her.

"In that case you'd better come to bed with me, and I'll see if I can find some of those buttons of yours."

The two weekends had worked out really well for me. The Minola factor was turning out to be quite a successful venture, and what with this new idea of his for the youth night, things seemed to be on the way up. This was just as well, as the bank balance had been getting dangerously low of late.

Tuesday afternoon came around quickly, and true to his word, Minola rang me to let me know that he managed to set everything up for tonight. I'd already stocked up on all of the soft drinks, removed the spirits from the shelves, and prepared the rest of the club ready for the Spanish teenagers. Minola was due to arrive with Mellissa at about 7.30 p.m., and as we didn't have anything else to do till then, we decided to grab something to eat and relax before the mayhem began.

It was getting quite late by the time we left the restaurant, so we headed straight back to the Stage Door and went inside. By the time I'd switched everything on, Minola and Mellissa had arrived.

"Hey, Minola, it's nice to see you're early for once."

"Always the joker, Kurt. You know I have a very good feeling about tonight."

"Well, I hope you're right," I said, shaking his hand.

"*Hola*, Kurt. How are you?" said Mellissa in her best English.

"*Hola*, Mellissa. You look *muy bonita* tonight." That means "very beautiful".

"*Gracias*," replied Mellissa, blushing profusely

"So if you would like to show Mellissa to the DJ booth, then maybe I can have a whisky to start the night off," said Minola.

"Unfortunately, as you can see, we've already removed all the spirits from the bar."

"But, Kurt, I need to have a drink before we start. Please, Kurt."

"Relax, Minola. I'm only winding you up. I have put a bottle by especially for you."

"Oh, I see. This is your British humour, but it was not funny."

"Trust me, it was worth it to see the look on your face," I said, laughing.

We opened the door at 8 p.m., and slowly but surely the teenagers arrived. Over the course of the night we let in approximately 180 kids paying £3 each to get in the door, and we took over £300 pounds over the bar. So all in all it wasn't too bad a night. Mellissa did a great job on the decks, and apart from one small incident with a lad lighting up a joint at the back of the club, the night went without any problems.

I gave Minola and Mellissa £250 of the door money, and after we locked up, Fallon suggested that we all go for a drink to celebrate as it was still only 12.30 a.m. We approached the port area. Fallon nipped into Tramps bar to grab a couple of grams, and we then went onto Linekers. As we approached the bar, the first face that I recognized was Luciana, who welcomed us with open arms. Once we'd received our drinks, Luciana led us over towards a vacant table.

Although a lot of the English work force had returned home for the winter, there were still enough British residents remaining to fill the main English bars like the London Bar and, of course, Linekers. Unfortunately, they no longer enjoyed the income that they were used to in the peak season, which is why I'd turned towards the Spanish crowd.

"So how did it go tonight?" asked Luciana.

"Great! It wasn't quite a full house, but we weren't far off it, thanks to Minola."

"No! I cannot take all of the credit. Without you this would never have happened."

"Thanks, Minola, but seriously, I appreciate all the hard work you must have done to make tonight happen, and I'd also like to raise my glass to Fallon and Mellissa for making tonight a great success."

Fallon passed me one of the wraps of cocaine and then took Luciana and Mellissa off to the loos, closely followed by myself and Minola. When we returned, the girls were already back at the table knocking back their drinks.

"So I take it you three would like another drink then?"

"That's okay. You sit down. Me and Fallon will get them in," said Luciana.

"So where's your jealous boyfriend tonight then?" I asked Mellissa.

"I do not see him now," she replied.

"They had a big row yesterday and broke up," said Minola.

"Oh, I'm sorry to hear that."

"I am not sorry," said Mellissa sharply.

"Still, it could be a good thing for you," said Minola.

"Why's that?" I asked him.

"Because Mellissa really likes you."

"Minola!" exclaimed Mellissa, walking off towards the bar looking very embarrassed.

"I'm flattered, but doesn't she realize that I'm with Fallon?"

"This is Spain, Kurt. So many different people come and go. There is very little long-term loyalty in relationships out here."

"Well, I won't disagree that there are many temptations to be had out here."

"Yes, and Mellissa is one of them."

"And a very pretty one at that," I said.

Mellissa was a lot different in a social atmosphere than she was when she was up confidently working behind the decks. Up close and personal, she seemed very shy yet extremely alluring and compelling, even more so now that I knew she had a thing for me. While we waited for the girls to return, I found out from Minola that it was Mellissa's birthday next week, and he made me promise to get her something nice.

Eventually the girls returned with the drinks and several rounds of vodka shots. We stayed in there until closing time and then walked up to the taxi rank to see Minola and Mellissa off before jumping in a cab ourselves and heading off to Fallon's apartment in Los Boliches.

We spent the next couple of days just relaxing and recovering from the weekend's activities. Soon it was Thursday evening. I'd already decided that if tonight was as slow as last Thursday, then it would definitely be our last until the new season began. Peter had rung me earlier to ask me if he could have the evening off, as he'd been offered some well-paid door work in one of the top Marbella clubs, and as I didn't expect it to be too busy that night, I was happy to grant his request.

We opened the gates at 1.00 a.m. with just me on the door and Danny on the decks, leaving Fallon working behind the bar on her own. As predicted, we were extremely quiet, with only a handful of customers to cater for.

At about 3.30 a.m., a group of about six Scousers entered the bar. Among them were Barry, Wilf, Ian, and the young Scouse lad called Steve who had been involved in the argument with the Spanish guy last week.

They walked up to the bar together, and the oldest of them, a man I hadn't met before, ordered the drinks.

"So, where's Peter tonight?" asked Ian sharply.

"He's not working tonight, so if you want to see him, you'll have to come back over the weekend sometime."

"Well, maybe we should take it out on you then, seeing as you're his employer" said Ian. He sounded threatening.

"Look, whatever your problems are with Peter, they are nothing to do with me, so why don't you calm down and let me get you all a drink. I'm not looking for any trouble here, lads, okay?"

"Is that right?" snapped Ian.

The young Scouser called Steve stepped forward. "Hey! Leave it out, Ian. They're all right in here."

"And what would you know?" asked one of the older Scousers.

"Kurt stood by me last week when I was needed his help. He's a good bloke. He doesn't deserve this, Francis. This isn't right," said Steve to the older man, who I now knew was called Francis.

"Okay, that's enough! We'll take that drink, thanks, and I'm sorry to have troubled you," said Francis.

Ian backed down immediately, and after Fallon had served them their drinks, Francis led them to a table at the back of the club. It was pretty clear to me that I'd had a narrow escape, as this Francis guy was obviously high up the pecking order of command.

Twenty minutes later Francis approached me again. This time he explained that Ian had seen Simon my ex DJ during the week, and he had told him that Peter had a vendetta against him and was going to cut him like he'd cut Simon for what happened in the bar the other week. He also told Ian that if any other Scousers got in his way, he'd cut them too. Naturally, they hadn't taken too kindly to this statement. I assured Francis that Simon was lying, probably to get him to do his dirty work for him. I also explained what Simon had done to deserve the attack from Peter in the first place. Once he was aware of these facts, he seemed to ease off a bit. Shortly afterwards he left, taking the lads with him, and as there were only a couple of customers left in the bar now, we decided to close early.

To be perfectly honest with you, it was quite a relief to get them out of the bar. If it had erupted in violence, I would have had a go at them, but obviously I was outnumbered. I would have lost and no doubt been seriously injured, not to mention the fact that Fallon and Danny would have also been drawn into it, and I really didn't want that to happen.

One thing was for sure. It would definitely be the last Thursday night I'd do for some time.

We slept through most of Friday, not waking until after 6 p.m. By the time we reached the London Bar, it was fast approaching 8.30 p.m. We hadn't eaten anything all day, so after a quick drink we left the bar to find somewhere to eat. As we walked out of the London Bar we ran straight into Geordie Andy, who was walking by with Kirby of all people.

"Hey, Kirby, long time, no see," I said.

"Hiya, Kurt. It's good to see you again," she said, greeting me with a hug.

"So where are you two off to then?" I asked Andy.

"Oh, my uncle's in town, and we're just on our way to meet him and some of his friends for a meal in town. What about you two?"

"Funnily enough, we were just on our way out to eat as well."

"Well, why don't you join us then? I'm sure my uncle won't mind."

"Sure, why not? Sounds like a great idea. So where's Nicola tonight then?"

"Oh, she's spending a week in England to attend a family wedding, and I was at a loose end, so Andy offered to take me out."

"So what's happening to the hairdresser's that you were going to open?"

"Actually, Rosa is finalizing the details now on a shop in Los Boliches. I'm sorry I haven't been down to the Stage Door to see you, but it's what Nicola wanted. I hope you understand."

I wished Kirby all the best, and we then followed Andy up to the high street and then down to a restaurant called London Town. It was situated close to the shop where I was ripped off for my noise limiter.

The restaurant had only recently been opened up by an ex-London chef and his wife. It wasn't a huge place, but it was very classy inside. Fortunately, they weren't too busy, so there wasn't any problem in adding us to the tables set aside for them. Andy introduced us to his uncle and friends, who all had strong London accents. This surprised me, as I half-expected them all to be from Newcastle.

They were quite a friendly bunch, and we spent the next couple of hours listening to Andy's uncle reminiscing over days gone by. Geordie told us that his uncle was a very close friend of the notorious "Jack the

Hat", who, I believe, was the guy that one of the infamous Kray twins shot dead. We were obviously sitting in influential company, to say the least!

Geordie's uncle told me that Andy was an amateur boxing champion and had been tipped to go all the way professionally. Unfortunately, he'd got involved in the social drug scene, which eventually destroyed a promising career, and he was still carrying the baggage of that around with him today. This explained many things about him.

Time was getting on now, so after inviting everyone down to the Stage Door later, I thanked everyone for letting us join then for the meal and then left. On the way back up to the Stage Door, I phoned Peter to tell him to round up the staff and meet us down there.

I'd arranged to open up at midnight, so we quickly set to the task of turning on the lights and music and getting the bar ready. We opened up dead on time and let in the first few customers.

Minola turned up an hour later with the beautiful Mellissa, followed by a steady flow of Spanish customers. Geordie's group arrived at about 2.30, and by this time we were in full swing. I walked them up to the bar and shouted over to Fallon to get a round of drinks in.

"Fallon! Fallon! Can we get a round of drinks over here, please, sweetheart?"

"I'm really sorry, babe, but as you can see we're rushed off our feet here. I'm afraid you're going to have to wait. Sorry."

I was going to argue with her, but I could see how busy she was, so I jumped behind the bar and personally served them myself. I decided to stay behind the bar for the next half hour or so to help the girls out just until it calmed down a bit. Just as I was about to return to the other side of the bar, an argument broke out between a young couple in front of me, and in the process several drinks got knocked over before Peter could get there to calm them down. The couple spent the next few minutes apologizing to me, and as there hadn't really been any harm done apart from soaking me and a teddy bear that Fallon liked to keep behind the bar, I decided to let them off with just a warning.

I mopped up the spilt drink from the bar and threw Fallon's lager-soaked teddy in the bin, and after changing my shirt, I went outside to get some fresh air. It wasn't long before I was joined by Mellissa, who had just been relieved from the decks by Minola.

"What happened to you? You are all wet," asked Mellissa.

"Oh, it's nothing. Some idiot knocked a drink over me. So are you enjoying yourself tonight?"

"Yes, very much, *gracias*."

"Minola told me that it was your birthday today. Is that true?"

"Yes, it is true. I am eighteen today."

"Congratulations, and happy birthday from me! Oh, and I've got you a little something," I said, passing her a wrap of coke.

"*Gracias*, Kurt, you shouldn't have," she said, giving me a hug.

"Well, I wasn't sure what to get you, so I hope it's okay. I'm not too good at choosing presents."

"There is one other thing that you could give me."

"Is there? And what would that be?"

"I would very much like to kiss you. Would that be okay?"

"Mellissa! You surprise me. And I thought you were the shy one."

"I cannot help myself. It's the gypsy blood in me. It makes me very passionate."

"Hmm, now you're turning me on."

"Then stop talking and kiss me."

Well who am I to argue with a passionate gypsy girl on her birthday? I embraced Mellissa and gently kissed her soft plump lips twice before giving her a long passionate kiss. It was a very erotic moment that seemed to last forever and most definitely left me full of desire for Mellissa.

"Hmm, you are a very sexy man, Kurt. I like to come home with you tonight."

"Mellissa, you are a very beautiful girl, but as much as I desire you, I don't want to do anything to upset Fallon."

"I say nothing to her."

"I would love to, Mellissa, but I can't at the moment, I have too much at stake right now."

"That's a shame, but if you change your mind, call me," she said, passing me a scrap of paper with her mobile number on.

"Thanks, I might just do that."

Mellissa kissed me once more and then made her way back inside, shortly followed by myself. As I re-entered the main bar area, I was collared by Fallon, who asked to speak to me urgently. She led me into the office and closed the door behind her.

"What's up, Fallon?"

She just looked at me and suddenly burst into tears.

"What's wrong, sweetheart? Has somebody upset you? Tell me!"

"I've fucked up. I'm in trouble," she kept saying.

"Fallon, calm down and tell me what's wrong. I'm sure we can sort it out."

After a few minutes and a lot of reassurance, I managed to calm her down. Once she'd regained some of her composure, she confessed to me that she'd owed £500 to a dealer and as a way of paying off the debt, he'd persuaded her to sell some cocaine for him. The problem was that the coke had gone missing from behind the bar, which put her in deep shit.

"What are you saying, Fallon? You mean to tell me you've been selling drugs from behind the bar without my knowledge? You stupid bitch! If you'd been caught, I'd have lost everything! I don't fucking believe this. And how the fuck did you manage to lose an ounce of fucking coke?"

"I'm sorry, I'm so sorry. I didn't know what else to do," she said, sobbing her heart out.

"Where did you see it last" I demanded to know.

"It was hidden in a teddy bear that I kept behind the bar, but it's not there anymore," she said through her tears.

"Well, it seems you're in luck. Someone spilt a drink over it earlier, so I threw it in the bin. Stay here and I'll go and get it."

I left the office and walked behind the bar and scoured through the rubbish bag that I'd thrown the bear into earlier. When I found it, I returned to the office and passed it to Fallon. She unzipped the back of the teddy bear only to find that unfortunately the powder was ruined.

"Shit! What am I going to do?" sobbed Fallon.

"Look, how much of it did you manage to sell?"

"I don't know, probably half of it."

"And how much have you got to pay him for it?"

"A thousand pounds! What am I going to do?" she said, sobbing uncontrollably.

"I can't believe how stupid you are. Look, you've sold half of it, right? So that makes you about £500 down. With the money you already owed him, that means that another grand will pay him off, right?"

"Yes, but I don't have the money."

"No, but I do, and I'll pay it for you because I wouldn't want to see you get hurt."

"Thank you, Kurt. Thank you."

"Look, you should know that I'm very disappointed in you, Fallon. I can't believe that you would risk my license just to pay off a debt. This has damaged my trust in you, Fallon. For now though you need to get back out there and finish the night off, and we'll deal with this after the weekend, okay?"

"Okay, I'm really sorry, and thank you," she said, kissing me on the cheek.

"Oh, and Fallon, no more dealing, all right?"

You know, life's a funny thing. One minute everything's going great, and then out of the blue life pops up and kicks you in the nuts just when you least expect it. Sorting out Fallon's misfortune was going to cost me money that I could ill afford to lose right now.

We finished off the last couple of hours and then after a short lock-in to celebrate Mellissa's birthday, we called it a night and headed back to the villa to get our heads down.

What Fallon had done had definitely put a strain on our relationship, but I couldn't hold it against her for long or it would most certainly have destroyed us, so I forgave her for her stupidity and made her promise never to do it again.

We slept for around five hours before getting up to head into Fuengirola to draw the money out of the bank for Fallon's dealer. Once we done that, we headed up to the Stage Door to clean up from last night and to restock the bar. This took us a few hours to complete, and afterwards we locked up and headed down to the local Burger King for something to eat. After that, Fallon rang her dealer and we met him in town and she squared him up. We then made our way down to Linekers, which is where we stayed with Luciana and Tony, slowly knocking back the drinks until it was time to open up once again.

I'd arranged to meet Peter and Danny at the club at around midnight. By the time we got there, they were already waiting outside with Minola and several other DJs. We all went inside, and after setting everything up, Minola introduced me to his fellow DJs.

"This is DJ Sanchez. He is very well known in the Spanish rave scene and had heard about the buzz being created from this new venue for the Spanish crowd, and he was wondering if it would be okay if he could play a set down here."

"It's good to meet you, and I'd be happy to let you play for us, although I can't really pay you anything for doing it."

"It's okay. I'm not looking to be paid. I just want to play, as do my friends, DJ Paul and Olli. They are down for the weekend from Madrid. They were playing at a rave with me last night."

"Pleased to meet you, lads. So are you two also going to play for us tonight?"

"Yes, we'd like that very much."

"And last but never least, the lovely Mellissa," said Minola.

"Hey, Mellissa, and how are you tonight?"

"*Muy bien, gracias,* Kurt" said Mellissa, giving me a hug.

Mellissa looked terrific tonight dressed in a lacy white blouse and a knee-high pleated skirt like the type that a gypsy girl might wear. She'd had her hair done to compliment her look.

"Wow, you look terrific tonight! Is there some special occasion that I should know about?"

"No, I just thought I'd show you what a real gypsy girl looked like so that you might see what you are missing."

"Well, you've certainly done that, but as I said yesterday I have too much to lose right now, more's the pity."

"Well, should you change your mind, then I am here for you," she said, kissing me on the cheek.

Mellissa's offer was very tempting, especially when she looked like that, but I had to concentrate on the night ahead if I was going to go anywhere near recuperating the £1,000 that I'd paid out to Fallon's dealer earlier. Minola took Mellissa and the other lads off the DJ booth, and at 12.30 a.m. we opened the doors.

We filled the club a lot quicker than usual that night, no doubt as a result of the extra DJs. In fact, I had to jump behind the bar to help Luciana and Kirby serve the customers for several hours. We started running out of bottled lager by 5 a.m., and by the end of the night we were also running short of whisky and vodka, but all in all it was probably the best night we'd had down here since turning over to the Spanish crowd. Once we'd locked the public out, the dozen or so of us that were left stayed behind for the ritual lock-in.

Once Fallon had served everyone who was left, she went off to the office with Luciana to have a line of coke, while most of the other guests who had stayed behind gathered around the captain's table to chat about the night's events, leaving Mellissa and Minola chatting to me at the bar. It had obviously been a very successful night, and I felt it only fair to reward

Minola accordingly, so I handed him £400 in cash. Minola insisted that he give something to the other DJs as a way of thanking them, so after giving Mellissa her cut, he made his way over to them, leaving me on my own with Mellissa.

"I think you are very handsome tonight, Kurt," said Mellissa, stroking my face with the back of her hand.

"Thanks, Mellissa, but I think you may have had a little too much to drink. Maybe you should have a line of this to help you sober up a little," I said, passing her a wrap of coke.

Mellissa took the coke from my hand and then embraced me and attempted to kiss me on the lips. As she did this, Fallon emerged from the office with the other girls.

"What's going on, Kurt?" she demanded to know.

"What do you mean? Nothing's going on!"

"Kurt, I'm not a fool, so please don't take me for one. Mellissa has been flirting with you all weekend, and now I find you kissing her in our bar! Are you seeing her behind my back?"

"First, this not our bar. It's my bar, and I don't appreciate being accused of things by you in front of everyone. Mellissa was feeling a little drunk, so I offered her some gear to try and sober her up. She was only thanking me for that."

"Yeah, so mind your own business, Fallon. Kurt does not belong to you," said Mellissa.

Well, you can imagine what happened next. All hell broke loose. Both girls grabbed hold of each other by the hair and started cussing and fighting each other. This was my fault for encouraging Mellissa. I should have seen it coming, but as usual I'd allowed my sexual desires to blind me from seeing the obvious.

It took several minutes to pull them both apart, and once we'd achieved it, Minola suggested that it would probably be best if he left and took Mellissa with him. Luciana comforted Fallon inside the bar, while I saw Minola's group out to the gates. It was pouring with rain outside, so he didn't want to hang around too long. I bid him goodnight and thanked him for intervening in the cat fight between the girls. I then said goodbye to Mellissa in the usual manor, and after a few protests, she left with Minola and his friends and headed for the taxi rank in the rain.

I locked the gates and went back inside to see if I could smooth over the ground with Fallon. Luciana left soon after I came back, leaving me and Fallon to sort out our differences. Fallon grabbed hold of me, spouting several obscenities at me.

"How could you do this to me? How could you cheat on me?" she demanded.

"Well, that's a bit hypocritical coming from you, don't you think?"

"And what's that supposed to mean?"

"Well, as I recall, you were the one who took advantage of me while I was seeing Nicola, without any concern for the consequences."

"Yes, but that was different"

"Why? Because the shoe is on the other foot now? Look, Fallon, it's true that she was flirting with me, and if I'm being honest with you, I enjoyed it. But I promise you that up to now I haven't had sex with her."

"Well, I'm still not happy with you."

"You know, you're very sexy when you're angry," I said, kissing her on the forehead.

"Then kiss me again and I'll show you how sexy I can really be," she said, smiling once again.

Fallon took my hand and led me over towards the captain's table. We proceeded to undress each other before passionately making love to one another on top of it. We were surrounded by mirrors that adorned the walls of the bar, and I couldn't help noticing our reflections in them, which made this sexual experience all the more erotic for me as well as for Fallon.

Once we'd regained our composure, we called it a night, locked up the bar, and headed back to the villa in the rain to carry on where we'd left off. Fallon seemed a lot happier now, and to be honest with you, so did I.

Chapter Ten

Winter Setbacks

We woke up at about 6 p.m. on Sunday evening. It was still raining quite hard, which was unusual in Spain, but I suppose we probably needed it, as it hardly ever rained out here anyway.

Once we'd got ourselves together, we left the villa and headed into Fuengirola. It had been quite a busy shift last night, and we'd no doubt have a lot of cleaning up to do. I parked up the jeep by the port and we made the short walk up to the Stage Door.

When we reached the gates, we were greeted by a heart-wrenching sight. It had been raining hard for over twelve hours, and as a result the walkway outside the Stage Door was several inches deep in rain water. And worst of all, the steps leading down towards the entrance doors were completely under water.

"Oh my god!" cried Fallon out loud.

"Noooo! I don't fucking believe this."

"What are we going to do?" asked Fallon.

"What can we do? We're fucked . . . completely fucked!"

Fallon did her best to console me, but I'd put everything I had into this venture, and I'm not just talking about money. Seeing my bar under water like that was soul-destroying, and the worse thing was that there was absolutely nothing that I could do about it. I was helpless, and I wasn't the only one.

Almost every underground shop and bar on the walkway was also under water, including the car park for the apartments above and the local supermarket. Not that that was any consolation.

While we were standing there talking to some of the other owners, the emergency services arrived, and shortly after that we were all advised to vacate the area while they attempted to pump the rain water out of the affected businesses. I unlocked the gates and gave the firemen a spare set of keys to the entrance of the bar. They assured me that once they'd pumped out the water, they would lock up behind them.

There was nothing else to do now but to drown our sorrows, so we headed into town. After making a late phone call to Rosa, my solicitor, to get her to contact my insurance company, we entered the London Bar. That is where we stayed until about 10 p.m., when Tony and Luciana turned up.

"Hey, Kurt, Fallon. What's up with you two? You look right down in the dumps."

"I take it you haven't heard yet then?"

"Heard what? What's happened?"

"The Stage Door's been flooded. We're fucked!"

"Don't say that, Kurt!" sobbed Fallon.

"What do you mean flooded? How?" asked Tony.

"The fucking rain! It's flooded every business in the walkway."

How much damage has it done?"

"Well, unless you've got a wetsuit and some breathing apparatus, then I can't tell you that right now."

"Oh my god, that's terrible!" said Luciana.

"So what are you going to do about it?" asked Tony.

"The emergency services are trying to pump the water out now, but to be honest with you, we're not going to be able to access the damage until the morning."

"We're really sorry to hear that, Kurt."

"Yeah, me too! Look, I think we're going to call it a night. I'm sorry, but I'm really not good company right now"

"Sure, no problem. That's understandable. We'll look in on you in the morning if that's okay with you," said Tony.

"Sure! Thanks, guys. We'll see you tomorrow then."

Fallon and I said goodnight and jumped in a cab and headed back to her apartment in Los Boliches to get our heads down for the night.

Up to now I'd suffered a few setbacks financially, and of course I'd lost Nicola through my own failings, but the one thing that always drove me on was the belief that I could get over just about anything. I'm a very positive guy as a rule, but this—how do I get over this?

Life's so unfair sometimes. Disaster always seems to hit those that don't deserve it. Why is that?

Monday morning arrived, and the rain that had fallen so hard was now replaced by glorious sunshine. We didn't waste any time getting ready, as we were eager to see what, if anything, was left of the Stage Door.

Once the taxi arrived, we drove down to Fuengirola, arriving outside the gates at about 10.30 a.m. The first thing we noticed was the crowd of people milling around the walkway and carrying what was left of their property out of the damaged businesses. The water that had engulfed the steps last night was now gone, so we walked down them towards the entrance of the bar.

My heart was racing as I unlocked the previously submerged entrance doors. I half-expected the water to flood out, but to my surprise, the only obvious sign that there'd been a flood was the wet carpet under foot.

"I'll turn the power on," said Fallon, reaching into the electric cupboard in the entrance hall.

"No! Don't touch anything. You might get a shock," I screamed at Fallon.

Fallon jumped back in fright at me shouting at her.

"Hey, it's okay, baby. I didn't mean to shout at you. I was just scared that you might hurt yourself. Leave it to me and I'll sort it out, okay?" I said, cuddling her.

I grabbed a beer crate from the cupboard and placed it on the floor outside the electric cupboard and told Fallon to wait outside. I then took a broom handle from the cupboard, stepped up onto the crate, and banged up the power switch on the fuse box. Several of the trip switches on the meter went bang and then flicked themselves back to the off position. Fortunately though, the light circuit wasn't one of them, and the bar immediately lit up.

I stepped off the crate and walked into the main bar, where the extent of the damage became apparent. The good news was that the water level had stopped about a foot short of the bar. I could tell this because it had left a dirty line along the strips of mirror that covered the bar front. The seating, lower walls, and floors were covered in a black sludge, and several manhole covers were missing from the floor, which was littered with unopened drinks bottles that had obviously floated around the bar.

The fridges behind the bar had also been destroyed, but my speakers and disco lights that were hanging from the ceiling and the TVs were fine. The only saving grace was that the steel doors had kept the water level down, and after closer inspection, I found that most of the electrical equipment had survived, so there was still a chance that I could salvage something from all this mess. The problem was that my finances were extremely low now.

"Well, I guess we'd better start cleaning up then," I said.

"We're never going to get this clean," sobbed Fallon.

"Sure we will, pumpkin. You know what they say. Never give up. Never surrender," I said, giving her a hug.

"Need any help," came a voice from behind us.

I turned around to find Tony, Luciana, Danny, and Peter standing in the doorway with several of the staff from Linekers.

"I thought you might need some extra help," said Tony.

"Thanks, guys. I really appreciate this."

"Right, we'd better get started then," said Luciana.

Whilst we drew up a plan of action, Tony and Danny went off to the hardware store with Fallon to pick up some mops, brooms, buckets, and various other cleaning products. We started by removing all of the cushions and throwing them outside, leaving the concrete seating and framework exposed. We then began collecting up all the bottles and other items that were scattered around the club, and while we were in the process of this, we discovered the missing manhole covers and put them back in their rightful places.

Tony, Fallon and Danny returned shortly afterwards with the cleaning products and a long hose pipe.

"What are you going to do with that? Don't you think we've had enough water in here already?" I said.

"Look, all this dirt and sludge came up from the various drains in the floor."

"Yeah, so tell me something I don't know."

"Well, I think the quickest way to clean this place is to hose it down, scrubbing it with the brooms as we go. We could flush away the excess water back down the storm drains and out of the doors," suggested Tony.

"You know, that's not a bad idea. But we'll have to be careful of the electrical equipment."

We started at the back of the club and slowly worked our way forward. While we were doing this, Fallon and a few of the others helped Danny take the equipment outside and load it into a van that Tony had borrowed from one of his mates.

By the end of the day we'd managed to hose down the whole bar, and although it was soaking wet, it was now starting to resemble the bar that it once was. There wasn't much else we could do today after hosing down the bar, so we left the front and back doors open to help dry the place out, locked up the gates, and headed back to Fallon's to drop off the equipment. Then we went on to Linekers to buy everyone a drink for helping us out.

"Well, I've got to say I didn't expect that! My faith in humanity has been restored once more, so without any more chat, I'd just like to raise my glass to say thanks to everybody that helped out. Thank you!"

We stayed in Linekers for a couple of hours before calling it a night and heading back to Fallon's for a well-earned rest.

When Tuesday morning came around, we once again made our way down to the Stage Door. The first thing I did was to ring the electrician, who promised me that he'd get to me as soon as he could. After that I called Pablo, my drinks supplier, to get him to chase up his friend to see if he had any more of those second-hand drinks fridges, and I also gave him an order for more stock.

It wasn't long before Tony and the others arrived, and we began the process of polishing the mirrors, tables, and bar area. While we were down there, Tony rang the local hire company and got them to deliver three large tubular hot air blowers that worked off of gas bottles. We positioned these around the main floor.

The electrician turned up at about midday and spent the next couple of hours attempting to dry out and test the system. Once he'd finished, he informed me that most of the sockets would have to be replaced and that we'd also blown out several of the main breakers in the fuse box. He told me that he would have to order the parts, as they didn't keep them in stock. They would take at least a few days to arrive, and he made arrangements to come back down on Friday to fit them.

Pablo arrived in the afternoon, and with the help of his friend he brought in the stock and a couple of replacement fridges. He also took the damaged fridges away for me. By 7 p.m. we'd managed to restock and clean the bar throughout. The girls had also removed all the cushion covers and bagged them up ready to go down to the launderette tomorrow. Finally, we began loading the foam cushions into the van that Tony had borrowed so that we could lay them out in the sun to dry in the garden of my villa over the next couple of days.

At 7.30 p.m. a familiar face came around the corner. It was Minola and a few of his little helpers carrying his record boxes. It dawned on me at that moment that I'd been so busy with what had happened that it had completely slipped my mind about the youth night tonight.

"Kurt, what has happened?" enquired Minola.

"Look, I'm really sorry. I should have rung you. The club's been flooded, and we've spent the last couple of days trying to clean up the mess."

"Kurt, this is terrible news. How bad is the damage?"

"Well, it's not good, but I think we will be open again soon."

"Is there anything I can do to help?"

"Well, to be honest, we've done just about all that we can do for now inside the bar, but I suppose we'd better put a sign up to say that tonight's event is cancelled, so if you could write one out for me in Spanish, that would help."

We finished loading the cushions into the van by 8 p.m. and then locked up the gates. By this time the Spanish teenagers had started to arrive, and they were quite disappointed to find out that the night had been cancelled. Once again I apologized to Minola for not calling him and told him that I'd be in touch about the weekend, as I wasn't really sure if it would be going ahead or not yet. After that we said our goodbyes and headed up to my villa in Mijas.

There wasn't anything else that we could do apart from running the gas heaters to dry out the club and, of course, washing all the seating covers.

By the time Friday came around the cushions were fully dried out, and we fitted them back into place. Everything inside the bar appeared to be dry now, so with Danny's assistance I refitted all the electrical equipment, and at midday the electrician turned up to fit all of the new sockets.

Disappointingly though, he still hadn't been able to acquire the replacement trip switches for the fuse box, which meant that we would not be able to open up that night. On the bright side of things, the bar was looking great again except for the strong smell of damp that was no doubt coming from the plaster on the walls. To get over that, we'd just have to run the air conditioning a little more often while we were open. It would probably be expensive, but at least we'd be open.

I rang Minola to give him the bad news and then put another cancellation notice up on the gate outside to explain our closure. This was an action that I was to repeat on the Saturday and following Tuesday night, as the trip switches didn't arrive until the Wednesday morning. This meant that I'd lost the whole weekend and two youth nights in a row. On top of that, the rent was due and it had cost me £3,000 in stock and repairs costs. This left me dangerously short of cash in the bank. This had been quite a damaging time for me mentally and financially, and to be quite honest with you, I'd be glad when we were open again.

I spent Thursday afternoon down at the Stage Door with the electrician as he fitted the new trip switches, and after a few other teething problems, I was fully operational again apart from the awful smell that the damp plaster was giving off. After the electrician had gone, I rang Rosa to find out what was happening with the insurance company. She told me that there was a problem with the policy and that they were refusing to pay anything out, as they considered the damage was caused by an act of god, which I wasn't covered for. She said she would fight their decision, but at the moment there was little that she could do to help me.

Although we'd temporarily managed to get the bar looking acceptable, it had cost me a considerable amount to achieve it, and on top of that, the strong smell of damp was a sure sign that the brickwork behind the plaster was saturated and would obviously have to be sorted out as soon as possible if I was to stop it getting any worse.

Unfortunately though, without the insurance company's help this was going to be difficult to achieve! At the moment the main thing was to try and survive and hopefully recuperate some of the money that I'd shelled out trying to keep this boat afloat, so to speak.

On the bright side of things, the bar was fully restocked and ready to open up once more, so I wasted no time in phoning Minola and the rest of the staff to let them know that we were back in business. Minola was pleased to hear the news, but he told me that there was a large organized rave taking place over the weekend in Malaga, which meant that we'd probably be a little quieter than usual. He also told me that he and Mellissa were scheduled to play tonight at the event, but that he would get down to me by 2 a.m. This was something that I really didn't want to hear right now, but the fact was that I had no choice but to open. I needed the money.

On Friday evening, after running the air-conditioner for some time, I opened up the doors once more, but by the time Minola got there at about 2.30 a.m., we'd only managed to attract about forty people into the bar.

"Hey Minola, am I glad to see you!"

"It's good to see you too, Kurt. I am sorry, but with this rave going on, I don't think we will be so busy tonight."

"Well, we can only do our best. Can I get you a drink?"

"I thought you'd never ask," said Minola, laughing.

"So where's the fiery Mellissa tonight then?"

"She's still working at the rave."

I got Minola a drink and he went up to join Danny on the decks.

Unfortunately, it didn't get much busier. In fact apart, from a handful of Brits arriving late on, we ended up with only about seventy people in the bar at the close of play. I could only hope that tomorrow would turn out a little better. We stayed behind for a short lock-in before closing up and heading for home.

Saturday evening started out the same way. The only difference was that I'd given Luciana the night off in expectation of a small crowd. Danny started the night off and was in full swing, when suddenly there was a flash of light in the DJ booth and the power to the club went off, plunging everyone into complete darkness aside from the emergency lighting. I immediately asked everyone to stay calm and tried to switch the power back on without success. The trip switches wouldn't stay on.

"Danny, unplug the equipment!" I shouted out to him.

Once he'd done that, I tried again and to my relief it came back on. The club lit up once more to the cheers of the thirty or so people inside.

"Okay, now start plugging in the equipment one piece at a time, please, Danny."

Danny proceeded to do this. Everything lit up until he tried to plug in the amplifier. As soon as he did this, the power tripped again. Danny pulled out the plug again, and I reinstated the electricity once more. It was pretty obvious to me now that the amplifier had blown. Next I had Danny turn the TVs on to the music channel and then turn up their internal speakers so that we had some background noise. The TV speakers weren't as loud as my amplifier, but it was better than nothing. I spent the next half hour ringing around trying to borrow a spare amp, but to no avail.

At 2 a.m. Minola arrived, followed by a large group of people who had followed him back from the rave. Suffice to say, they weren't too impressed at what they found.

"What has happened?" asked Minola.

"You're not going to believe this, but the amplifier has blown and I can't replace it until tomorrow."

"You are not having too much luck, Kurt."

"You can say that again! Someone up there really doesn't like me."

"I am sorry for you, but these people won't stay without the music."

Minola explained the problem to the customers, and as predicted, most of them left. A handful of his friends stayed behind for a drink before leaving to catch up with the others. It didn't take long before we were practically empty, and I didn't see any reason to carry on, so I paid Danny and Peter for half a shift and closed up early.

Minola was right. The last few weeks had been terrible, and I still wasn't out of the woods yet. My bank balance was now pretty non-existent, and on top of everything else, the rent on the villa was due next week. I had to make a decision about whether to continue renting it or not. It seemed like everything was against me right now, and I wasn't sure if I could recover from it!

We spent the Sunday at the villa just relaxing. There was very little that I could do about the amplifier until the Monday, and even then to replace it would practically wipe me out of cash. I had to do something to resolve my situation and fast!

The way I saw it, I had only one option left open to me. I'd have to borrow some money. The problem I had was that I had already sold my house in England, and as far as the Stage Door was concerned, without at least a year's accounts on the business, it would have little or no collateral value.

The only other choice I had was to borrow some money from a friend. There were only a few people I knew who would be in a position to help me, and one of those was Nicola. She'd already told me that she'd put extra money by, and although it would be difficult to ask her, I had to hope that we still had enough friendship between us to allow her to consider helping me out.

As soon as we were up and had eaten breakfast on Monday morning, I rang Nicola's mobile, which was answered by Kirby.

"Hi, Nicola's not available right now. Can I take a message?"

"Hey, Kirby, it's Kurt. Can you get Nicola for me? It's important."

"Hi, Kurt. I'm sorry, but as I just said, she not here. She's staying in England until the end of the week."

"Great! It just keeps getting better and better."

"What do you mean by that?"

"Oh, nothing. Don't worry about it. Just tell her that I called when you hear from her, okay?"

"Sure, no worries. Bye then, Kurt."

"Yeah, bye, Kirby, and thanks anyway."

Well I guess I had to go to plan B. The next person on my list was my old friend Alan who had originally come out with us but had now returned to England to live with Peta. I managed to get through to Alan straight away, and he was quite pleased to hear my voice. He told me that he and Peta were doing quite well and had recently put a deposit down on a house and were waiting for the mortgage to complete.

I explained to Alan what had been happening out here and told him about the cash crisis that I had at the moment. The problem that he had was that he'd just used up most of his savings on the deposit and the costs of buying this new house. He told me that the best he could do for me would be a couple of grand, which would leave them short of cash, but he was happy to do that for me if I thought it would help.

I was extremely grateful for his offer, as it would definitely get me out of the shit in the short term, but it wasn't going to be enough to get me through to the summer season when all the tourist trade would return. Alan promised to transfer the money into my bank that day and wished me luck. I thanked him for his help and hung up the phone.

By the afternoon the money was in my bank. I went out and bought a new amp straight away and then went back down to the Stage Door to install it.

I had two more phone calls that afternoon, one from Minola to tell me that the youth night wouldn't be happening as they'd found another venue to stage it in. He was very apologetic, but I'd missed two evenings already, and you can't expect people to wait around forever. I thanked him for his call and hung up feeling even more frustrated at my misfortune.

The second phone call came from the beautiful Keeley.

"Hi, Kurt, guess who it is."

"Hiya, Keeley. It's great to hear your voice. How are you?"

"Terrific, thanks, and I've got some great news. I'll be flying in to Spain tomorrow for that photo shoot that I told you about."

"I didn't think that was happening until next week."

"It wasn't, but they brought it forward as a few other things have come up now. I'll be arriving at Malaga airport at 10 a.m., and I'd like you to meet me. I can't wait to see you. I've got so much to tell you."

"Well, it's rather short notice, but sure, of course I'll meet you."

Keeley went on to tell me the flight number amongst other things and then blew me a kiss and hung up.

Well that was all I needed! What with all the goings on over the last few weeks, I'd completely forgotten that Keeley was coming out here. Still, under the circumstances, maybe this distraction was something that I needed right now. It would probably do me a power of good to get away from all the stress that I was under right now. Besides, I had no more work until next Friday, and I'd already told Keeley that I'd be there for her.

I took Fallon out for a meal that evening and told her that I needed to fly back to England to see if I could borrow some money from my family. I told her that I'd leave first thing in the morning so as to get back in time for the weekend. Fallon didn't question my decision to fly back, as she knew the financial situation that I was in. I didn't like deceiving her, but this was something that I needed to do.

In the morning I packed a bag, kissed Fallon goodbye, and then left for the airport. I timed it so that when I arrived, Keeley's plane would be just landing. At 10.30 a.m. she walked through the arrivals gate looking more stunning and vibrant than I'd ever seen her before. As soon as she spotted me, she ran over and flung her arms around my shoulder, planting kisses all over my face.

"I'm so pleased to see you," she said.

"Hey, gorgeous, I'm pleased to see you too. You look fantastic. This modelling stuff is definitely doing you good."

"And what of you? You look a little tired. I think maybe you've been working too hard."

"You know me, Keeley. I'm a workaholic, and . . . I've had a few hiccups recently."

"What you need is a little rest and relaxation, and I've got just the thing for you. The magazine that I'm working for has booked me into a top hotel for my stay here, so I'd like you to stay there with me while I'm out here."

"And how long are you going to be here for?"

"I fly back on Thursday, so let's not waste any more time talking. You can tell me all about these hiccups of yours on the way," she said, kissing me once more.

I took Keeley's hand, walked her to the jeep, and then followed her entourage's coach to the hotel in Malaga. Once Keeley had checked in, we were shown up to the suite that had been reserved for her. Internally it was like a penthouse, luxurious and spacious in its design. It even had its own hot tub. I could see we were going to have a lot of fun in here.

"Wow, look at this place! How much are these people paying you for this photo shoot?"

"Enough. I told you that I was doing well. These people, as you call them, represent a top magazine. Money is no object to them. I'm really enjoying my life right now, but there's still one thing missing for me, Kurt, and that's you."

"Keeley, we've been over this before."

"Look, why don't we talk about this later? I haven't seen you for so long, and I'm eager to make up for lost time," she said, unbuttoning my shirt.

It had been a long time since I'd tasted the fruit from her bountiful tree, and I intended to take my time enjoying every inch of her incredible body. We spent most of the afternoon fooling around, moving from the bedroom to the hot tub and back again. In those few hours I completely forgot about my troubles.

"Mmm, I've missed this so much," said Keeley, cuddling up to me in the king-size bed that they'd provided.

"Yeah, I must admit I haven't felt this relaxed for quite a while."

"So tell me about these hiccups of yours. I want to hear about everything that you've been up too."

I explained to her about the problems that I'd been having and told her that I was still seeing Fallon and that my association with Nicola was all but over. I also briefly told her about my financial trouble. I felt quite awkward mentioning it, as I didn't want it to seem that I was only seeing her for money.

"So how does Fallon feel about you being here with me then?"

"She doesn't know. She thinks I'm in England trying to raise some cash."

"Good! Then we shouldn't be disturbed over the next couple of days."

Keeley was feeling a little exhausted after the travelling and, of course, having her wicked way with me, and it wasn't long before she fell asleep in my arms. In the brief amount of time that I'd known Keeley, she'd become very special to me, and as I stroked her hair, I couldn't help wondering again whether or not I'd made the right choice in not going with her the last time she'd asked. I felt so relaxed and content lying here with the feel of Keeley's warm body pressed up against me. It made me think long and hard about the path that I'd taken.

Keeley eventually opened her eyes at about 8 p.m. that evening, and as soon as we were showered and dressed, we left the hotel and headed into town. Keeley's photo shoot wasn't due to start until the following afternoon, so tonight she was intent on partying. She'd come out here with an entourage of photographers, makeup artists, and several other fashion models, and she'd arranged to meet up with them at an exclusive club in town.

Once we got there, she introduced me to her friends and colleagues and then left me with them while she went off to speak to her employers. Over the next few hours I found myself involved in conversations with people that I had very little in common with. Don't get me wrong, they were very friendly towards me, but I never was one for flower talking, and although Keeley was flitting back and forth between me, her employers, and her mates, it did make me feel like a bit of a gooseberry. It was sort of like I didn't belong.

We called it a night and headed back to the hotel at about 1 a.m. as Keeley needed her beauty sleep if she was going to look her best for tomorrow.

"I'm really pleased you met my friends. They were all talking about you."

"Yeah, I'm sure. They were probably wondering what you were doing with a guy like me now that you're on your way up the ladder of success."

"No, don't say that. You're worth ten of them. I'd much rather be with you. In actual fact, they all really liked you."

"Is that right? Strange how you spent more time with everyone else than you did with me then, eh?"

"Kurt, it was a promotional party. I had to spend some time with them."

"I thought you wanted to spend some time with me. You're with these people 24/7."

"Please don't be like that, Kurt. Look, I've got a proposition for you that will fix all that."

"Oh, and what's that then?"

"Well, it will cost you to find out."

"Yeah? And what exactly did you have in mind?"

"Take me to bed and we'll discuss terms," she said in a very naughty voice.

Well, who was I to argue with a girl whose sole intention was to wear me out? I happily followed her into the bedroom for yet another round of sexual passion.

We were woken up about at about midday to the sound of the room's telephone ringing. It was Keeley's wake-up call. She was due on location at the beach in an hour's time. She spent the next twenty minutes rushing around getting ready before being picked up at the front of the hotel with the other girls. I didn't want to get in the way, so I'd persuaded her to go on her own and told her to ring me when she'd finished.

Once she'd left, I gave Fallon a ring to let her know that I was okay and that I'd be back tomorrow afternoon. She was very pleased to hear my voice and left me feeling quite guilty about lying to her, but I had to see this through if only to discover in myself whether I still wanted this life out here.

I spent the rest of the afternoon just walking around Malaga town sightseeing and mulling things over in my head.

At about 7 p.m. Keeley rang me to let me know that she'd finished work and asked me to meet her at a restaurant in town. By the time I got there, she had already sorted out a table.

"Hey, baby," she said, hugging me.

"So how did you get on?"

"Really good, thanks. It makes the work at lot easier when the sun's shining."

"So what's this proposition you were talking about last night then? We never did get around to talking about it."

"Well, there's something you should know first. I've been offered a run of work in America. The money would be really good, but I'd have to move out there permanently."

"Well, that's great. I'm pleased for you, but what's that got to do with me?" I asked her.

"The thing is, I want you to come with me."

"But . . ."

"Look, you said yourself that you're struggling out here, and I know you like being with me or you wouldn't have left Fallon to be here now, so why not leave with me? You could sell the bar and start again over there."

"You're absolutely right. I love being with you, and I am struggling at the moment, but it's the path I chose and I have to see it through. Besides, what would I do out there?"

"I'm sure a man with your drive and capabilities could make something of yourself wherever you go. Kurt, I want you to come with me. We could live off my money until you get on your feet."

"Or you could help me out now and I could visit you once you're settled in."

"That's not what I want, Kurt. If that happens, you'll still be here sharing your life with Fallon or whoever else comes along, and I'll end up doing the same. Don't you see? This is an opportunity for both of us to be happy. We could make a great life for ourselves in America—a fresh start, so to speak."

"Keeley, it's a big thing you're asking me to do. What if it doesn't work out between us? I'll be the one that stands to lose the most. I could end up with nothing."

"Kurt, I want you in my life on a full-time basis. I don't want to share you with anyone. I know it will work out between us. You just have to take a leap of faith."

"Don't take this the wrong way, Keeley. You're a very beautiful girl, and my feelings do run deep for you. I'd be a liar if I said I wasn't tempted by your offer, but I still don't know what to tell you. I need time to think about your proposal."

"Look, you know my feelings for you, so here's the choice. Leave all this crap behind you and start a new life with me, or stay and I'll be out of your life for good. It's your decision, but I'll need an answer by the morning so that I can book you a flight back with me."

"Keeley, don't be like that. You've got to let me make my own mind up without pressurizing me, okay?"

"Okay, I'll leave it in your hands for now, but I will need an answer soon."

We finished our meals and then after going back to the hotel to get changed, we went back out again, just the two of us this time. We spent the evening checking out the music bars in town and generally having a great time before returning to the hotel to crash for the night.

It was quite an offer that Keeley had made to me, and to be quite honest with you, I didn't expect her feelings for me would still be that strong. What was more surprising was the feelings that I felt for her. But to give up everything that I'd worked towards as soon as the going got tough and to uproot and move to the States and have to live off her money and probably in her shadow at least to start with . . . I wasn't not sure that I could do that.

I knew that with the way things were going out here it was possible that the Stage Door could go belly up at any time, but that's the challenge. Life would be pretty boring if everything was served up on a plate for you. And I was never one to walk away from a challenge.

To me, owning the Stage Door was like achieving a lifelong ambition, so giving it up didn't come easy for me. I knew it would upset Keeley if I turned her down, but I couldn't let that affect my decision.

Thursday morning came around, and after breakfast Keeley was quickly on my case for a decision.

"So what have you decided, Kurt? Please tell me that you're coming with me."

"Look, I've thought long and hard about your offer, and I'm probably about to make the biggest mistake of my life, but I can't walk away from what I've achieved out here. You're a great girl, one that any man would be proud to be with. I am very tempted by your offer, but I'm afraid that I've got to turn you down. I'm sorry, Keeley."

Keeley's heart sank when she heard my decision, and her eyes welled up with disappointment.

"Are you sure I can't convince you to change your mind?" she said with tears running down her face.

"Hey, princess, we can still talk on the phone and visit each other once things settle down. I'd only be in your way out there anyway."

"You wouldn't! I want you to be with me. Don't you understand that?"

"I'm sorry, sweetheart, really I am. The last thing I want is to see you unhappy. I have to do this for my own sanity. Please understand."

"Well, I'm sorry too, but if that's your choice, then I think you should go now."

"Keeley, don't be like that, please."

"Just get your things and go. The sooner you're out of my life the better!" she screamed at me.

"Fine! If that's what you want, then I'll go"

I grabbed my stuff and walked out of the door without saying goodbye. Whichever way I'd decided, I would have had a similar scene. Worst of all, because of the way this had ended, I couldn't ask her to lend me any money either. So I returned to Mijas empty-handed.

If the time I'd spent with Keeley had taught me anything, it had been to renew my determination to succeed with the Stage Door. It was just a shame that we'd finished the way we did. As I've said before, I had strong feelings for Keeley, and I very much hated seeing her hurt. It was the last thing that I wanted. I was pretty sure that Keeley was just speaking out of disappointment, but now was obviously not the time to reason with her.

I arrived back at the villa at around midday to find Fallon waiting for me, and although she was disappointed to hear that I hadn't managed to secure any funds, she was still very pleased to see me back home.

We weren't due to open up again until the next night, and as neither of us fancied sitting in, we decided that we'd go into town for a drink and to spend a little time together.

After getting changed, we jumped into the jeep and headed into Fuengirola. We spent the next few hours just walking up and down the high street, mostly just window shopping. I did splash out on a few tops for Fallon, which seemed to cheer her up.

It wasn't anywhere nearly as hot as it was in the summer, but the temperature was still up around the high sixties. All that walking around made us feel parched, so we popped into the London Bar for a drink to quench our thirst.

We hadn't been in the bar more than ten minutes before Tony and Luciana walked in with several other members of the Linekers staff.

"Hey, Tony, what are you lot up to then?"

"Hiya, Kurt, Fallon. We're all off down to the go-karting track. Scott arranged it for everyone a couple of weeks ago."

"Sounds like fun. How much does it cost?"

"Well, as I said, we didn't pay for it, but I think it's about £40 a head. Why? Do you fancy joining us?"

"Yeah, why not? What do you think, Fallon? Do you fancy going?"

"Are you kidding? I'd love to!"

"Well that settles it then. We're going karting."

After a couple of drinks in the bar, we all left and headed up to the track, which was situated just outside of town.

When we arrived we went inside, paid our money, and followed Tony and the others over to the pits to collect our go-carts. Before we were allowed to get in them, we had to go through a short induction on how it all worked and the basic ground rules. After that we got into the carts and began to race each other. It was the first time that I'd been carting, and I've got to say that it was quite exhilarating. Fallon really enjoyed herself too, and much to the surprise of everyone else including me, she managed to win two of the races that we were in. This made her very happy, and she wasn't about to let me forget it.

In the end I was glad we'd come. It had turned out to be a lot of fun. It was just what we needed to give us both a much-needed lift.

After we'd finished at the track we all went on to a restaurant for a meal and something to drink. Fallon spent most of the meal teasing me over her victories, which was fair enough, I suppose, as I'd have done the same to her. To the victor go the spoils, as they say.

"You seem to be in a very good mood tonight, Fallon."

"Well, I'm just pleased to have my honey bunny back again. I really missed you, and I've got something to ask you."

"Oh, and what's that then, princess?"

"Well, I know you're struggling with money right now, and the cost of the villa isn't helping. So why don't you give it up and move in with me? It's what I really want."

"I think that's a great idea, kitten, as long as you're sure that that's what you want."

"Are you kidding? I love you!" she said, hugging me as tightly as she could.

I didn't have to think for too long about Fallon's request, as it really was the obvious solution to my problems, besides which, I quite liked being with her too. Fallon jumped for joy at hearing my response and then threw her arms around me, repeatedly kissing me on the face.

"This calls for a celebration," said Fallon, looking very pleased with herself.

"Oh, and what did you have in mind?" I asked her.

"Mmm, I can think of lots of things that we can do when we get home, but for now I think we should party."

"I'll drink to that," I said, raising my glass.

All of the Linekers crew who weren't working that night were also up for a night out, so we left the restaurant, and after nipping home to get washed and changed, we went back out again and met up with the others at Linekers to start the night off. Then we moved on to the Underground, which is where we stayed dancing and drinking the night away and generally having a great time. At the end of the night we said our goodnights to the others and then jumped into a cab and headed back to Fallon's apartment for some fun and games before crashing out in each other's arms.

We both got up at about midday and spent the afternoon ferrying my stuff back and forward to Fallon's place, before handing back the keys for the villa to Rosa at about 8 p.m. Once we were finished, I rang Minola to remind him that we were opening tonight. After eating, we headed down to the Stage Door to finish off preparing everything for later.

As we entered the bar, the first thing that hit us was the strong smell of damp once again, so I immediately fired up the air conditioning and opened up the rear doors to let some fresh air in. Then I left Fallon preparing the bar area while I sorted out the equipment and music.

Minola had told me earlier that he'd done his best to put the word about that we were back in business, so hopefully we'd get a bigger crowd tonight. He'd also told me that Mellissa wanted to know if she could come back down again. Apparently, she'd promised to apologize to Fallon and to behave herself. Fallon wasn't too enthusiastic about this, but she recognized that Mellissa was extremely popular with the customers, so she reluctantly agreed as long as she didn't try to come on to me again.

Luciana, Danny, and Peter turned up together at about 11.30 p.m., and we opened the Stage Door at midnight. By about 1 a.m. we'd managed to attract over sixty customers, which was quite a promising start. Minola was due to arrive at any moment, so I joined Peter at the door and waited for him to arrive.

I didn't have to wait too long. He turned up fifteen minutes later, followed by Mellissa and a large group of people.

"Hey, Kurt, I've brought some friends with me," said Minola.

"Yes, so I see. Thanks. It's much appreciated. So how are you tonight?"

"I'm very good, thanks, and you? How are you tonight?"

"All the better for seeing you, Minola, and of course, let's not forget the beautiful Mellissa. How are you tonight? Promise me that you're going to behave yourself tonight, sweetheart."

"Don't worry. I behave tonight for you, Kurt."

"Thanks, I appreciate that," I said, giving her a hug.

I left Peter on the door to let in the customers and took Mellissa and Minola inside. Mellissa stayed true to her word and immediately went up to apologize to Fallon. After that everything seemed to go quite well, apart from the odd complaint about the smell. By 4 a.m. we must have had around 160 people in the bar, and they were still trickling in.

As I stood at the door talking to Peter, Minola came over to warn me that there were a couple of undercover policemen in the bar tonight. He quickly pointed them out to me. He'd already taken the liberty of warning all of his friends to be careful not to use any drugs while they were about. He also told me that you can always spot the Spanish undercover cops; more often than not they wore shiny black shoes and generally didn't quite fit in with the punters in the bar.

I must admit it was quite worrying having them in the bar, and I kept a close eye on them for the next hour until they left. Apart from that, the night couldn't have gone better. We'd generated quite a lot of cash and had a trouble-free night.

We closed up just before 6 a.m. as I didn't want to provoke any problems with the police, especially as they'd been milling around in here earlier. For the moment at least, it was better to be safe than sorry, especially as I was obviously on their radar right now.

We did have a short lock-in afterwards just for the staff and a few friends. Happily, the tension between Fallon and Mellissa seemed to have dissipated, and they were now actually sitting together laughing and chatting. We stayed for another hour or so before locking up and grabbing the customary breakfast at Jimmy's. Soon after this we said our goodbye's and headed for home to grab some much-needed sleep.

Chapter Eleven

The Final Days

I didn't open my eyes until late that afternoon. Fallon had left me a note to say she'd gone down the gym to attend one of her many classes.

Once showered and dressed, I left the apartment and headed down to the Stage Door to begin cleaning and restocking the bar. Fallon joined me about an hour later to help me finish up, and soon after that we headed into town to get something to eat.

"So how did your workout go in the end?"

"Great, thanks. It's just a shame that you couldn't join me."

"Yeah, sorry about that, darling, but I was obviously still hung over from last night."

"Yeah, I sympathize with you. I felt a little bit rough myself earlier."

"I noticed you were getting on a lot better with Mellissa last night."

"Well, she's quite a nice girl once you get to know her, but I still wouldn't trust either of you to be alone together," she said, smiling.

"That's rich! Judging by the way you two were getting on last night, I don't think I'd trust you two be alone together either," I said sarcastically.

"Oi, you cheeky bastard!" she said, punching me on the arm.

We stayed on in the restaurant for a while longer before heading up to the London Bar to meet up with the rest of the staff. As we entered the bar, I was surprised to find Nicola and Kirby sitting at the table with Danny, Peter, and Luciana.

"Hey, Nicola, Kirby! What brings you two down here then? Not that we're not pleased to see you, of course," I said, greeting them both.

"Well, two things really. First, we're out celebrating, as we've just got our opening license through, and second, Kirby told me that you'd phoned when I was in the UK, and I wondered what you wanted," said Nicola.

"Oh, it doesn't matter anymore, I was just trying to raise a little money, that's all."

"So is it okay if me and Kirby come down the Stage Door tonight then?"

"Girls, you should know that you're always be welcome to come down. In fact, I insist that you do so that I can buy you both a bottle of bubbly to celebrate your opening license."

"Yeah, and I'll second that," said Fallon, hugging them both.

"Well, we've still got a while to kill yet, so why don't I get the next round in?"

This brought cheers from everyone at the table, and we spent the next couple of hours just drinking and messing about until it was time to head up to the Stage Door to prepare it for the night ahead.

As I opened the door to the bar, the strong smell of damp hit me straight away, and I wasted no time in switching on the air conditioning to full power. It was probably going to cost me a fortune when the electric bill came in, but what choice did I have?

The strong smell that was in the air slowly cleared, and on the stroke of midnight we opened the doors once more. This would be our last working weekend before Christmas Eve, which fell on the Tuesday. The good thing about that was that we could be out celebrating it as opposed to working! We still hadn't decided what to do about New Year's Eve, but we'd no doubt discuss it once we'd got Christmas out of the way.

Minola and Mellissa arrived at around 1 a.m. After getting a drink, they took their rightful places behind the decks, and the bar slowly filled up with paying customers. I wasn't sure how busy we'd be tonight, what with Christmas fast approaching, but to my surprise we had a full house in no time. I had to run the air-conditioner on full for most of the night, as we were receiving quite a few complaints about the smell.

As I was standing at the entrance talking to Peter, Fallon beckoned me over to her. She was trying to serve a couple of Spanish guys who were standing there arguing with her at the bar.

"What's up, Fallon?"

"Can you speak to these two and find out what they want, please?"

I turned around to look at the two guys. They were dressed fairly casually, but there was something about them that just didn't sit right with me.

"So, how can I help you?" I asked them in broken Spanish.

"We would like some coke please. How much do you charge?"

It was obvious to me that these were undercover coppers and it wasn't the liquid coke that they were after!

"Sure, no problem. Fallon, can you pour these two gentlemen a glass of coke each, please?"

"No, you misunderstand. We want coke, the Columbian kind. How much is it?" they asked again.

"Hey, mate, we don't sell drugs in here. It's a bar. We sell alcohol."

"Sorry, but we were told we could get some in here."

"Well you can't! So I think it's time you both left"

I beckoned Peter over to escort them to the door, but as he put his hand on one of their shoulders, they both immediately produced their police badges. I didn't want any trouble from them, so I sent Peter back to the door in an attempt to take the sting out of the situation.

"Look, guys, I'm sorry about the misunderstanding, but you can't just come in here asking for drugs. This is something that we just don't accept in here."

"You are the owner, no?"

"Yes, I am."

"We have received several complaints about drug use in this bar. If we find this to be true, make no mistake. We will close you down!" he said in a very stern voice.

"I promise to keep my eyes open, but as I said, as far as I'm aware, there isn't a drug problem in here. You are of course welcome to stay as long as you like to monitor the activity in here."

"You should also know that we have had several complaints from concerned residents about the smell of damp in here, and we have decided to send a health inspector down to you on Monday morning to determine whether or not it is safe to open to the public."

"Okay, thanks for letting me know. Now, can I get you both a drink" I asked them with a false smile on my face.

They took their drinks and began to mingle with the crowd who were by now well aware of the fact that these two were police officers. This was the second weekend in a row that we'd had the filth in here, and I was beginning to wonder whether or not someone had it in for me. We were, after all, by far the busiest music bar in town right now, which was no doubt pissing the other club owners off.

One thing was for certain, though. I didn't need these Muppets milling around my bar every night! I thought it would be wise to let Minola know about the police presence, so I made my way over to him.

"It's okay, Kurt. I know they are here. Mellissa has already been around to inform everyone. They won't find or see anything. I make sure of that."

"Thanks, Minola, and thanks to you too, Mellissa. I really appreciate that," I said, giving her a hug.

"For you it's no trouble," she said, stealing a kiss from me.

"Hey, behave yourself. Fallon will kill me if she catches you doing that."

"I don't care. I would like you to spend the night making love to me," she said. She was looking extremely seductive. I paused for a moment, slightly taken aback by her directness.

"Jesus Christ! Don't get me wrong. I'd love to fuck you, Mellissa. I think you're very sexy, but if Fallon found out, it would cause me too many problems."

"Well, if you change your mind . . ." She pressed herself against me and kissed me once more.

"I think I better leave now while I still can," I said to Minola.

"Yes, I think if you stay here any longer, Mellissa will eat you up."

"Hmm, now there's a thought," I said, laughing.

I left the two of them to the music and made my way back over to Fallon, who was now talking to Peter at the bar.

"Hey, Fallon, what's up?" I asked, hoping that she hadn't spotted Mellissa's advances.

"You'll be glad to know our resident police officers have now left the building."

"Yes, I'm very pleased to hear that, poppet," I replied, relieved to know that she hadn't noticed Mellissa's antics.

"Oh, and they left this piece of paper for you to confirm that a health inspector is coming out at 11 a.m. on Monday morning."

"Yeah, they did mention that to me. I guess we'll just have to make sure this place is spotlessly clean for when they arrive."

The rest of the evening went off okay, although the police did keep up a strong presence outside the bar. We closed the gates just before 6 a.m. and soon followed the customers out of the doors. I'd decided against a lock-in, what with all the police activity we'd been getting and the blatant come-on that I was receiving from Mellissa that night.

Before Minola left, he invited us down to his for Christmas Eve. As we weren't intending to work again until after the Christmas break, we happily accepted his offer. It would make a change for someone to entertain us for once. The rest of my staff was also invited, including Nicola and Kirby.

Once we'd said goodbye to Minola and the flirtatious Mellissa, we headed down to Scottie's for breakfast, before taking the twenty-minute walk along the beach back to Fallon's apartment.

We only had one more weekend left this year and maybe New Year's Eve if we could arrange something in time. After that we'd be starting the build-up to the next summer's trade bonanza. It had been quite a struggle lately, but we'd survived against all the odds.

I must admit that when I first came out here with Nicola, I thought that things would be simple and everything would fall into place so easily. The truth is that I couldn't have been further from the truth. The pressures and temptations of living out here had definitely taken their toll on the path that I thought I was on. Running this bar had been extremely hard work with long hours and few financial rewards. I'd had to deal with many idiots and become an agony aunt to my staff, but even with these setbacks, I've got to say that the benefits of the lifestyle were worth every second of the time I'd spent out here.

The rest of the weekend passed by quickly. On Monday morning I met the health inspector as arranged and waited down the club as he performed his inspection. After he'd completed his tests, he told me that I would be informed of the results over the next week or so and that a decision about what action if any would be made at that time.

I spent the rest of the day traipsing around the shops with Fallon trying to find her a Christmas present and an outfit for the following night. Once we'd finished shopping, we headed for home and spent a peaceful night in together.

We didn't get up until early afternoon the next day, and we spent the rest of the day lazing around the communal pool until it was time to make a move. Minola's party wasn't due to start until 10 p.m., but we'd arranged to meet the others at Linekers bar at around 8.30 p.m. to give us time to drive up there. It was quite busy on the roads, and as a result, it took us just over an hour to get there.

We arrived at Minola's just before 10 p.m. and found him still in the process of setting everything up with the help of a few friends.

"Hey, Minola, Happy Christmas to you. You're running a little late, aren't you?"

"Yes, it's a big panic here, but no matter. Happy Christmas to you too," he said, giving us all a hug.

"Is there anything we can do to help you?"

"No, no, you just relax. We have it all under control. Tonight I entertain you for a change. You are my special guests, so please enjoy."

By 10.30 p.m. Minola had got his act together, and he opened the doors to let in the handful of customers who were waiting outside. It didn't take too long for his small bar to fill up. The girls wasted no time in heading for the dance floor, leaving Tony, Danny, and me chatting and drinking at the bar with Minola.

There seemed to be no shortage of DJs waiting to get on the decks, all of whom were happy to play for free, such was the friendship between them and Minola. Mellissa turned up at about midnight to play her set, and I welcomed her in the usual way. I tried not to be overly flirtatious with her, as I didn't want to encourage her advances. The last thing I needed tonight was another cat fight!

Minola refused to take any money from me for any of the drinks that I ordered for myself and Fallon, and of course the Charlie flowed freely all night. At about 5 a.m. Tony, Luciana, Danny, and Peter all decided to make a move. After saying their goodbyes, they jumped into a taxi and headed back to Fuengirola, leaving Nicola, Kirby, Fallon, and me to finish the night off at Minola's.

It had been a really busy night. What with all the alcohol and powder that we'd consumed, we were now definitely starting to feel the effects. Once Minola had locked the bar up, he invited us back to his house next door along with a few friends and his staff.

We'd only been sitting down in his front room for about twenty minutes when we saw a couple of figures passing by his front window and heading for the front door.

"Who's that?" I asked Minola.

"Oh, it's okay. It's probably just my landlord. I owe him some money on the lease, but don't worry, I'll sort it out"

The next thing we noticed was at least six more figures passing the window, followed by a loud bang on the door.

"This doesn't look like a friendly landlord to me. It looks more like a raid," I said to Fallon.

Before Minola had time to open the door, everyone in the room immediately began stashing anything illegal that they had on them down the back of the couch and behind whatever piece of furniture they could find. Minola opened the front door and was immediately pushed to one side as several of the men walked into his house.

It quickly became apparent to all of us that they were indeed police officers.

We were all told to sit down and not to move while they went about searching his house. They found most of the drugs that we'd stashed, but surprisingly enough, they didn't seem to be too bothered about that. The truth was they had their own agenda in mind, and it wasn't too long before they found what they were looking for.

It turned out that a couple of Minola's friends had burgled a time-share property and sold Minola a few of the stolen items, two of which were a couple of small paintings. Minola had sold one of the paintings to a dealer for £500, and the dealer in turn put the painting up for sale at a local auction house. The upshot of it all was that the painting turned out to be worth £100,000, and the police were monitoring the auctions for stolen goods. As a result, the dealer was arrested and gave Minola's name to them.

Once they'd found the second painting, they immediately arrested Minola for the burglary and carted all of us down to the police station in Fuengirola. They held us there for questioning for most of the day, not releasing us until later that evening.

Minola wasn't so lucky. He told them that he'd brought the items in good faith from a guy that had come into his bar, but they didn't believe his story, and after charging him for burglary, they remanded him in custody to await trial. The police told us that once he'd been to court he would probably be given a financial bail, but they couldn't say when or what that would be.

By this time we were all feeling pretty tired and not at our best, so Fallon and I walked down to the taxi rank with Nicola and Kirby, and after seeing them off, we also jumped in a cab and headed for home to crash out for the rest of the evening.

We woke up on Boxing Day at around 10.30 a.m. both feeling extremely hung over. It was our last day off before the final weekend of the year, and we decided that we'd spend the day trying to come up with ideas to boost the weekend's takings. There seemed to be a lot more tourists arriving this week, so it seemed obvious to us that we should try to encourage some of them into our bar. Don't get me wrong. The Spanish trade had served us well of late, but it has to be said that they don't spend money like the English.

The other factor that we had to take into account was, of course, the arrest of my most influential DJ Minola! I wasn't quite sure how this would affect the size of the Spanish crowd.

Eventually, after much deliberation we decided to run with the Spanish night on the Friday, but on the Saturday night we'd cater mainly to the English with a disco-type theme, offering discounted drinks to anyone that made the effort to dress up. It was a bit of a risk to do this, as it would more than likely deter the Spanish trade, but with the influx of Christmas tourists in town, we both felt that it was a risk worth taking.

I took the liberty of phoning the printer's. To my relief, they were open for business and happy to take my order to make the posters and fliers for the Saturday night. I informed the printer that we'd only just come up with the idea, so he'd have to use his imagination on the designs, which he agreed to do. He informed us that they would be ready to pick later that evening.

We still had a few hours to kill before the printers would be ready, and we were now feeling quite hungry, so we decided to take the opportunity to grab a belated Christmas dinner in town.

After we ate, I received a phone call from Danni, Minola's girlfriend, to tell me that the police intended to hold him in custody until after the New Year. This was obviously a very stressful time for Danni, and I took the liberty of consoling her. She then passed the phone to Mellissa, who was sitting there with her.

"Hey, Mellissa, terrible news about Minola then."

"Yes, it's very upsetting."

"Look, I don't mean to sound insensitive, but I do need to know what's happening tomorrow night. Will you still be coming?"

"Don't worry, Kurt. I take care of the music for you if that's what you want."

"Of course it's what I want. And thanks, I owe you one."

"I think you'll find you owe me two now," she said, giggling down the phone.

"Okay, I'll see you tomorrow night then. *Adios*, sweetheart!"

""Yes, I look forward to it," she said and blew me a kiss before hanging up.

The next thing Fallon did was to ring around her friends and rustle up a few girls to hand out the fliers for us for Saturday night's event. We picked up the posters and fliers from the printer's at about 9.30 p.m., and I've got to say that he'd made a terrific job on the artwork. Once I'd settled the bill with him, we went around with Fallon's friends giving out fliers and putting up as many posters as we possibly could until about 1 a.m., when we all met up again at Linekers to wind down over a drink.

It had been quite a hectic day in the end, but it had left us all looking forward to Saturday night. It would be good to cater for the English once again.

Friday evening was soon upon us. After eating, Fallon and I met up with the rest of the staff at the London Bar for a few drinks before heading up to the Stage Door to get ready for the last Friday of the year. As I've said, I wasn't quite sure what sort of response we'd get that night. Minola was very well liked and would be sorely missed.

After running the air-conditioner for half an hour, we opened the doors. Danny started on the decks, and at around 1 a.m. Mellissa and a couple of other DJs arrived, followed by a large group of about forty Spanish kids.

"Hey, Kurt, I brought some customers for you," said Mellissa, hugging me tightly.

"Hiya, gorgeous! Wow, you look great tonight, and thanks for bringing down the customers," I said, giving her a kiss.

We had about eighty punters in the bar now, and it wasn't long before we filled up completely. The crowd was split fifty-fifty between English and Spanish, and it was quite noticeable that the tills were definitely up. We'd put up several posters in the bar advertising Saturday night, and it had created quite a buzz amongst the English punters.

As far as the Spanish night was concerned, it pretty much went off without a hitch. I've got to say that Mellissa had done a great job tonight, and I wasted no time in telling her that. The other good thing was that there hadn't been any police presence in the bar, which was great news.

Of course, we had the usual lock in to celebrate the evening, and as everyone said goodnight, I pulled Mellissa to one side and personally invited her to tomorrow night's event. I asked her to bring Danni down as a guest of honour out of respect to Minola and as an attempt to cheer her up.

The next afternoon we headed into town, as we'd decided to meet up with the staff to go on a shopping trip. Well, it seemed only right that if we were going to ask the customers to dress up, then we should do the same.

There were many back-street shops and stalls scattered around the town, and we had a lot of fun searching through them, choosing the right outfits for everyone. Danny went for a brown flared suit and a white shirt with large white collars and cuffs, topped with an afro wig. This brought fits of laughter from everyone and earned him the nick name Disco Stu.

I didn't want to look like a complete twat, so I went for a white suit, black shirt, and white tie. The girls both dressed in silver shiny mini-dresses with white boots, and we dressed Peter up like one of the Blues Brothers. It was very comical to see.

It was now approaching 6 p.m. After all that walking around, we were all feeling quite thirsty, so we headed down to Linekers still dressed in our 70s gear.

Shortly after we'd got the first round in, three familiar faces walked into the bar. It was Geordie Andy with Nicola and Kirby. They were both dressed in gold hot pants, boob tubes, and pigtails. They'd also finished off their outfits with a set of roller-skate boots.

"Fuck me, it's like *Saturday Night Fever* in here," I said, laughing out loud.

"Hey, Kurt, how the fuck are you?" said Andy.

"I'm great, thanks, but what the hell's going on?"

Fallon had rung them to tell them that we were all coming down here in fancy dress, so she wondered if they were up to joining us and maybe giving us a hand in the bar tonight.

"Hey, Nicola and Kirby, first I have to say thanks to Fallon for inviting you. I definitely didn't see that coming. And second, I've got to say that I'm loving the roller skates and pigtails. In fact, the three of you look terrific. And of course I'd be honoured to have you helping out tonight," I said, giving them both a big hug and a kiss.

We stayed in Linekers for the next few hours, generally being very loud and, of course, attracting quite a lot of attention dressed as we were.

Eventually, though, we had to depart, as we'd decided to open up a little earlier than usual, and, of course, we had to run the air-conditioner again to try and reduce the smell inside the bar.

There was a strange feeling in the air of anticipation and excitement, as if it was our opening night all over again. I wasted no time in opening the doors at just after 11 p.m. to reveal a queue of people waiting to get inside. Many of them were dressed in 70s outfits. It was a very colourful sight, and it seemed to put everyone in a really good mood.

We had plenty of staff inside and Fallon had the bar well under control, so I went outside to join Peter on the door. The bar filled up very quickly with mostly English tourists, although a certain amount of Spanish punters had also arrived and decided to stay.

At around 1 a.m. Mellissa turned up arm-in-arm with Danni and a couple of lads. I'd like to say what they were dressed in, but my answer would have to be "very little indeed". Both had on the shortest of mini-skirts and the slinkiest of tops.

"Wow, look at you two! I'm lost for words. You look fantastic . . . very sexy!"

"Thank you, Kurt, you're looking very smart yourself. Oh, and thanks for inviting me," said Danni, giving me a hug.

"You're more than welcome, and try not to worry about Minola. I'm sure that everything will work out okay. I want you to enjoy yourself tonight, so no sadness, all right? Oh, and keep your money in your pockets because tonight the drinks are on me."

Danni hugged me again and then headed inside with the lads they'd arrived with.

"So you like what I'm wearing then?" said Mellissa.

"That's a bit of an understatement, isn't it? I think you look very sexy tonight."

Mellissa didn't need any more encouragement than that and practically pounced on me, planting kisses all over me.

"Whoa! Slow down, Mellissa. You're like a wild animal."

"Do I not excite you?" she asked, pressing her body against me.

"Oh, yeah! You definitely turn me on in a big way, but I can't just fuck you at the door of the club, can I?"

"Well, I'm happy to go around the corner if it makes you feel better."

"Mellissa, behave yourself, will you, for fuck's sake? You're like a fucking time bomb waiting to go off. I do find you attractive, and the thought of have a tumble with you is very appealing to me, but I'm not about to jeopardize my relationship with Fallon to do it, okay?"

"Okay, I'm sorry if I have upset you," she said, pulling away from me.

"Look, don't get upset, okay? You've just got to be a little more discreet. Otherwise a lot of people will get hurt in the process."

I gave her another hug, kissed her on the forehead, and then walked her inside to join the others. It was now heaving inside. The dance floor was in full swing, and the theme night seemed to be going down like a storm with everyone. Nicola had jumped behind the bar to help with the demand, and Kirby was busy skating around collecting glasses. Geordie Andy was mingling with the crowd and generally helping keep order in the bar. Everybody seemed to be mucking in, so I decided to relieve Danny on the decks and announce that we were going to have a disco dancing competition with the winner receiving a £50 prize. We'd taken a fortune on the door, so that more than covered it.

I appointed Danni and Mellissa as judges and told everyone that if they were tapped on the shoulder, then they had to leave the dance floor. The last person or couple standing would win the prize.

We weren't short of applicants, and before long the competition was under way. Some of the contestants were really good dancers, while others unfortunately reminded me of a funky chicken. But all in all it was very entertaining, and it was good to see Danni enjoying herself too.

Eventually we got down to the winners, who turned out to be a young couple who blew us away with their dance coordination. The crowd cheered them on as they collected their prize.

I carried on playing the music for the next hour or so until Danny jumped back on the decks to relieve me, assisted by Mellissa. I then took the opportunity to check up on Fallon and the girls. They had been working flat out behind the bar to keep up with the demand.

"Hey, baby, you look worn out. I'll make it up to you later, okay?"

"Well, I think we're over the worst of it, but I'll hold you to that making-up part of it later, honey bunny," she said, kissing me.

I gave Fallon a big hug and thanked both Luciana and Nicola for helping out. Then I made my way over to the other side of the bar to mingle with the crowd and to make sure Danni was okay. Tonight couldn't have possibly gone any better for me, and at that moment I felt terrific. It felt like nothing could possibly go wrong tonight.

Famous last words! No sooner had the thought crossed my mind than I felt a tap on my shoulder. As I turned around, I was greeted with a hug and a kiss from Keeley of all people.

"What the hell are you doing here? I thought you'd gone back to the UK."

"I did go back. I was very upset and angry at you after what happened between us, but I decided I couldn't leave it like that, so I flew back to make it right. I love you, Kurt."

"Look, give me a call tomorrow and we'll meet up and talk. Now's not the time to do this," I said, hoping that she'd agree to leave before creating a scene.

"That's where you're wrong. Now is the perfect time!"

"Go home, Keeley. I'll talk to you tomorrow when you're sober," I said, slightly raising my voice.

"But I don't want to wait. I want to talk now," she demanded.

"For fuck's sake, Keeley, you're going to get me into trouble."

"I don't care about Fallon. She's not good enough for you, and you know it. You were destined to be with me, not her!"

"Okay, you're starting to scare me a little right now. Look, if you won't leave on your own account, then I'll have Peter escort you out of here by force. It's your choice, sweetheart."

"What's going on here then, Kurt? Why are you arguing with Keeley?" said Fallon, who was now standing next to me.

"Tell her, Kurt. She has a right to know!"

"A right to know what?" replied Fallon angrily.

"That he's leaving you and this place behind him and coming to live with me in America."

I don't believe this, I thought. She was going to fuck me over again! I quickly beckoned Peter over before it developed into an all-out war and asked him to escort Keeley out of the bar.

"Kurt, why are you doing this? I thought you loved me!"

"You're making a fool of yourself, Keeley, and embarrassing me in the process. The best thing you can do right now is to go home, sober up, and I'll talk to you later."

"Yeah, go on, fuck off, and don't come back! You're not welcome here anymore, you trouble-making bitch!" shouted Fallon.

"Who the fuck are you to talk to me like that? You're nothing more than a stand-in for Kurt. He doesn't want to spend the rest of his life with a cheap tart like you!"

"Please, Keeley, just go. You're not welcome here right now," I pleaded with her.

"Well, that's funny, because that's not what you said when you were fucking me the other week."

"Tell me that's not true. Tell me she's lying, Kurt!" Fallon demanded.

"We'll talk about it later, Fallon. Now get that bitch out of here!" I shouted to Peter.

He didn't waste any more time in removing her from the bar. She continued to scream obscenities at both me and Fallon as she went.

"What's going on, Kurt? Is it true what she said? Tell me. I need to know," demanded Fallon.

"Not now. I've told you we'll talk about it later. Now leave it alone, please."

"Fuck you, Kurt! How could you do that to me?" she said, bursting into tears and storming out of the club.

"Kurt, don't worry. She'll calm down. For now though you've got a club to run," said Peter.

"You're right of course. Chasing her now wouldn't achieve anything. What the hell was Keeley thinking?"

I took Peter's advice and went back behind the bar to help Luciana and Nicola out, as they were still quite busy serving the customers.

"What was all that about?" asked Nicola.

"Nothing. It was just a misunderstanding, that's all."

"Funny, that's what you said to me when we broke up. You blokes will never learn, will you?" I just smiled at Nicola and then turned around to serve a customer.

The pressure at the bar continued right up until we called last orders, at which point I left the girls to it and re-joined Peter at the door to thank everyone for coming as they began to drift out of the bar. Once we'd seen the last of them out, I got Luciana to pour me a large drink and sat down to relax at the captain's table. I hadn't been there long when Mellissa came over and sat down beside me.

"Poor Kurt, your woman has walked out on you and now you are all alone. Why don't you come back to mine tonight and I will try to cheer you up?" she said, sliding a hand inside my shirt.

"You don't give up do you?"

"I am Spanish. We are a very stubborn race of people."

"So I noticed," I said, laughing.

A few minutes later Danni came over to thank me for a great night out and to say goodnight as she'd called a taxi to take her home. I stood up and gave her a big hug. Both Mellissa and I walked her outside to see her off. When I got to the top of the steps, I found Fallon waiting there.

"Kurt, can you let me in please? I'm sorry I ran out on you."

"To be honest with you, Fallon, I'm a little disappointed. You shouldn't believe everything that you hear."

"So nothing happened between you then?"

"It's a bit more complicated than that, but nothing happened that you need to worry about."

"So she was lying then?"

"Yes, she was lying, okay? That's what you want to hear, isn't it?" I said to her.

I couldn't tell her the truth; it would have broken her heart. Beside which, Keeley and I were now history. That was one thing I was pretty sure of. It wouldn't serve any purpose to admit to cheating on her now.

After kissing and making up, Fallon went back inside, and I saw Danni to her waiting taxi. Mellissa decided to join her in the taxi. It was obvious now that she wasn't going to score with me tonight, more's the pity. Still, perhaps it was for the best; I'd had enough drama tonight to last me for a lifetime.

I went back inside to re-join Fallon and the others for a final drink before calling it a night myself. The good news was that my gamble on the disco night had paid off and the tills were now bulging with cash. So after bagging up the money, we finished off our drinks, locked up the Stage Door, and headed straight home. Fallon was eager to make up for her earlier tantrums.

The last two weeks had totally turned my fortunes around. I'd gone from being practically skint to having several thousand pounds back in the bank. Hopefully, this was a sign of things to come. The only negative was the incident with the troublesome Keeley. Her actions were unforgivable. I mean, I know she was disappointed, but now she was starting to feel like some kind of stalker.

I woke up on Sunday afternoon at around 2 p.m. with Fallon's warm silky body still wrapped around me. I wasn't in too much of a rush to get up, so I just cuddled up to her and dozed back off to sleep for another hour. Eventually we got up at about 3.30 p.m. and set off for the Stage Door to clean up and restock the bar.

As we approached the bar, I noticed a yellow form attached to the one of the gates. It soon became apparent on closer inspection that it was an official notice from the town hall. I couldn't understand most of what it said, but the one thing that did stand out to me was the word *cerrada*, meaning closed!

"Fuck it!" I cursed as I ripped the notice off of the gate.

"What's up? What does it say?" Fallon asked, looking worried.

"It's a fucking closure notice!"

"What about Rosa? Can't she help?"

"Yes, of course. Well done, sweetheart. I'll call her straight away."

Rosa asked me to pop the form down to her so that she could go through it and then work out what action was necessary. It turned out that we'd officially been closed down due to health and safety issues arising from the damp problem, and on top of that they'd also received a written complaint from a member of the public. Rosa set up a meeting with one of the officials in the town hall for tomorrow morning to try to resolve the situation for me. I thanked her for her time and then returned to the Stage Door where I'd left Fallon earlier to finish cleaning up while I went to see Rosa. The only saving grace was that we weren't actually intending to open up for New Year's Eve, so we still had a few days to try to resolve the issues that were now facing us

We took an early night that evening, as neither of us were in the mood to go out. Before we knew it, Monday morning came around and I was back on the phone to Rosa once again. She didn't want to say too much over the phone apart from asking us to come down to her office as soon as possible. Suffice to say, we wasted no time in complying with her request, and before long we were sitting down in front of her.

"*Hola,* Kurt, I'm afraid it is not good news. The health and safety officer is being very stubborn. Their test has come back showing a high risk to the public due to the damp in the plaster."

"So what do they want me to do about it?"

"They are insisting that the walls be fully stripped of plaster and allowed to dry out properly before being treated with a sealant and then re-plastered. They also want to oversee the work with regular inspections, and it must be carried out by a Spanish building firm"

"But that could take months!"

"I understand your concerns, but my hands are tied. The truth is that if you want to reopen for the new season, then you must comply with their request."

I thanked Rosa for trying to help us, but ultimately I left her office feeling devastated at the news that I'd just received. I couldn't believe it. After everything that we'd been through, what with the noise limiter, Minola getting arrested, and the flood, this seemed to be the final straw!

Naturally Fallon tried her best to console me, but she was wasting her time. I was totally heartbroken, and the more I thought about it, the worse it felt.

"Don't worry, Kurt, we'll sort it out," she said, desperately trying to lift me.

"You don't get it, do you? It will take months to sort this out, not to mention the cost."

"Yes, but the summer season will help you recover your losses."

"And in the mean time I'll have to pay the lease, the cost of repairs, and our living costs. Fallon, I don't have that kind of money, and with the bar closed, I'll have no income!"

"We could both get jobs to help us pay for things."

"What jobs? In case you didn't notice, we're out of season now. There are no jobs! I have to face facts; it's not looking good right now."

"Don't say that!" she said, raising her voice.

"Look, I can't do this right now. I've got no fight left in me. I just need to go and get drunk, okay?"

"And how's that going to help?" she screamed at me.

"Just go home, Fallon. I need to be on my own right now"

"Fine, suit yourself! Give up if that's what you want to do," she said angrily.

I turned my back on her, got into the jeep, and drove off towards the town, leaving her crying in the road. I knew that she was trying to help me, but I just wasn't in a place where she could reach right now. This was just something that I had to sort out in my head on my own.

I headed into town and entered the first bar that I came across, and for the next few hours that's where I stayed. Not surprisingly, by the time I left the bar, I was pretty slaughtered and still feeling extremely sorry for myself. I climbed back into to jeep, turned on the engine, and managed to drive for four or five minutes before stalling the motor in the middle of the street.

Unfortunately for me, at that moment a police car pulled up behind me, and it didn't take them to long to realize how drunk I was. The next thing I knew, I was being dragged out of the jeep and bundled into the back of the police car. I don't remember much after that apart from waking up in a police cell with no shoes on my feet and a major headache to boot.

After pulling myself together, I managed to get the attention of the officer on duty. Using a mixture of broken English and broken Spanish, I was able to communicate with him, and he allowed me to make the statutory phone call.

I called Fallon. She was still very angry with me but eventually agreed to come down with my passport to get me released. The police had decided not to charge me on this occasion, although I was given an official caution, and once Fallon arrived with my passport, they agreed to release me.

"What the fuck do you think you were playing at last night?" screeched Fallon angrily.

"I'm sorry, babe. I just lost it for a while."

"I knew I should have gone with you."

"I can look after myself, you know."

"Oh, yeah? Because it doesn't fucking look like it from where I'm standing."

Fallon hugged me tightly and then pulled away. As she did that, I noticed a bruise on the side of her face.

"What the hell's that?"

"Well I'm glad you asked, because while you were off gallivanting around getting drunk, I bumped into your recent bed buddy!"

"What are you talking about? Tell me what happened!"

"I bumped into Keeley. She was more than happy to tell me every explicit detail about your little visit to her when you were supposed to be in England raising money for the bar. You lied to me Kurt!"

"Fallon, I can explain"

"Don't bother! If you can't be honest with me now, then what future could we possibly have?"

"Okay, cards on the table. I did go and see her when she said, but it wasn't solely with the intention of jumping into bed with her. I genuinely went to see her out of desperation to raise some cash to save what we had. What you may or may not know is that I have a history with her. She wanted me to give up everything in Spain and live as a couple with her in the UK at first and then in the USA, but I refused, and she didn't take to kindly to the rejection. Once she realized I wasn't going to leave you for her, she started screaming obscenities at me, and I left. That was the last time that I saw her until the other night, honestly."

"Well, it all makes sense now."

"What do you mean? And you still haven't told me how you got that bruise on your face."

"What you don't know is that it was your precious Keeley who got you shut down! She was the one who made the written complaint and applied pressure on the town hall to have you closed down."

"What? That's quite a leap for you to make, don't you think?"

"Is it? Well, let me tell you how I got this bruise on my face. As you can imagine, I wasn't in the best of moods when I ran into Keeley, and believe me, the last thing I needed was to have her in my face. It didn't take too long before we were trading insults and eventually punches. You see, she told me herself that she'd done her best to set you up so that you'd be closed down. She also told me that she'd sent a letter to the town hall and made phone calls via her solicitor to threaten them with legal action. She said it wouldn't be long now before you're living with her, and then I flipped!"

I didn't know what else to say to Fallon. What she'd told me had left me feeling a little shocked and stunned, but the more I thought about it, the more it made sense.

"Oh, finally sinking in now, is it? That bitch has fucked us both over, and she still thinks that you're going to sail off into the sunset with her."

"I can't believe it. Why would she do that? I made it perfectly clear to her that we were over. She's fucking crazy if she thinks I'm going anywhere with her. Look, it's you I want. And you're right, I shouldn't have lied to you. It's you I want, not her."

"Well, I'm not sure whether I want this any more. I'm sorry, Kurt, but I think you should stay somewhere else tonight. I need some time to think."

"Sweetheart, it's New Year's Eve. We can work this out, I promise, okay?"

"No, Kurt, it's not okay. I don't know if I can trust you, and to be perfectly honest with you, I don't know if I want to," she said, cupping my cheek in her hands. With tears running down her face she turned and walked away from me.

Well, you handled that well, I said to myself sarcastically! I finally seemed to have hit rock bottom. I was on the verge of losing my bar and possibly my girlfriend again, and at the root of it all was that crazy bitch Keeley who had well and truly fucked me over. Still, they do say that if you play with fire, then you're bound to get burnt.

As far as Keeley was concerned, I intended to let her know that we were never going to be a couple. Naturally, I was extremely angry with her, but I suppose ultimately that I was responsible for my own downfall. Fallon had every right to be angry with me, although it has to be said that our relationship had always been a little open. Still, I had no right to lie to her.

I gathered my things from the police station and made my way into the area of town where I had been arrested to try and find the jeep. Apparently, the police had parked it up on the side of the road where they'd found me. Unfortunately, on the police report they'd only stated the area where they'd found me and not the road, so it took me quite a while to find it. Once I'd located the jeep, I headed back to the centre of town and booked into a local hotel. I tried several times to call Keeley to give her a piece of my mind, but she never picked up the phone. All I could do was leave an angry message. I also tried to call Fallon to see if she was alright, but she too didn't answer her phone.

I did, however, receive a call from Rosa. She had taken the liberty of doing a costing for the work that needed to be done to reopen the Stage Door. She said that I would have to use Spanish builders and that the approximate cost of the work would be around £16,000, with a schedule of work that would be stretched over twelve weeks. Rosa told me to think about what she'd said and to let her know as soon as I'd decided on my course of action.

I hung up the phone and sat down on the terrace of the hotel room and just looked out towards the beach. It was obvious to me now that there was no way possible that I could raise that kind of money. I'd already sold my house, and with the Stage Door in the state it was, I wouldn't be able to generate any cash from that either.

I didn't have much left in the bank now, and £2,000 of that I owed to Alan. With no income coming in and the monthly lease on the bar to pay, not to mention my general living costs, it didn't take a genius to work out that I was finally sunk! Things had definitely gone against me lately, what with Minola's incarceration, the flood, and my own infidelities which had caused me to lose Nicola and now Fallon. When I first came out here with Nicola, I had so many dreams of how it was going to be. Most of them had come true, but I'd also had so much temptation put in front of me that I'd ended up taking advantage of the situation.

If I hadn't got involved with Keeley, then who knows? Maybe I'd still be with Nicola and things would have been different. It was obvious to me now that it really was over, and as much as I didn't want to admit it, I had to make the decision to call it a day.

I needed to recoup as much cash as possible now to try and cut my losses, so I decided to park the jeep up and remove all the equipment and stock from the bar and transfer it to my hotel, so as to sell it to the highest bidder. This job took me about three hours. Crazy, isn't it? It took me months of hard work to put this bar together, and I spent many more months trying to hold it all together, only to dismantle it in three hours.

No doubt, when I got back to England, many would say that I wasted my time and money coming out here, but the truth is that it truly was the best time of my life. Although I'd now lost the material side of things, I'll always have the memories in my head. And who knows? Maybe I'll learn from my mistakes and try again someday. But for now I had to try and sell the stock and equipment so that I would have some cash to go back with.

It was early evening now, so my first port of call was to see Scott at Linekers. He was, of course, full of questions and because it was New Year's Eve, he was also very busy, but he was more than happy to buy my stock off of me with a fairly generous offer. I also managed to get him to agree to buy the glass washer and the pair of glass-front fridges. I thanked him for the offer, and he wished me all the best for the future.

After that I went around a few of the music bars in town and managed to sell my lighting, noise limiter, and record decks. I sold the rest of the equipment to a dealer out of the local paper. He didn't give me the best price for it, but you know what they say, every penny counts.

In total I'd managed to raise just over £4,000, which was no mean feat at this time of year. I wasn't in the mood to celebrate, so I decided to call it a day and to leave the New Year's Eve revellers to it, and I headed back to the hotel to get some much-needed sleep.

I got up at 2 p.m. on New Year's Day. There was no going back now, so after taking one final look around the Stage Door, I locked up the gates for the last time and put the keys in an envelope with a letter to Rosa giving her instructions to hand them back to the landlord, and I posted them through her office door.

There wasn't much else to do now other than to gather my things from Fallon's place and book my flight home. This would be one of the hardest things I'd have to do. Ending it with Fallon was not something that I really wanted to do, but I felt that it was a necessary step to take. I didn't want to take her away from the life she loved out here, and I wasn't sure what future awaited me in the UK. The way I saw it was that it was the right thing to do for her sake. I owed it to Fallon to let her know that I was calling it a day out here. It would be the coward's way out to leave without saying goodbye, and that's something that I wouldn't be able to live with!

I parked up outside Fallon's apartment, walked up to her front door, and rang the bell. I did have a key, but I thought that it would have been disrespectful to just let myself in after all that happened. After about thirty seconds Fallon opened the door.

"Kurt! What are you doing here? I thought you were going to give me some time to think. I'm still angry with you," she said, looking surprised to see me.

"I'm sorry, Fallon, but there's something that I have to do."

"Why? What's happened?" Fallon led me into the front room and we sat opposite each other. "Well what's going on, Kurt?"

"I'm not sure how to say this, but I'm not going to reopen the club."

"What do you mean? What's happened?"

"The cost of the repairs is way beyond me. I simply can't afford it."

"Surely there must be some way of saving it? You're just not thinking straight right now."

"You're wrong, Fallon. For the first time in ages I'm as level-headed as I could possibly be. I've decided to cut my losses and give up the bar."

"But what will you do? How will you live?"

"I'm going back to England on my own."

"No! You can't! What about us? We can still work it out, can't we?" she asked, sounding very upset at the news she'd just received.

"Fallon, you yourself asked me to move out. It's okay. I lied and cheated on you! You were perfectly within your rights to do that. Look, I for one am truly sorry for what happened. I'm a fucking idiot, so I'm here to pick up my stuff and say goodbye to you. I owe you that much at least."

"I never said that we were over. I just needed some space to think. I want you to stay with me. Please, Kurt," she pleaded, hugging me through her tears.

"Fallon, please don't make this any harder for me than it is. I'll never forget you. You'll always be close to my heart, but this is something that I have to do."

"I don't want you to do this," she whispered in my ear.

"I'm sorry, sweetheart, but it's for the best. I'm not going to change my mind," I said, kissing her on the forehead.

Fallon burst into a flood of tears and told me that she couldn't stay there and watch me walk out of her life. Fallon kissed me one more time and then walked out of the apartment in tears, closing the door behind her. I felt absolutely terrible seeing her so upset, and I'm not embarrassed to say that I shed a few tears myself once she'd left.

I gathered my stuff, and after leaving Fallon's key on the kitchen counter, I left her apartment. On the way back to the hotel I rang the airport and booked a flight out for the morning.

I hadn't been back in the hotel room long before the mobile started to ring. It seems that bad news travels just as fast out here. I spoke to Danny, Peter, and Tony in the space of an hour or so. All of them tried to encourage me to come out tonight, but I just couldn't face them, so I gratefully declined their offers. I said my goodbyes on the phone to them, and they of course wished me well.

I did receive a call and several texts from that bitch Keeley, but I decided not to answer her. I had nothing but contempt for her now, and to be honest with you, I just couldn't bear to listen to her crap any longer.

I took an early night to try and make the time pass more quickly, but the more I tried to get to sleep, the more awake I felt. In the end it must have been the longest night of my life, but eventually the morning came around, and after loading my stuff into the jeep, I headed for the airport, checked in, and after a long wait I boarded the plane and headed back to jolly old England.

My dream was over. I'd lived the life of a king in what seemed like a fairy-tale world that went by in a flash. I didn't know what the future held for me, but it was clear that this chapter of my life was well and truly over.

Who knows what life has in store for me next? I guess I'll just have to wait and see.

The only thing that I would add to this story is that if you are fortunate enough to have the opportunity in life to do something that you've always wanted to do, then my advice would be to take it. Although I'd lost everything that I'd worked towards out here, I certainly don't regret it. If someone asked me whether I'd do it all again tomorrow given the chance, my answer would always be yes! Without a shadow of doubt, I'd definitely do it again! How many people do you hear saying, "I wish I had the courage to do that"? Well, I did have the courage, and it's something that will stay with me for the rest of my life!

So if you get the chance, take it, but promise me one thing—try to learn from my mistakes. Do your best not to be too indulgent when temptation finds you.

Good luck!